Towards a Standards-Based Curriculum 2014

A Toolkit for the New Primary Curriculum

Amazon Edition published   ited

Printed by Crea

Copyright © Ja

About the Author

Jazz C Williams holds Qualified Teacher Status (QTS) and has experience as a classroom teacher and in school leadership and management. He currently holds a leadership position within a state primary school where he is responsible for curriculum and assessment. In addition, he is a qualified and registered specialist teacher for literacy difficulties and dyslexia. Jazz C Williams has written for the peer-reviewed journal, *Literacy* (UK Literacy Association, Wiley-Blackwell) and has a professional and academic background in literacy, language and learning holding a variety of postgraduate qualifications in these areas. He continues to develop academically and professionally, currently engaged in research into the construct of reading comprehension and inference in assessment tools.

Preface

Moving Towards a Standards-Based Curriculum 2014 is written to offer school leadership, management and classroom teachers a source of support and guidance when implementing the revised National Curriculum effective from September 2014. The significant challenge for primary schools is the move from a conventional approach to the curriculum to a standards-based way of working.

When I was tasked with preparing long-term and medium-term planning for the revised National Curriculum, I found several commercial publications offering schemes for Reading and Mathematics matched to the new programmes of study. Disappointingly, none of these materials seemed to communicate much about the curriculum and assessment model underpinning the renewed National Curriculum. At best, I found them to be supplementary materials opposed to a solution to implementing new statutory requirements. I became aware of the need for a book explaining the core principles of a standards-based curriculum that primary schools in England are faced with establishing. I felt a personal and professional obligation to share insights into a standards-based model, the theoretical underpinnings and how these translate into practice. *Towards a Standards-Based Curriculum* offers examples of how the revised programmes of study can be converted into curriculum and assessment maps and medium-term planning. This book will give the reader a sound understanding of a standards-based curriculum for primary schools, key areas that need to be considered and starting points for professionals to engage in their own development of curriculum and assessment. The materials in this book may be adopted or adapted. They form part of a book intended to be a key reference work for experienced professionals in primary school and those entering teaching in the near future.

It should be made clear that I have written *Towards a Standards-Based Curriculum* to be positive and constructive. The demands of the revised National Curriculum can be debated as excessive or too challenging; the removal of level descriptors lamented or celebrated. What remains is the need for primary schools to implement statutory requirements in the programmes of study and make it work for them and the children they educate. Consequently, this book avoids arguments over the adequacies or limitations of the National Curriculum and favours a constructive and pragmatic approach.

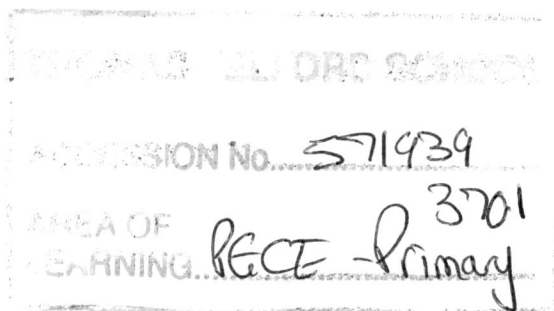

Acknowledgements

The writing of *Towards a Standards-Based Curriculum* would not have been possible without help and support from many individuals.

I extend my thanks to Lynn Livesey who gave me the precious resource of time to engage with the revised National Curriculum. Her encouragement to publish and disseminate the work is appreciated. I must thank Pat Arnold for placing an immense amount of professional trust and confidence in my ability to lead the development of the new programmes of study. I am sure the work that has been started will bring benefits within the years to come.

Over the last three years, I have been blessed to work alongside an outstanding Upper Key Stage 2 teacher, Cath Law, who has provided support, acted as a critical friend and we have shared much laughter together. Cath- I thank you for having the confidence, faith and trust in my work on the Mathematics curriculum. I hope that we will work alongside one another once again in the not too distant future.

During the last two years, the desire to author a book and see it published moved me. If everyone has at least one book in them, this may very well be mine. It is the product of events coinciding and converging, a sense of the right time arising- fate, perhaps. I extend my thanks and appreciation to Steve Lawrence, who has recognised my drive to write and publish the body of work contained *Towards a Standards-Based Curriculum*.

Michelle Robinson dedicated much of her time to reading and engaging with this book to ensure it was fit for purpose. Thank you for everything.

There are individuals who deserve mention for the day-to-day encouragement and support from those I have the pleasure to know: Susan Lee and Carol Valentine- I thank you for your friendship.

Using *Towards a Standards-Based Curriculum*

This book is written with school leadership and management in mind as well as the classroom teacher who are at the forefront of delivering a standards-based curriculum on a daily basis. The book can be read from the beginning, chapter-by-chapter, or navigated according to need and interest. It is advisable to engage with Chapter One if you do not have a sound working knowledge of a standards-based model and the essential principles underpinning it.

Professionals in primary education are encouraged to interact with this book, annotate it, highlight it and make frequent reference to it as a means of supporting classroom practice. It is intended for active use in schools rather than read and consigned to a bookshelf, or tucked away in a classroom cupboard! To facilitate engagement with the content of the book, chapters tend to follow a generic structure.

A brief introduction to the chapter is featured as italicised text. This is followed by **Outcomes**. These indicate what a reader should learn from the content. They are also a convenient means of surveying some of important aspects covered in the chapter's main body. **Critical Questions** tend to appear towards the end of a chapter. They encourage reflection on a chapter's content or offer guidance for teachers making the move towards a standards-based system. **Essentials** conclude the chapters in *Towards a Standards-Based Curriculum*. The main points, ideas or concepts are reiterated and summarised. Chapter Six through to Chapter Eight deviate from the structure of previous chapters, presenting a wealth of curriculum and assessment resources for Mathematics, English and Science.

It is important to bear in mind this book provides examples of how the programmes of study in English, Mathematics and Science can be translated into curriculum, assessment and classroom practice. Professionals in primary schools should feel free to adopt or adapt ideas in *Towards a Standards-Based Curriculum* as they see fit.

Introduction

A review of the National Curriculum in England commenced in January 2011 with the intention of placing 'the principles of rigour, fairness and freedom at its core' (Department for Education, 2011, p. 3). In June 2013, the Department for Education confirmed assessment against level descriptors would be abolished and not replaced. It was announced that an 'assessment framework should be built into the school curriculum, so that schools can check what pupils have learned and whether they are on track to meet expectations at the end of the stage'. With level descriptors as indicators of achievement and progress abolished, the attainment targets in the National Curriculum have become the sole focus of what is taught and assessed. A further draft version of the programmes of study in July 2013 was accompanied by comments that the best performing schools teach what is assessed, a principle of the renewed National Curriculum. Without ever being explicitly named as such, the curriculum for 2014 brings a standards-based model to England; what is assessed gets taught and what gets taught is assessed (Johnston and Costello, 2009).

In Chapter One, the standards-based curriculum is contrasted with what can be considered a conventional approach. The first chapter of *Towards a Standards-Based Curriculum* outlines the core principles and concepts in a standards-based model. Chapter Two considers curriculum and assessment mapping as the starting point for building an assessment framework into the school curriculum. Examples of mapping, or long-term planning, are provided for Mathematics and Science. These first two chapters give a broad, overall picture of what a standards-based curriculum is and what it involves.

Chapter Three shifts towards understanding standards. The emphasis is on unpacking and decoding standards so classroom teachers are able to devise appropriate teaching sequences with adequate depth and breadth. Taxonomies of the cognitive domain are offered as a tool whereby primary school staff can decode the demands of standards and consider how these will be reflected in classroom practice. As part of Chapter Three, developing progressive teaching sequences is discussed and some instructional strategies appropriate to a standards-based mode of working outlined.

Across Chapter Four and Chapter Five, assessment in a standards-based curriculum is addressed. A range of assessment tools and means of scoring children's progress against standards are outlined. Chapter Five makes the case for Assessment Plans as a standards-based form of short-term planning. These chapters are likely to be of intense interest to school leadership, management and classroom teachers who are contemplating how to assess children's learning without level descriptors.

The final three chapters offer unit plans, or medium-term planning, for Mathematics, Science and English. These standards-based resources cover the programmes of study across Key Stage 1 and Key Stage 2.

When engaging with a standards-based curriculum, the following has particular resonance and will be frequently paraphrased in the book.

'What gets assessed is what gets taught' is a common assertion whose meaning is often underestimated. It is not just *what* gets assessed, but *how* it is assessed that has implications for what is learned.

(Johnston and Costello, 2009, p. 145)

The first three chapters in *Towards a Standards-Based Curriculum* are mainly concerned with 'what gets assessed is what gets taught' whereas Chapter Four and Five focus on '*how* it is assessed'.

Contents

'What gets assessed is what gets taught' is a common assertion whose meaning is often underestimated. It is not just *what* gets assessed, but *how* it is assessed that has implications for what is learned.

(Johnston and Costello, 2009, p. 145)

Chapter 1: Defining a Standards-Based Curriculum

A standards-based curriculum effectively sets a series of expectations for what children should know, understand and be able to do by set points in their primary education. It is a performance model where assessment drives teaching and learning against targets stipulating what all children must achieve mastery of. In Chapter One, the features of a standards-based curriculum are outlined and the key principles in such a curricular model identified. Congruency as a central concept in a standards-based curriculum is defined. The need for alignment of standards at national, school and classroom level is considered.

Outcomes

By the end of this chapter, you should be able to:

- Define what is meant by a standards-based curriculum.

- State the key principles underpinning the organisation and design of a standards-based curriculum.

- Summarise the differences between a conventional approach to the curriculum and a standards-based model.

- Explain the differences between standards-based and standards-embedded models.

Any curriculum document indicating what is taught and assessed as one and the same is 'standards-based'. This is embodied in the revised National Curriculum programme of study for English, Mathematics and Science where what is taught and assessed is set out year-by-year or by phases; Key Stage 1, Lower Key Stage 2 and Upper Key Stage 2. In the context of the USA, the expected knowledge and understanding for a year group is referred to as 'grade-level standards' (Rakow, 2008, p. 46). The National Curriculum prefers the terms 'end of year expectations' or 'end of key stage expectations'. This book will tend to use the term 'grade-level standards' because it is somewhat more concise than the English equivalent

The notion of all children meeting grade-level standards involves a mastery model. There is generally less content to be taught and assessed, but it is addressed in more depth to ensure all children secure knowledge and understanding expected by the end of an academic year. A mastery approach does give rise to several questions or issues with the answers requiring whole-school agreement: *At what point should a class move on when a small minority continue to make limited progress towards grade-level standards? What mechanisms will be in place to move this minority to the expected level of achievement if the vast majority is ready to progress? Should more able children be given enrichment tasks linked to current grade-level standards or begin work on more advanced standards?*

It is not appropriate to suggest answers in this chapter; individual schools are best placed to contemplate the questions and devise a response knowing both the human and financial resources they have at their disposal.

Conventional Practice vs Standards-Based Practice

So far it has been established a standards-based curriculum provides landmarks for learning. There is an expectation children will achieve mastery of knowledge and understanding. Accountability is intensified. Classroom teachers are responsible for children meeting grade-level standards. A standards-based model therefore involves much higher stakes at classroom level for each year group teacher. To respond to the challenge, a subtle yet significant shift in the way in which teaching and learning is planned is required.

Since the introduction of the National Curriculum in 1988, a typical approach to teaching and learning has been to select a topic. Once chosen, a series of teaching and learning activities are devised. The teaching sequence would progress and terminate with an assessment before moving on to the next topic from the curriculum. A topic-teach-assess tendency is at odds with a standards-based approach. The conventional practice of topic-teach-assess is reversed when dealing with a standards-driven curriculum. In the latter model, teachers begin by analysing the standards and what knowledge, understanding and skills they encapsulate and assessment activities are then set. The curriculum therefore becomes the pathway to children demonstrating that they have achieved the standards. The curriculum is dictated by standards and assessment. Information from assessments indicates whether children are ready to move on to the next set of standards or require further immediate teaching of skills, knowledge and understanding before this is feasible (CAPP, 2009). A standards-based model can be viewed as an inversion of conventional practice, taking assessment as a more profound start and end point. Some readers may recognise elements of a standards-based approach within their current practice in the conventional paradigm. For example, the use of *Assessing Pupils' Progress* (APP) materials emerging in 2008 and dispensed with by the coalition government just two years later.

Curriculum and assessment against standards was a feature of the APP initiative where achievement of Reading, Writing and Mathematics criteria was exemplified in a series of Standards Files. Published in 2008, APP was the result of the Department for Children, Schools and Families (DCSF) and Qualifications and Curriculum Authority (QCA) attempting to promote greater assessment for learning in primary schools. Despite this good intention, APP as a standards-based tool was problematic. When implemented in addition to existing assessment arrangements rather than a replacement, workload concerns and bureaucratic burdens became an issue. Furthermore, the APP materials were being inserted into a conventional model of practice rather than explicitly reframing curriculum and assessment as one and the same. The National Curriculum for 2014 achieves what APP could not: a clear standards-based model making the curriculum and assessment inseparable.

To reiterate the difference between conventional practice and the standards-based approach, features of the two models have been tabulated to aid in comparing and contrasting them.

Comparing Conventional and Standards-Based Approaches

(Adapted from CAPP, 2009)

Conventional	Standards-Based
A topic is taken from the curriculum as given in long-term planning at whole-school level for a year group.	Standards are identified and clustered together and these determine what children should know and understand.
Teaching and learning activities are designed around the topic.	Assessment is designed to determine how children are progressing towards standards.
Assessment is designed and conducted.	Teaching is planned in line with the assessment tasks and activities; multiple opportunities to acquire knowledge and understanding are provided. Multiple measures of achievement are built into units of work. This is addressed in Chapter Four and Five.
The next topic is selected.	Data from assessment indicates what needs to be retaught or provides evidence for moving on.

The process in a standards-based curriculum is markedly different; it involves a backward design in comparison to the conventional approach. Assessment is planned first and shapes the curriculum that children will follow to achieve specified standards. Topics are secondary to what children are expected to know, understand and be able to do. At this stage, it is appropriate to focus more intensely on the features of a standards-based curriculum.

Features of a Standards-Based Approach

Starting Point	The standards specified in the National Curriculum programme of study for English, Mathematics and Science.
Pre-assessment	This is focused on the grade-level standard being addressed in a teaching sequence.
Acceleration and Enrichment	The corresponding standard from the next year group may be introduced.
	Children may be given tasks where they demonstrate achievement of standards in a variety of situations and apply it to different contexts while those who have not yet achieved mastery receive further direct teaching.
Teaching	Lessons are planned from the standards.
	There are sequential lessons tightly focused on children achieving the specified standard(s).
	Strategies are used to ensure knowledge and concepts and ideas are introduced and revisited so mastery of grade-level standard(s) is achieved.
Assessment	Short-cycle assessment carefully monitors progress towards the standard(s) in a subject area.

Role of the Teacher

Monitoring progress towards mastery of the standard that drives the curriculum, teaching and assessment.

Managing time so ensure standards mapped into a half term or term are taught and assessed. This pace setting stems from whole-school level mapping of the curriculum standards, the long-term plan.

Adapted from Snow et al (2001) and CAPP (2009).

The term 'pace setting' refers to standards being clustered into units of work and assigned to a particular half term or period of time for teaching and learning. By setting the expectation for what is taught and assessed and when this occurs, school leadership and management can obtain a clear overview of what children are learning and achieving in relation to grade-level standards.

A central concept in a standards-based model is congruency. This refers to assessment and teaching focusing on standards so all classroom activities are aligned to the essential knowledge, skills and understanding children must acquire. Congruency, or alignment of standards, assessment and teaching, must be intentional and highly explicit. It is useful to conceive of congruency as a triad in understanding the importance of the relationship between standards, teaching and learning. The congruency triad visually represents the key elements in a standards-based approach to teaching and learning. It is applicable at classroom level within and between units of work.

The Congruency Triad in a Standards-Based Curriculum

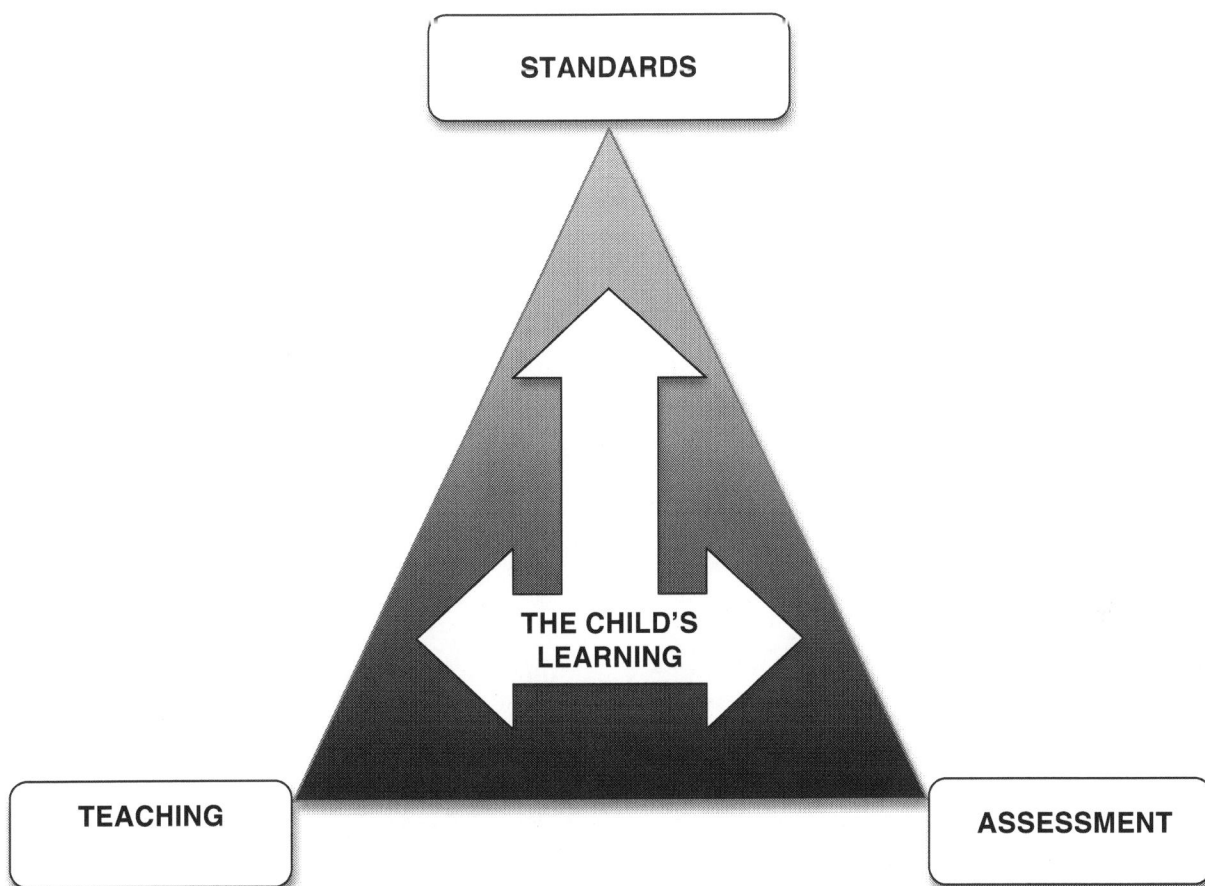

Congruency aligns classroom practice to grade-level standards as mapped out at school level in the form of long-term planning. There is an alignment between school level planning and classroom practice stemming from national expectations. Taking the notion of congruency and alignment of standards translated from national to school and classroom level, it is possible to build a model or framework for understanding how this operates.

National and School Level Alignment

National Level	
National Curriculum (2014) Programmes of Study and Attainment Targets	Assessment and reporting arrangements; national mechanisms for ensuring standards

School-Level
Constructing a locally-articulated curriculum achieved by mapping of standards within the National Curriculum programmes of study
Establishing a comprehensive local assessment system with expected practices embedded in policy *The local assessment system tracks progress and achievement of National Curriculum standards.*

Professional development and training on the standards-based curriculum	**Pace-setting** of standards and regular reviews of children's progress and achievement	**Monitoring and evaluating quality of teaching and assessment** within the principles of a standards-based curriculum

The starting point are the programmes of study setting statutory expectations for grade-level standards to be met by the end of a child's time in a year group or end of a phase. At school level, national expectations are translated into a locally-articulated curriculum. This means individual schools decide on the sequence in which grade-level standards are taught, assessed and how they are clustered into units of work. Inextricably linked to this is a means of whole-school tracking to identify achievement and progress towards meeting standards. It is worth briefly considering how achievement can be given a label in a standards-based curriculum.

The expectation is that all children achieve mastery of grade-level standards. A simple four-way distinction could be made drawing on a similar terminology used by the revised Early Years Foundation assessment in 2012: Well Below, Emerging, Expected and Exceeding The distinction can be made in relation to specific standards addressed in a unit of work. At the end of an academic year, the categories can be used to judge overall achievement against the full range of grade-level standards in Reading, Writing, Mathematics and Science. Examples of tracking grids are provided as supplementary materials in this book or within the main body of a chapter where appropriate. For now, let us return to the national and school-level alignment.

As part of establishing a locally-articulated curriculum and assessment system, teaching and support staff will need access to continued professional development to promote whole-school understanding of a standards-based model. This should not only involve understanding what standards mean, which is the focus of Chapter Three, but also set the expectation for how achievement will be assessed and monitored. Overarching policy, principles and general features of standards-based practice should become part of the collective consciousness within a school to ensure consistency.

School and Classroom Level Alignment

School-Level
Constructing a locally-articulated curriculum achieved by mapping of standards within the National Curriculum programmes of study
Establishing a comprehensive local assessment system with expected practices embedded in policy *The local assessment system tracks progress and achievement of National Curriculum standards.*

Professional development and training on the standards-based curriculum	**Pace-setting** of standards and regular reviews of children's progress and achievement	**Monitoring and evaluating quality of teaching and assessment** within the principles of a standards-based curriculum

Classroom Level
Implementation of the locally-articulated curriculum and assessment

Implementation of Standards-Based Curriculum	Implementation of Standards-Based Units of Work	Implementation of Standards-Based Teaching and Learning Opportunities

Standards-Based Assessment Plans for English and Mathematics feeding into the locally-articulated curriculum and assessment system. In turn, this feeds into national level expectations and requirements.

At classroom level, the locally articulated curriculum and assessment mapping translates into unit plans or medium term planning. Continued professional development received by staff is put into practice and standards-based practice becomes the day-to-day mode of working. School-level monitoring and evaluation ensures principles of a standards-based approach are implemented and acts as the mechanism for determining impact on children's learning.

There must be a clear through-line between national grade-level standards, their organisation at school level and translation into classroom teaching and learning. Such alignment must be intentional, explicit and the high-stakes clearly communicated to teaching staff. All classroom work links directly back into a school level curriculum and assessment system and this in turn reflects school effectiveness against overall national.

The difference between a standards-based curriculum and standards-embedded approach is now considered. This book is preoccupied with the former and discrete teaching of the core subject programmes of study. However, it is useful to be aware of an alternative way of using grade-level standards.

A standards-embedded approach involves thematically linking content. It is reminiscent of the creative curriculum. Placing the models opposite one another highlights some of the differences.

Comparing Standards-Based and Standards-Embedded Models

	Standards-Baseds	Standards-Embedded
Starting Point	The standards specified in the National Curriculum programmes of study for English, Mathematics and Science.	Questions and content relevant to individuals and groups.
Pre-assessment	This is focused on the grade-level standard being addressed in a teaching sequence.	Background knowledge.

	Standards-Based	**Standards-Embedded**
Acceleration and Enrichment	The corresponding standard from the next year group may be introduced. Children may be given tasks where they demonstrate achievement of standards in a variety of situations and apply it to different contexts	To a corresponding standard as well as thematically connected content.
Teaching	Lessons are planned from the standards. There are sequential lessons tightly focused on children achieving the specified standard(s). Strategies are used to ensure that knowledge and key ideas are introduced and so mastery of grade-level standard(s) is achieved.	Lessons are planned around key questions, topics and themes that make connections to standards across curriculum areas.
Assessment	Short-cycle of assessment to carefully monitor progress towards the standard(s) in a subject area.	Variety of assessments.
Role of the Teacher	Monitoring progress towards mastery of the standard(s) driving the curriculum, teaching and assessment. Managing time so ensure standards mapped into a half term or term are taught and assessed.	Facilitates children's learning and engagement as well as assessing achievement.

In terms of the starting point, there is no reason why a standards based approach should exclude children from formulating questions they would like to find the answer to in a unit of work. There is also no reason why their current knowledge and understanding is not elicited. Assessment in both models should ideally involve multiple opportunities to demonstrate learning and multiple measures of children's achievement. The significant difference between the two is that a standards-embedded approach involves classroom teachers having the freedom to move grade-level standards into clusters for a unit of work. These could be drawn from English, Science and Mathematics so teaching and learning occurs within a theme. Particular challenges are posed by a standards-embedded model in respect to ensuring appropriate coverage. It is perhaps useful to keep a standards-embedded approach in mind as an alternative way to implementing the revised National Curriculum.

Critical Questions

There are a multitude of questions that need to be considered when establishing a standards-based curriculum. The following bank of questions is related to various features of a standards-based model. They are broad and overarching questions intended to support the formation of individual responses and professional perspectives.

Standards

What are the standards that need to be taught and assessed?

How many standards can reasonably be addressed in a unit of work or across a year?

Have component parts of the standards been analysed to support teaching, learning and assessment?

Individual Strengths and Areas for Development

What standards have already been achieved and how will this be established and evidenced?

What do the children need to achieve standards that are the focus of a unit or programme of study?

What individual or group needs should be taken into account? How will these be accommodated?

For accommodations, how will assessment and the curriculum be linked?

Teaching and Learning Activities

Are planned teaching and learning activities sequenced logically and progressively to move children towards achieving the standard(s)?

What experiences do all children need to meet the standards or aspects of these?

Are the teaching and learning activities designed to give products and performances?

Assessment

What assessments are needed to provide children with feedback on their progress towards the standard(s)?

Have clear assessment criteria and tasks been planned and devised to move children towards the standard(s)?

Are multiple measures of learning and progress planned for during the course of a unit?

Can the products and performances be used to assess progress and achievement of the standard(s)?

Essentials

From this chapter, the key points to take away are:

- A standards-based curriculum involves a tight focus on all children achieving grade-level standards specified for their year group or by the end of a particular phase in primary education.

- The standards-based model differs from a conventional approach. Assessment drives the curriculum and is the start and end point in a unit of work.

- Congruency between standards, teaching, learning and assessment is a central concept; what gets assessed is taught and what taught gets assessed.

- A clear, intentional and explicit through-line must exist between national, school and classroom levels when adopting a standards-based curriculum.

- The locally-articulated curriculum sets the pace for what is taught and assessed, including when this is expected to happen.

- A standards-based model can be contrasted with a standards-embedded approach. However, there are commonalities between the two.

Chapter 2: Curriculum & Assessment Mapping

In this chapter, the notion of "what gets assessed is what gets taught" (Johnston and Costello, 2009, p. 145) is brought sharply into focus when curriculum and assessment in a standards-based model is considered. The Department for Education (2013) has asserted the need for the 'assessment framework [...] built into the school curriculum'; curriculum and assessment mapping are addressed here as the first steps in establishing this. Curriculum and assessment mapping outlines a pathway through standards within and between year groups and key stages. School leadership, management and classroom teachers will have a firm overview of what is expected to be assessed and when.

Outcomes

By the end of this chapter, you should be able to:

- Distinguish between topic mapping and curriculum and assessment mapping.

- Consider a means of identifying standards using coding.

- Identify how curriculum and assessment mapping fit into the concept of congruency and alignment required in a standards-based model.

In conventional practice, the curriculum is typically mapped according to topics. Long-term planning specifies the topic or theme taught at various stages of the academic year. A conventional topic map is partially reproduced below with title of each topic drawn from the revised National Curriculum programme of study; (black cells indicate no topic is planned for a half term).

Year Group/Term	KEY STAGE 1 SCIENCE					
	Autumn 1	Autumn 2	Spring 1	Spring 2	Summer 1	Summer 2
Year 1	Everyday Materials	Light	Plants	Animals including humans	Seasonal Changes	
Year 2	Use of Everyday Materials	Sound	All Living Things and their Habitats	Plants Animals, including humans		

Other than specifying topics and offering an at-a-glance overview of these, the key issue is that the map contains no indication of what is going to be learnt and assessed each half term. In a standards-based curriculum, it is preferable to be far more explicit about what knowledge, skills and understanding are being taught, learned and assessed. This means considering setting the pace at long-term planning level. Consider the following example.

Year Group /Term	Autumn 1	Autumn 2	Spring 1
Year 1	**Everyday Materials** EM1.1 Distinguish between an object and the material from which it is made EM1.2 Identify and name a variety of everyday materials, including wood, plastic, glass, metal, water and rock EM1.3 Describe the simple properties of a variety of everyday materials EM1.4 Compare and group together a variety of everyday materials on the basis of their simple physical properties EM1.5 Find out how the shapes of solid objects made from some materials can be changed by squashing, bending, twisting and stretching	**Light** LT1.2 Observe and name a variety of sources of light, including electric lights, flames and the Sun LT1.2 Associate shadows with a light source being blocked by something	**Plants** PL1.1 Identify and name a range of common plants, including garden plants, wild plants and trees, and those classified as deciduous and evergreen PL1.2 Identify and describe the basic structure of a variety of common flowering plants, including roots, stem/trunk, leaves and flowers
Year 2	**Use of Everyday Materials** EM2.1 Identify and compare the uses of a variety of everyday materials, including wood, metal, plastic, glass, brick/rock, and paper/cardboard EM2.2 Compare how things move on different surfaces	**Sound** SND2.1 Observe and name a variety of sources of sound, noticing we hear with our ears SND2.2 Recognise that sounds get fainter as the distance from the sound source increases	**All Living Things and their Habitats** ALT2.1 Explore and compare the difference between things that are living, dead, and things that have never been alive ALT2.2 Identify that most living things live in habitats to which they are suited and describe how different habitats provide for the basic needs of different kinds of animals and plants, and how they depend on each other ALT2.3 Identify and name a variety of plants and animals in their habitats, including micro-habitats ALT2.4 Describe how animals obtain their food from plants and other animals, using the ideas of a simple food chain, and name and identify different sources of food

It is possible to immediately see what a child is expected to know and understand. The time frame for this learning is specified by standards indicated for each half term. Curriculum and assessment mapping can be achieved in a similar way for Mathematics, which is shown in the partially produced Lower Key Stage map.

MATHEMATICS CURRICULUM AND ASSESSMENT MAP		
Year Group / Unit	**Autumn 1** **Unit 3A Number, Place Value & Shape**	**Autumn 2** **Unit 3B Add and Subtract Three-Digit Numbers**
	NPV3.2 Recognise the place value of each digit in a three-digit number (hundreds, tens, ones)	AS3.1 Add and subtract mentally a three-digit number and ones
	NPV3.3 Compare and order numbers up to 1000	AS3.2 Add and subtract mentally a three-digit number and tens
	NPV3.5 Read and write numbers to at least 1000 in numerals and in words	AS3.3 Add and subtract a three-digit number and hundreds
	NPV3.1 Count from 0 in multiples of 4, 8, 50 and 100; finding 10 or 100 more or less than a given number	AS3.4 Add and subtract numbers with up to three digits, using the efficient written methods of columnar addition and subtraction
	NPV3.6 Solve number problems and practical problems involving these ideas	AS3.5 Estimate the answer to a calculation and use inverse operations to check answers
	NPV3.4 Identify, represent and estimate numbers using different representations	AS3.6 Solve problems, including missing number problems, using number facts, place value, and more complex addition and subtraction.
	GPS3.1 Draw 2-D shapes and make 3-D shapes using modelling materials; recognise 3-D shapes in different orientations; and describe them with increasing accuracy	M3.3 Add and subtract amounts of money to give change, using both £ and p in practical contexts
	M3.2 Measure the perimeter of simple 2-D shapes	

Curriculum and assessment mapping is specific about the content that is taught in each year group. Such transparency makes this form of mapping ideal for publishing curriculum information online as required by The School Information (England) (Amended) Regulations 2012. It is possible for parents and carers to immediately see what is taught and when therefore they are able to have clear expectations about what their children should be achieving.

It will have been noted that each of the standards from a programme of study is given an alphanumerical reference in the extracts of mapping contain in this chapter. By coding standards alphanumerically, a shorthand means of referencing them is created. The coding must be consistent across whole-school curriculum and assessment mapping, unit plans and tracking systems. This book uses alphanumerical codes in the following way: capital letters indicate the strand of a programme of study to which a standard belongs; the first numeral shows which year group it belongs to; the final numeral denotes the number of standards. For example, NPV3 is used to refer to grade-level standards related to number and place value in the Year 3 programme of study. NPV3.2 indicates it is the second of several standards in the strand. There is no set way of coding standards for ease of reference or any statutory requirement to do so. Standards-based documents in jurisdictions such as Massachusetts and Vermont utilise references to ensure consistency within and between schools..

The following tables contain the alphabetic codes used in *Towards a Standards-Based Curriculum*.

Mathematics

NPV	Number, place value, estimation and approximation
AS	Addition and subtraction
MD	Multiplication and division
M	Measures
D	Data and working with statistics
GPS	Geometry- properties of shape
GPD	Geometry- position and direction
F	Fractions
DF	Decimals and Fractions
PDF	Percentages, decimals and fractions
RP	Ratio and proportion
AL	Algebra

Science

EM	Materials
LT	Light
SND	Sound
ALT	All Living Things
PL	Plants
AH	Animals including humans
E&S	Seasonal Changes / Earth and Space
ELEC	Electricity
FM	Forces and Magnets
FO	Forces
EV	Evolution and Inheritance
ScKS1	Working and thinking scientifically at Key Stage 1
ScLK	Working and thinking scientifically at Lower Key Stage 2
ScUK	Working and thinking scientifically at Upper Key Stage 2

English

S	Spelling
WS	Word Structure
H	Handwriting
SS	Sentence Structure
P	Punctuation
TS	Text Structure
SP	Spelling and Punctuation
RC	Reading Comprehension
WR	Word Reading
WC	Writing Composition

For describing a child's achievement of standards, the following codes appear in examples of tracking and recording sheets throughout the book:

WB	Well Below
EM	Emerging
E	Expected
EX	Exceeding

The next stage in this chapter examines long-term plans, examples of curriculum and assessment mapping for Science and Mathematics. Several questions can be used to guide the reading of the mapping.

Critical Questions

There are four questions relevant to reflecting on the content of this chapter.

Standards

Would you agree with how the standards have been clustered in terms of procedural and conceptual knowledge? If not, how could they be arranged to be more cohesive?

Are there any standards that should be introduced earlier or later? What is the rationale for this?

Is the number of standards reasonable in each half term block? Are there any adjustments that could be made?

Individual Strengths and Areas for Development

Will organisation of standards in the curriculum and assessment map facilitate teachers revisiting those not yet achieved before the end of an academic year?

Mathematics Curriculum and Assessment Mapping

YEAR 1 CURRICULUM AND ASSESSMENT MAP FOR MATHEMATICS	
YEAR 1 AUTUMN 1	**YEAR 1 AUTUMN 2**
NPV1.4 Identify and represent numbers using concrete objects and pictorial representations including the number line, and use the language of: equal to, more than, less than (fewer), most, least NPV1.3 Given a number, identify one more and one less NPV1.5 Read and write numbers from 1 to 20 in digits and words. GPS1.1 2-D shapes (e.g. rectangles (including squares), circles and triangles) GPD1.1 Order and arrange combinations of objects and shapes in patterns	AS1.3 Add and subtract one-digit and two-digit numbers to 20 (9 + 9, 18 - 9), including zero AS1.1 Read, write and interpret mathematical statements involving addition (+), subtraction (-) and equals (=) signs AS1.2 Represent and use number bonds and related subtraction facts within 20 AS1.4 Solve simple one-step problems that involve addition and subtraction, using concrete objects and pictorial representations, and missing number problems
YEAR 1 SPRING 1	**YEAR 1 SPRING 2**
M1.10 Sequence events in chronological order using language such as: before and after, next, first, today, yesterday, tomorrow, morning, afternoon and evening M1.11 Recognise and use language relating to dates, including days of the week, weeks, months and years M1.12 Tell the time to the hour and half past the hour and draw the hands on a clock face to show these times M1.8 Measure and begin to record time (hours, minutes, seconds) M1.4 Compare, describe and solve practical problems for time (quicker, slower, earlier, later	M1.5 Measure and begin to record lengths and heights M1.6 Measure and begin to record mass/weight M1.7 Measure and begin to record capacity and volume M1.11 Compare, describe and solve practical problems for lengths and heights (e.g. long/short, longer/shorter, tall/short, double/half) M1.2 Compare, describe and solve practical problems for mass or weight (e.g. heavy/light, heavier than, lighter than) M1.3 Compare, describe and solve practical problems for capacity/volume (full/empty, more than, less than, quarter)
YEAR 1 SUMMER 1	**YEAR 1 SUMMER 2**
NPV1.1 Count to and across 100, forwards and backwards, beginning with 0 or 1, or from any given number M1.9 Recognise and know the value of different denominations of coins and notes GPD1.2 Describe position, directions and movements, including half, quarter and three-quarter turns	NPV1.2 Count, read and write numbers to 100 in numerals, count in different multiples including ones, twos, fives and tens MD1.1 Solve simple one-step problems involving multiplication and division, calculating the answer using concrete objects, pictorial representations and arrays with the support of the teacher. F1.1 Recognise, find and name a half as one of two equal parts of an object, shape or quantity F1.2 Recognise, find and name a quarter as one of four equal parts of an object, shape or quantity

YEAR 2 CURRICULUM AND ASSESSMENT MAP FOR MATHEMATICS

YEAR 2 AUTUMN 1	YEAR 2 AUTUMN 2
AS2.3 Recall and use addition and subtraction facts to 20 fluently, and derive and use related facts up to 100	PV2.1 Count in steps of 2, 3, and 5 from 0, and count in tens from any number, forward or backward
AS2.8 Show that addition of two numbers can be done in any order (commutative) and subtraction of one number from another cannot	MD2.1 Recall and use multiplication and division facts for the 2, 5 and 10 multiplication tables, including recognising odd and even numbers
AS2.4 Add and subtract numbers using concrete objects, pictorial representations, and mentally, including a two-digit number and ones	MD2.2 Calculate mathematical statements for multiplication and division within the multiplication tables and write them using the multiplication (x), division (÷) and equals (=) signs
PV2.2 Recognise the place value of each digit in a two-digit number	
PV2.6 Use place value and number facts to solve problems	MD2.3 Recognise and use the inverse relationship between multiplication and division in calculations
AS2.5 Add and subtract numbers using concrete objects, pictorial representations, and mentally, including a two-digit number and tens	MD2.4 Show that multiplication of two numbers can be done in any order (commutative) and division of one number by another cannot
AS2.6 Add and subtract numbers using concrete objects, pictorial representations, and mentally, including two two-digit numbers	MD2.5 Solve one-step problems involving multiplication and division, using materials, arrays, repeated addition, mental methods, and multiplication and division facts including problems in contexts
AS2.7 Add and subtract numbers using concrete objects, pictorial representations, and mentally, including adding three one-digit numbers	
AS2.9 Recognise and use the inverse relationship between addition and subtraction and use this to check calculations and missing number problems	
AS2.1&2 Solve simple one-step problems with addition and subtraction applying their increasing knowledge of mental and written methods	
GPS2.1 Identify and describe the properties of 2-D shapes, including the number of sides and symmetry in a vertical line	
GPD2.1 Order and arrange combinations of mathematical objects in patterns	

YEAR 2 SPRING 1	YEAR 2 SPRING 2
NPV2.3 Identify, represent and estimate numbers using different representations, including the number line NPV2.4 Compare and order numbers from 0 up to 100; use <, > and = signs NPV2.5 Read and write numbers to at least 100 in numerals and in words M2.6 Compare and sequence intervals of time M2.7 Tell and write the time to five minutes, including quarter past/to the hour and draw the hands on a clock face to show these times	M2.1 Choose and use appropriate standard units to estimate and measure length/height in any direction (m/cm); mass (kg/g); temperature (°C); capacity (litres/ml) to the nearest appropriate unit, using rulers, scales, thermometers and measuring vessels M2.2 Compare and order lengths, mass, volume/capacity and record the results using >, < and = M2.3 Read relevant scales- nearest numbered unit AS2.1&2 Solve simple one-step problems with addition and subtraction including those involving numbers, quantities and measures GPS2.2 Identify and describe the properties of 3-D shapes, including the number of edges, vertices and faces GPS2.3 Identify 2-D shapes on the surface of 3-D shapes, for example a circle on a cylinder and a triangle on a pyramid GPS2.4 Compare and sort common 2-D and 3-D shape and everyday objects

YEAR 2 SUMMER 1	YEAR 2 SUMMER 2
M2.4 Recognise and use symbols for pounds (£) and pence (p); combine amounts to make a particular value and match different combinations of coins to equal the same amounts of money; add and subtract money of the same unit, including giving change M2.5 Solve simple problems in a practical context involving addition and subtraction of money D2.1 Interpret and construct simple pictograms, tally charts, block diagrams and simple tables D2.2 Ask and answer simple questions by counting the number of objects in each category and sorting the categories by quantity D2.3 Ask and answer questions about totalling and compare categorical data	F2.1 Recognise, find, name and write fractions $\frac{1}{3}$, $\frac{1}{4}$, $\frac{2}{4}$ and $\frac{3}{4}$ of length, shape, set of objects or quantity F2.2 Write simple fractions e.g. $\frac{1}{2}$ of 6 = 3 and recognise the equivalence of two quarters and one half. GPD2.2 Use mathematical vocabulary to describe position, direction and movement, including distinguishing between rotation as a turn and in terms of right angles for quarter, half and three- quarter turns (clockwise and anti-clockwise), and movement in a straight line.

YEAR 3 CURRICULUM AND ASSESSMENT MAP FOR MATHEMATICS

YEAR 3 AUTUMN 1	YEAR 3 AUTUMN 2
NPV3.2 Recognise the place value of each digit in a three-digit number (hundreds, tens, ones)	AS3.1 Add and subtract mentally a three-digit number and ones
NPV3.3 Compare and order numbers up to 1000	AS3.2 Add and subtract mentally a three-digit number and tens
NPV3.5 Read and write numbers to at least 1000 in numerals and in words	AS3.3 Add and subtract a three-digit number and hundreds
NPV3.1 Count from 0 in multiples of 4, 8, 50 and 100; finding 10 or	AS3.4 Add and subtract numbers with up to three digits, using the efficient written methods of columnar addition and subtraction
100 more or less than a given number	AS3.5 Estimate the answer to a calculation and use inverse operations to check answers
NPV3.6 Solve number problems and practical problems involving these ideas.	AS3.6 Solve problems, including missing number problems, using number facts, place value, and more complex addition and subtraction.
NPV3.4 Identify, represent and estimate numbers using different representations	
GPS3.1 Draw 2-D shapes and make 3-D shapes using modelling materials; recognise 3-D shapes in different orientations; and describe them with increasing accuracy	M3.3 Add and subtract amounts of money to give change, using both £ and p in practical contexts
M3.2 Measure the perimeter of simple 2-D shapes	

YEAR 3 SPRING 1	YEAR 3 SPRING 2
MD3.1 Recall and use multiplication and division facts for the 3, 4 and 8 multiplication tables	F3.1 Count up and down in tenths; recognise that tenths arise from dividing an object into 10 equal parts and in dividing one-digit numbers or quantities by 10
MD3.2 Write and calculate mathematical statements for multiplication and division using the multiplication tables that they know, including for two-digit numbers times one-digit numbers, using mental and progressing to efficient written methods	F3.2 Recognise, find and write fractions of a discrete set of objects: unit fractions and non-unit fractions with small denominators
	F3.3 Recognise and use fractions as numbers: unit fractions and non-unit fractions with small denominators
MD3.3 Solve problems including missing number problems, involving multiplication and division including integer scaling problems and correspondence problems in which n objects are connected to m objects.	F3.4 Recognise and show, using diagrams, equivalent fractions with small denominators
	F3.5 Add and subtract fractions with the same denominator within one whole
D3.1 Interpret and present data using bar charts, pictograms and tables	F.3.6 Compare and order unit fractions with the same denominator
D3.2 Solve one-step and two-step questions such as 'How many more?' and 'How many fewer?'- scaled bar charts and pictograms and tables	F3.7 Solve problems that involve all of the above

YEAR 3 SUMMER 1	YEAR 3 SUMMER 2
GPS3.2 Recognise angles as a property of shape and associate angles with turning GPS3.3 Identify right angles, recognise that two right angles make a half-turn, three make three quarters of a turn and four a complete turn; identify whether angles are greater than or less than a right angle GPS3.4 Identify horizontal, vertical, perpendicular and parallel lines in relation to other lines	M3.1 Measure, compare, add and subtract: lengths (m/cm/mm); mass (kg/g); volume/capacity (l/ml) M3.4 Tell and write the time from an analogue clock, including using Roman numerals from I to XII, and 12-hour and 24-hour clocks M3.5 Estimate and read time with increasing accuracy to the nearest minute; record and compare time in terms of seconds, minutes, hours and o'clock; use vocabulary such as a.m./p.m., morning, afternoon, noon and midnight M3.6 Know the number of seconds in a minute and the number of days in each month, year and leap year M3.7 Compare durations of events, for example to calculate the time taken by particular events or tasks

YEAR 4 CURRICULUM AND ASSESSMENT MAP FOR MATHEMATICS

YEAR 4 AUTUMN 1	YEAR 4 AUTUMN 2
NPV4.4 Recognise the place value of each digit in a four-digit number (thousands, hundreds, tens, and ones)	NPV4.1 Count in multiples of 6, 7, 9, 25 and 1000
NPV4.5 Order and compare numbers beyond 1000	NPV4.3 Count backwards through zero to include negative numbers
NPV4.6 Identify, represent and estimate numbers using different representations	MD4.1 Recall multiplication and division facts for multiplication tables up to 12 × 12
NPV4.2 Find 1000 more or less than a given number	MD4.2 Use place value, known and derived facts to multiply and divide mentally, multiplying by 0 and 1; dividing by 1
NPV4.7 Round any number to the nearest 10, 100 or 1000	MD4.3 Use place value, known and derived facts to multiply and divide mentally, multiplying together three numbers
NPV4.8 Solve number and practical problems that involve all of the above and with increasingly large positive numbers	MD4.5 Multiply two-digit and three-digit numbers by a one-digit number using formal written layout
AS4.1 Add and subtract numbers with up to 4 digits using the efficient written methods of columnar addition and subtraction where appropriate	GPS4.1 Compare and classify geometric shapes, including quadrilaterals and triangles, based on their properties and sizes
AS4.2 Estimate and use inverse operations to check answers to a calculation	GPS4.2 Identify acute and obtuse angles and compare and order angles up to two right angles by size
AS4.3 Solve addition and subtraction two-step problems in contexts, deciding which operations and methods to use and why	GPS4.3 Identify lines of symmetry in 2-D shapes presented in different orientations
	GPS4.4 Complete a simple symmetric figure with respect to a specific line of symmetry

YEAR 4 SPRING 1	YEAR 4 SPRING 2
MD4.4 Recognise and use factor pairs and commutativity in mental calculations	F4.1 Count up and down in hundredths; recognise that hundredths arise when dividing an object by a hundred and dividing tenths by ten
MD4.6 Solve problems involving multiplying and adding, including using the distributive law and harder multiplication problems such as which n objects are connected to m objects	DF4.1 Recognise and write decimal equivalents of any number of tenths or hundredths
F4.2 Solve problems involving increasingly harder fractions to calculate quantities, and fractions to divide quantities, including non-unit fractions where the answer is a whole number	DF4.2 Recognise and write decimal equivalents
	DF4.3 Find the effect of dividing a one- or two-digit number by 10 and 100, identifying the value of the digits in the answer as units, tenths and hundredths
F4.3 Identify, name and write equivalent fractions of a given fraction, including tenths and hundredths	DF4.4 Round decimals with one decimal place to the nearest whole number
F4.4 Add and subtract fractions with the same denominator	DF4.5 Compare numbers with the same number of decimal places up to two decimal places
M4.2 Measure and calculate the perimeter of a rectilinear figure (including squares) in centimetres and metres	DF4.6 Solve simple measure and money problems involving fractions and decimals to two decimal places
M4.3 Find the area of rectilinear shapes by counting	M4.1 Convert between different units of measure (e.g. kilometre to metre; hour to minute)
	M4.5 Estimate, compare and calculate different measures, including money in pounds/pence

YEAR 4 SUMMER 1	YEAR 4 SUMMER 2
M4.6 Read, write and convert time between analogue and digital 12 and 24-hour clocks	NPV4.9 Read Roman numerals to 100 (I to C) and understand how, over time, the numeral system changed to include the concept of zero and place value
M4.7 Solve problems involving converting from hours to minutes; minutes to seconds; years to months; weeks to days.	GPD4.1 Describe positions on a 2-D grid as coordinates in the first quadrant
D4.1 Interpret and present discrete data using bar charts and continuous data using line graphs	GPD4.2 Describe movements between positions as translations of a given unit to the left/right and up/down
D4.2 Solve comparison, sum and difference problems using information presented in bar charts, pictograms, tables and simple line graphs	GPD4.3 Plot specified points and draw sides to complete a given polygon

YEAR 5 CURRICULUM AND ASSESSMENT MAP FOR MATHEMATICS

YEAR 5 AUTUMN 1	YEAR 5 AUTUMN 2
NPV5.1 Read, write, order and compare numbers to at least 1 000 000 and determine the value of each digit	F5.1 Compare and order fractions whose denominators are all multiples of the same number
NPV5.2 Count forwards or backwards in steps of powers of 10 for any given number up to 1 000 000	F5.2 Recognise mixed numbers and improper fractions and convert from one form to the other
NPV5.3 Round any number up to 1 000 000 to the nearest 10, 100,1000, 10 000 and 100 000	F5.3 Add and subtract fractions with the same denominator and related fractions; write mathematical statements >1 as a mixed number
AS5.1 Add and subtract whole numbers with more than 4 digits, including using efficient written methods (columnar addition and subtraction)	F5.4 Multiply proper fractions and mixed numbers by whole numbers, supported by materials and diagrams
AS5.2 Add and subtract numbers mentally with increasingly large numbers	DF5.1 Read and write decimal numbers as fractions
AS5.3 Use rounding to check answers to calculations and determine, in the context of a problem, levels of accuracy	DF5.2 Recognise and use thousandths and relate them to tenths, hundredths and decimal equivalents
AS5.4 Solve addition and subtraction multi-step problems in contexts, deciding which operations and methods to use and why	DF5.3 Round decimals with two decimal places to the nearest whole number and to one decimal place
NPV5.4 Solve number problems and practical problems that involve all of the above	DF5.4 Read, write, order and compare numbers with up to three decimal places
GPS5.1 Identify 3-D shapes, including cubes and cuboids, from 2-D representations	DF5.5 Solve problems involving number up to three decimal places
GPS5.8 State and use the properties of a rectangle (including squares) to deduce related facts	MD5.8multiply and divide whole numbers and those involving decimals by 10, 100 and 1000
GPS5.9 Distinguish between regular and irregular polygons based on reasoning about equal sides and angles	M5.1 Convert between different units of measure (e.g. kilometre and metre; metre and centimetre; centimetre and millimetre; kilogram and gram; litre and millilitre)

YEAR 5 SPRING 1	YEAR 5 SPRING 2
MD5.1 Identify multiples and factors, including finding all factor pairs	MD5.5 Multiply numbers up to 4 digits by a one- or two-digit number using an efficient written method, including long multiplication for two-digit numbers
MD5.3 Know and use the vocabulary of prime numbers, prime factors and composite (non-prime) numbers	MD5.7 Divide numbers up to 4 digits by a one-digit number using the efficient written method of short division and interpret remainders appropriately for the context
MD5.4 Establish whether a number up to 100 is prime and recall prime numbers up to 19	
MD5.9 Recognise and use square numbers and cube numbers, and the notation for squared and cubed	MD5.2 Solve problems involving multiplication and division where larger numbers are used by decomposing them into their factors
MD5.6 Multiply and divide numbers mentally drawing upon known facts	MD5.11 Solve problems involving multiplication and division, including scaling by simple fractions and problems involving simple rates.
M5.3 Measure and calculate the perimeter of composite rectilinear shapes in centimetres and metres	
M5.4 Calculate and compare the area of squares and rectangles including using standard units, square centimetres and square metres and estimate the area of irregular shapes	MD5.10 Solve problems involving addition, subtraction, multiplication and division and a combination of these, including understanding the meaning of the equals sign
M5.5 Recognise and estimate volume	

YEAR 5 SUMMER 1	YEAR 5 SUMMER 2
PDF5.1 Recognise the per cent symbol (%) and understand that per cent relates to "number of parts per hundred", and write percentages as a fraction with denominator hundred, and as a decimal fraction	M5.2 Understand and use basic equivalences between metric and common imperial units and express them in approximate terms
PDF5.2 Solve problems which require knowing percentage and decimal equivalents of 1/2 , 1/4 , 1/5 , 2/5 , 4/5 and those with a denominator of a multiple of 10 or 25	M5.6 Solve problems involving converting between units of time
GPS5.2 Know angles are measured in degrees; estimate and measure them and draw a given angle, writing its size in degrees (o)	M5.7 Solve problems involving addition and subtraction of units of measure (e.g. length, mass, volume, money) using decimal notation
GPS5.3 Identify multiples of 90 degrees	D5.1 Solve comparison, sum and difference problems using information presented in line graphs
GPS5.4 Identify angles at a point on a straight line and ½ a turn (total 180 degrees)	D5.1 Complete, read and interpret information in tables, including timetables.
GPS5.5 Identify angles at a point and one whole turn (total 360 degrees)	
GPS5.6 Identify reflex angles, and compare different angles	
GPS5.7 Draw shapes using given dimensions and angles	
GPD5.1 Identify, describe and represent the position of a shape following a reflection or translation, using the appropriate language, and know that the shape has not changed	

YEAR 6 CURRICULUM AND ASSESSMENT MAP FOR MATHEMATICS

YEAR 6 AUTUMN 1	YEAR 6 AUTUMN 2
NPV6.1 Read, write, order and compare numbers up to 10 000 000 and determine the value of each digit	ASMD6.8 Use estimation to check answers to calculations and determine, in the context of a problem, levels of accuracy
DF6.1Identify the value of each digit to three decimal places and multiply and divide numbers by 10, 100 and 1000 where the answers are up to three decimal places	ASMD6.1 Multiply multi-digit numbers up to 4 digits by a two-digit whole number using the efficient written method of long multiplication
NPV6.2 Round any whole number to a required degree of accuracy	ASMD6.2 Divide numbers up to 4 digits by a two-digit whole number using the efficient written method of long division, and interpret remainders as whole number remainders, fractions, or by rounding, as appropriate for the context
NPV6.3 Use negative numbers in context, and calculate intervals across zero	
NPV6.4 Solve number problems and practical problems that involve all of the above.	
ASMD6.5 Use their knowledge of the order of operations to carry out calculations involving the four operations	ASMD6.7 Solve problems involving addition, subtraction, multiplication and division
ASMD6.3 Perform mental calculations, including with mixed operations and large numbers	GPS6.1 Recognise, describe and build simple 3-D shapes, including making nets
ASMD6.6 Solve addition and subtraction multi-step problems in contexts, deciding which operations and methods to use and why	M6.6 Recognise when it is necessary to use the formulae for area and volume of shapes
GPS6.2 Compare and classify geometric shapes based on their properties and sizes and find unknown angles in any triangles, quadrilaterals, and regular polygons	M6.7 Calculate, estimate and compare volume of cubes and cuboids using standard units including cm cubed, cubic metres and extend to other units (mm/km)
M6.4 Recognise that shapes with the same areas can have different perimeters and vice versa	
M6.5 Calculate the area of parallelograms and triangles	

YEAR 6 SPRING 1	YEAR 6 SPRING 2
ASMD6.4 Identify common factors, common multiples and prime numbers	PDF6.1 Solve problems involving the calculation of percentages of whole numbers or measures such as 15% of 360 and the use of percentages for comparison
F6.1 Use common factors to simplify fractions, use common multiples to express fractions in the same denomination	PDF6.2 Recall and use equivalences between simple fractions, decimals and percentages, including in different contexts.
F6.2 Compare and order fractions, including fractions >1	AL6.1 Express missing number problems algebraically
F6.3 Associate a fraction with division to calculate decimal fraction equivalents (e.g. 0.375) for a simple fraction	AL6.2 Use simple formulae expressed in words
F6.4 Add and subtract fractions with different denominators and mixed numbers, using the concept of equivalent fractions	AL6.3 Generate and describe linear number sequences
F6.5 Multiply simple pairs of proper fractions, writing the answer in its simplest form	AL6.4 Find pairs of numbers that satisfy number sentences involving two unknowns
F6.6 Divide proper fractions by whole numbers	RP6.1 Solve problems involving the relative sizes of two quantities, including similarity
DF6.2 Multiply one-digit numbers with up to two decimal places by whole numbers	RP6.2 Solve problems involving unequal sharing and grouping
DF6.3 Use written division methods in cases where the answer has up to two decimal places	
DF6.4 Solve problems requiring answers to be rounded to specified degrees of accuracy	
GPS6.4 Find unknown angles where they meet at a point, are on a straight line, and vertically opposite	

YEAR 6 SUMMER 1	YEAR 6 SUMMER 2
M6.2 Use, read, write and convert between standard units, converting measurements of length, mass, volume and time from a smaller unit of measure to a larger unit, and vice versa, using decimal notation to three decimal places	D6.1 Interpret and construct pie charts and line graphs and use these to solve problems
	M6.3 Convert between miles and kilometres
	D6.2 Calculate and interpret the mean as an average
M6.1 Solve problems involving the calculation and conversion of units of measure, using decimal notation to three decimal places where appropriate	GPS6.3 Illustrate and name parts of circles, including radius, diameter and circumference
	GPD6.1 Describe positions on the full coordinate grid (all four quadrants)
	GPD6.2 Draw and translate simple shapes on the coordinate plane, and reflect them in the axes

Science Curriculum and Assessment Mapping

CURRICULUM AND ASSESSMENT MAP FOR SCIENCE: AUTUMN	
YEAR 1 AUTUMN 1	**YEAR 1 AUTUMN 2**
Everyday Materials EM1.1 Distinguish between an object and the material from which it is made EM1.2 Identify and name a variety of everyday materials, including wood, plastic, glass, metal, water and rock EM1.3 Describe the simple properties of a variety of everyday materials EM1.4 Compare and group together a variety of everyday materials on the basis of their simple physical properties EM1.5 Find out how the shapes of solid objects made from some materials can be changed by squashing, bending, twisting and stretching	**Light** LT1.2 Observe and name a variety of sources of light, including electric lights, flames and the Sun LT1.2 Associate shadows with a light source being blocked by something
YEAR 2 AUTUMN 1	**YEAR 2 AUTUMN 2**
Uses of Everyday Materials EM2.1 Identify and compare the uses of a variety of everyday materials, including wood, metal, plastic, glass, brick/rock, and paper/cardboard EM2.2 Compare how things move on different surfaces	**Sound** SND2.1 Observe and name a variety of sources of sound, noticing we hear with our ears SND2.2 Recognise that sounds get fainter as the distance from the sound source increases
YEAR 3 AUTUMN 1	**YEAR 3 AUTUMN 2**
Rocks EM3.1 Compare and group together different kinds of rocks on the basis of their simple physical properties EM3.2 Describe in simple terms how fossils are formed when things that have lived are trapped within rock EM3.3 Recognise that soils are made from rocks and organic matter	**Light** LT3.1 Notice that light is reflected from surfaces LT3.3 Find patterns that determine the size of shadows

YEAR 4 AUTUMN 1	YEAR 4 AUTUMN 2
States of Matter	**Sound**
EM4.1 Compare and group materials together, according to whether they are solids, liquids or gases	SND4.1 Identify how sounds are made, associating some of them with something vibrating
EM4.2 Observe that some materials change state when they are heated or cooled, and measure the temperature at which this happens in degrees Celsius	SND4.2 Find patterns between the pitch of a sound and features of the object that produced it
EM4.3 Identify the part played by evaporation and condensation in the water cycle and associate the rate of evaporation with temperature	SND4.3 Find patterns between the volume of a sound and the strength of the vibrations that produced it

YEAR 5 AUTUMN 1	YEAR 5 AUTUMN 2
Properties of Everyday Materials & Reversible Change	**Forces**
EM5.1 Compare and group together everyday materials based on evidence from comparative and fair tests, including their hardness, solubility, conductivity (electrical and thermal) and response to magnets	FO5.1 Explain that unsupported objects fall towards the earth because of the force of gravity acting between the Earth and falling object
EM5.2 Understand how some materials will dissolve in liquid to form a solution, and describe how to recover a substance from a solution	FO5.2 Identify the effects of air resistance, water resistance and friction, that act between moving surfaces
EM5.3 Use knowledge of solids, liquids and gases to decide how mixtures might be separated, including through filtering	FO5.3 Understand that force and motion can be transferred through mechanical devices such as gears, pulleys, levers and springs
EM5.4 Give reasons, based on evidence from comparative and fair tests, for the particular uses of everyday materials, including metals, wood and plastic	
EM5.5 Demonstrate that dissolving, mixing and changes of state are reversible changes	
EM5.6 Explain that some changes result in the formation of new materials, and that this kind of change is not usually reversible, including changes associated with burning, oxidisation, and the action of acid on bicarbonate of soda	

YEAR 6 AUTUMN 1	YEAR 6 AUTUMN 2
	Light LT6.1 Understand light appears to travel in straight lines LT6.2 Use the idea light travels in straight lines to explain that objects are seen because they give out or reflect light into the eye LT6.3 Explain that we see things because light travels from light sources to our eyes or from light sources to objects and then to our eyes LT6.4 Use the idea that light travels in straight lines to explain why shadows have the same shape as the objects that cast them, and to predict the size of shadows when the position of the light source changes

CURRICULUM AND ASSESSMENT MAP FOR SCIENCE: SPRING

YEAR 1 SPRING 1	YEAR 1 SPRING 2
Plants	**Animals, including humans**
PL1.1 Identify and name a range of common plants, including garden plants, wild plants and trees, and those classified as deciduous and evergreen	AH1.1 Identify and name a variety of common animals that are birds, fish, amphibians, reptiles, mammals and invertebrates
PL1.2 Identify and describe the basic structure of a variety of common flowering plants, including roots, stem/trunk, leaves and flowers	AH1.2 Identify and name a variety of common animals that are carnivores, herbivores and omnivores
	AH1.3 Describe and compare the structure of a variety of common animals (birds, fish, amphibians, reptiles, mammals and invertebrates, and including pets)
	AH1.4 Identify, name, draw and label the basic parts of the human body and say which part of the body is associated with each sense
YEAR 2 SPRING 1	**YEAR 2 SPRING 2**
All Living Things	**Animals, including humans**
ALT2.1 Explore and compare the difference between things that are living, dead, and things that have never been alive	AH2.1 Notice that animals, including humans, have offspring which grow into adults
ALT2.2 Identify that most living things live in habitats to which they are suited and describe how different habitats provide for the basic needs of different kinds of animals and plants, and how they depend on each other	AH2.2 Find out about and describe the basis needs of animals, including humans, for survival (water, food and air)
	AH2.3 Describe the importance for humans of exercise, eating the right amounts of different types of food, and hygiene
ALT2.3 Identify and name a variety of plants and animals in their habitats, including micro-habitats	**Plants**
ALT2.4 Describe how animals obtain their food from plants and other animals, using the ideas of a simple food chain, and name and identify different sources of food	PL2.1 Observe and describe how seeds and bulbs grow into mature plants
	PL2.2 Find out and describe how plants need water, light and a suitable temperature to grow and stay healthy

YEAR 3 SPRING 1	YEAR 3 SPRING 2
Plants	**Animals, including humans**
PL3.1 Identify and describe the functions of different parts of flowering plants: roots, stem, leaves and flowers	AH3.1 Identify that animals, including humans, need the right types and amounts of nutrition, and that they cannot make their own food, they get nutrition from what they eat
PL3.2 Explore the requirements of plants for life and growth (air, light, water, nutrients from the soil, and room to grow) and how they vary from plant to plant	AH3.3 Identify that humans and some animals have skeletons and muscles for support, protection and movement
PL3.3 Investigate the way in which water is transported within plants	
PL3.4Explore the role of flowers in the life cycle of flowering plants, including pollination, seed formation and seed dispersal	

YEAR 4 SPRING 1	YEAR 4 SPRING 2
All Living Things	**Animals, including humans**
ALT4.1 Identify and name a variety of living things (plants and animals) in the local and wider environment, using classification keys to assign them to groups	AH4.1 Describe the simple functions of the basic parts of the digestive system in humans
ALT4.2 Recognise that environments are constantly changing and that this can some times pose dangers to living things	AH4.2 Identify the different types of teeth in humans and their simple function
	AH4.3 Construct and interpret a variety of food chains, identifying producers, predators and prey

YEAR 5 SPRING 1	YEAR 5 SPRING 2
All Living Things	**Animals, including humans**
ALT5.1 Explain differences in the life cycles of a mammal, an amphibian, an insect and a bird	AH5.1 Describe the changes as humans develop from birth to old age
ALT5. 2 Describe the life process of reproduction in some plants and animals	

YEAR 6 SPRING 1	YEAR 6 SPRING 2
All Living Things ALT6.1 Describe how living things are classified into broad groups according to common observable characteristics and based on similarities and differences, including plants, animals and microorganisms ALT6.2 Give reasons for classifying plans and animals based on specific characteristics	**Animals, including humans** AH6.1 Identify and name the main parts of the human circulatory system and explain the functions of the heart, blood vessels and blood. AH6.2 recognise the impact of diet, exercise, drugs and lifestyle on the way their bodies function AH6.3 Describe the ways in which nutrients and water are transported within animals, including humans

CURRICULUM AND ASSESSMENT MAP FOR SCIENCE: SUMMER

YEAR 1 SUMMER 1	YEAR 1 SUMMER 2
Seasonal Changes E&S1.1 Observe changes across the four seasons E&S1.2 Observe and describe weather associated with the seasons and how day length varies	

YEAR 2 SPRING 1	YEAR 2 SPRING 2

YEAR 3 SUMMER 1	YEAR 3 SUMMER 2
Forces and Magnets FM3.1 Notice that some forces need contact between two objects and some forces act at a distance FM3. 2 Observe how magnets attract or repel each other and attract some materials and not others FM3.3 Compare and group together a variety of everyday materials on the basis of whether they are attracted to a magnet, and identify some magnetic materials FM3.4 Describe magnets as having two poles FM3.5 Predict whether two magnets will attract or repel each other, depending on which poles are facing	

YEAR 4 SUMMER 1	YEAR 4 SUMMER 2
Electricity ELEC4.1 Identify common appliances that run on electricity ELEC4.2 Construct a simple series electrical circuit, identifying and naming its basic parts, including cells, wires, bulbs, switches and buzzers ELEC4.3 Identify whether or not a lamp will light in simple series circuit based on whether or not the lamp is part of a complete loop with battery ELEC4.4 Recognise that a switch opens and closes a circuit and associate this with whether or not a lamp lights in simple series circuit ELEC4.5 Recognise some common conductors and insulators and associate metals with being good conductors	

YEAR 5 SUMMER 1	YEAR 5 SUMMER 2
Earth and Space E&S5.1 Describe the movement of the Earth relative to the Sun in the solar system E&S5.2 Describe the movement of the Moon relative to the Earth E&S5.3 Describe the Sun, Earth and Moon as approximately spherical bodies E&S5.4 Use the idea of the Earth's rotation to explain day and night	

YEAR 6 SUMMER 1	YEAR 6 SUMMER 2
Evolution and Inheritance	**Electricity**
EV6.1 Recognise that living things produce offspring of the same kind, but normally offspring vary and are not identical to their parents	ELEC6.1 Associate the brightness of a lamp or the volume of a buzzer with the number and voltage of cells used in the circuit
EV6.2 Recognise that living things have changed over time and that fossils provide information about living things that inhabited the Earth millions of years ago	ELEC6.2 Compare and give reasons for variations in how components function, including the brightness of bulbs, the loudness of buzzers and the on/off position of switches
EV6.3 Identify how animals and plants are adapted to suit their environment in different ways and that adaptation may lead to evolution	ELEC6.3 Use recognised symbols when representing a simple circuit in a diagram

Essentials

From this chapter, the key points to take away are:

- Long-term planning should move away from preoccupation with topics to specifying the knowledge, skills and understanding taught and assessed across an academic year.

- Curriculum and assessment mapping begins to establish a framework for knowing what is taught and when it should have been learned. This builds the assessment framework into the curriculum from the outset.

- Mapping standards involves thinking about clustering those that share close procedural and conceptual knowledge and understanding into blocks of learning. These will form the basis for medium-term planning.

- A curriculum and assessment map can evolve as teachers work with the suggested pathway through an academic year, identifying where standards may need to be clustered differently.

- Grade-level standards can be given codes so they can be easily referenced. These need to be consistent across a whole school if they are to provide common shorthand for use by staff.

Chapter 3: Unpicking Standards & Teaching Sequences

Standards in the National Curriculum programme of study for English, Mathematics and Science represent a substantial body of knowledge and understanding. They are the basis for developing a teaching sequence and establishing assessments to capture a child's achievement. In order to work effectively with the standards in the National Curriculum, it is imperative to decode what they involve. This chapter draws attention to the importance of unpicking standards to identify their components. Grade-level standards that seem relatively simple on the surface can be complex when unpicked. This has implications for what needs to be taught and assessed to be able to confidently report that children have achieved them. Later in the chapter, attention is focused on development of teaching sequences in a standards-based curriculum. Some instructional strategies are suggested for checking content, procedural and other types of learning are taking place.

Outcomes

By the end of this chapter, you should be able to:

- Recognise the importance of unpicking standards in the National Curriculum programmes of study.

- Identify how deconstructing standards supports the planning of teaching sequences and assessment.

- Devise progressive teaching sequences ensuring skills, knowledge and understanding are introduced logically.

Standards represent a significant knowledge and understanding, usually condensed into a single statement. On the surface, many of the standards in the National Curriculum appear relatively simple and straightforward. However, unpicking what they mean and actually involve can reveal greater complexities that have implications for what is taught and what children must demonstrate in order to achieve them.

There can be a range of interpretations of what skills, knowledge and understanding are contained within a standard. Classroom teachers may interpret a standard differently based on their experience and subject-knowledge. It is unlikely teachers with limited subject-knowledge would identify all the elements in a standard necessary for children to fully achieve it. If the specifics of what is being taught are not established, it follows that what is assessed will be limited. Consequently, quality of achievement could be called into question and considered inflated. A process of unpicking standards and decoding what they entail is an important stage in implementing the National Curriculum programme of study in core subjects.

Deconstructing standards enables school leadership, management and classroom teachers to become familiar with the content of the curriculum in terms of depth and breadth. Later, this translates into ensuring assessment collects a depth and breadth of evidence showing achievement of grade-level standards. There are several advantages and benefits for dedicating time to unpicking standards.

By bringing staff together to unpick standards, an increasingly common understanding of what a broad statement in the curriculum involves can be established. Through doing this collaboratively, teachers can share their interpretation and begin to reach an agreement on the key elements of learning involved. This is the start of establishing a whole-school understanding. Furthermore, teachers in need of developing their subject-knowledge or hold low expectations of what children can achieve are exposed to deeper and more thorough ideas about what standards involve. As the standards are decoded and broken into their key elements and components, the resulting list of skills, knowledge and understanding can be used to form the basis for teaching sequences. The components also offer benchmarks of achievement supporting the focus of assessments.

The major drawback when considering unpicking standards is that a large investment of time is necessary if it is to be done thoroughly. It is worthwhile considering making decoding of standards an on-going process. For example, identifying particular points in the academic year where groups of teachers meet to review how they have unpicked standards giving them an opportunity for them to engage in professional dialogue on whether adequate depth and breadth has been identified.

Standards can be decoded in terms of cognitive demand with taxonomies of the cognitive domain acting as useful tools. Bloom's Taxonomy (1956) is likely to be familiar to many readers. This taxonomy sought to identify verbs that correlated with levels of knowledge elicited through questions, tasks and activities. Devised in 2000 and published in 2001, two associates of Bloom amended the original taxonomy. Here, the original and revised versions are presented alongside one another. They can offer a basis for professionals in primary education conducting their own decoding and deconstruction of grade-level standards.

Taxonomy of the Cognitive Domain for Standards Analysis

Bloom (1956)	Anderson and Krahwohl's Taxonomy (2000, published 2001)
Knowledge This involves remembering or retrieving previously learned material. The following verbs relate to this: *know; identify; relate; list; define; recall; acquire; name; record; recognise.*	**Remembering** Retrieving and recalling knowledge from memory. According to this taxonomy, remembering is when memory is used to produce definitions, facts, lists or recite material.
Comprehension The ability to construct meaning from material. These verbs indicate this cognitive function: *locate; explain; describe; infer; conclude; illustrate; interpret; draw; represent; differentiate.*	**Understanding** Constructing meaning by interpreting, giving examples, classifying, summarising, inferring or comparing and explaining.
Application This refers to the ability to use learned material in new situations. Some verbs related to this are: *apply; relate; develop; use; organise; interpret; demonstrate; calculate; show.*	**Applying** Carrying out or using a procedure taught. Material that has been learned is used to create products (such as models or presentations).

Analysis

Breaking down or distinguishing parts of a whole into its components. Verbs relating to this are: *analyse; compare; examine; contrast; categorise; investigate; classify; deduce; discover; discriminate; separate.*

Analysing

This involves determining how parts relate to one another or an overall idea and purpose. Attributes must be differentiated and distinguished. Graphic representations are often associated with undertaking analysis. For example, constructing graphs, diagrams and charts.

Synthesis

This involves the ability to put components together into a coherent whole. Verbs indicative of this mental function are: *produce; compose; design; assemble; create; prepare; plan; generalise; combine; relate; develop; arrange; construct; derive; write; propose.*

Evaluating

This involves critiquing. In the taxonomy by Anderson and Krahwohl, the ability to evaluate comes before the act of creation or synthesis. It is the precursor to being able to select components to form part of a product.

Evaluation

Material is judged, checked and critiqued. Verbs related to this aspect of the taxonomy are: *assess; evaluate; conclude; argue; decide; rate; select; consider; infer.*

Creating

This involves putting elements together to form a coherent and successful whole. Parts are synthesised to arrive at a new product. In the revised taxonomy, this represents the highest level of mental functioning. For Anderson and Krahwohl, this is akin to synthesis,

The advantage of the updated taxonomy lies in the fact it offers a slightly more logical progression in cognitive demands. For instance, there is a slight reordering of the original taxonomy by Bloom (1956) with Creating (Synthesis in Bloom's version) coming after Evaluation. The revised taxonomy makes greater sense. For example, an individual must recognise elements that need to be combined in order to successfully create a piece of written composition. Note that the verbs identified by Bloom (1956) correlate to the revised taxonomy by Anderson and Krahwohl (2000) despite the amended order of mental functions. National Curriculum standards can therefore be understood using either of the taxonomies.

Let us look at how the taxonomies can shed light on demands placed on children and implications for teaching and assessment using examples of standards from the programme of study for Science. In this worked example of unpicking and decoding standards, the thought process is italicised.

Example of Unpicking and Decoding a Science Standard

> EM4.3 Identify the part played by evaporation and condensation in the water cycle and associate the rate of evaporation with temperature.

This standard uses the verb 'identify' meaning children are expected to know and remember the scientific concepts of evaporation and condensation. These concepts- evaporation and condensation- are substantial ideas when referring to changes of state. Each will need to be explicitly taught so children understand the processes before encountering them in the context of the water cycle. The second substantial element in the standard is children associating rate of evaporation with temperature. A series of benchmarks for a unit of work including this standard will need to include the following:

- *The same material can exist as a liquid and a gas*

- *Evaporation is the process by which liquid changes state and becomes a gas*

- *Recognise that drying involves evaporation of water*

- *Identify increased temperature leads to a greater rate of evaporation*

- *Condensation is when a gas turns into a liquid*

- *Condensation is the reverse of evaporation*

- *Air contains water vapour and it condenses when it comes into contact with a cold surface*

- *Water evaporates from oceans, seas and lakes then condenses to form clouds*

The benchmarks suggested above are by no means exhaustive. It is clear from this example the verbs in a standard are important sources of information relating to cognitive demands. Remembering is suggested in EM4.3 along with understanding when children must explain the water cycle using the conceptual knowledge of evaporation and condensation. Additionally, identification of key terms enables conceptual knowledge to be extracted from the broad language of a standard to inform teaching, learning and assessment. Unpicking standards has formed the basis for the following Year 4 sample unit of work, 'States of Matter'.

Year 4 Autumn 1	SCIENCE UNIT OF WORK: STATES OF MATTER	
Thinking and Working Scientifically Standards	**Content Standards for Science**	**Benchmarks**
ScLK1.1 Asking relevant questions **ScLK1.2 Setting up simple practical enquires, comparative and fair tests** **ScLK1.3 Making accurate measurements using standard units, using a range of equipment for example thermometers and data loggers** **ScLK1.4 Gathering, recording, classifying and presenting data in a variety of ways to help in answering questions** **ScLK1.5 Recording findings using simple scientific language, drawings, labelled diagrams, bar charts and tables** **ScLK1.6 Reporting on findings from enquiries, including oral and written explanations, displays or presentations of results and conclusions** **ScLK1.7 Using results to draw simple conclusions and suggest improvements, new questions and predictions for setting up further tests** **ScLK1.8 Identifying differences, similarities or changes related to simple scientific ideas and processes** **ScLK1.9 Using straightforward scientific evidence to answer questions or to support their findings**	EM4.1 Compare and group materials together, according to whether they are solids, liquids or gases EM4.2 Observe that some materials change state when they are heated or cooled, and measure the temperature at which this happens in degrees Celsius EM4.3 Identify the part played by evaporation and condensation in the water cycle and associate the rate of evaporation with temperature	Identify solids and liquids
		There are liquids other than water
		Liquids do not change in volume when they are poured into a different container
		The same material can exist as both solid and liquid
		Liquids can be changed to a solid by cooling and this is freezing or solidifying
		A solid can be changed to a liquid by heating and this is melting
		Different solids melt at different temperatures
		Melting and solidifying or freezing are changes that can be reversed and are the reverse of each other
		Evaporation is when a liquid turns to a gas
		Explain 'disappearance' of water in a range of situations as evaporation
		Liquids other than water evaporate
		Explain everyday examples of 'drying' in terms of factors affecting evaporation
		Condensation is when a gas turns to a liquid
		Condensation is the reverse of evaporation
		Air contains water vapour and when this hits a cold surface it may condense
		The boiling temperature of water is 100°C
		Water evaporates from oceans, seas and lakes, condenses as clouds and eventually falls as rain
		Water collects in streams and rivers and eventually finds its way to the sea
		Evaporation and condensation are processes that can be reversed
		Interpret the water cycle in terms of the processes involved

Within this unit of work, or medium term plan, the benchmarks derived from unpicking EM4.3 have been included to identify the scope of the standard. It will be noted this example of a unit overview also contains benchmarks arising from a process of breaking down EM4.1 and EM4.2. Clearly, the three standards involve a substantial body of conceptual knowledge and understanding. Let us apply the taxonomy introduced earlier to understanding the demands of EM4.1.

EM4.1 Compare and group materials together, according to whether they are solids, liquids or gases.

The phrase 'compare and group' involves the children engaging in analysis. They will need to recognise the properties of a solid, liquid and gas, which involves an element of remembering. If the children are asked to group a set of materials according to their own criteria, perhaps as an assessment for learning task, they are creating therefore engaged in using higher cognitive functions.

After unpicking the components of standards and cognitive demands, it is necessary to produce a logical teaching sequence with a clear progression in how knowledge and understanding is accumulated. For instance, the order of benchmarks in the 'States of Matter' unit overview may be changed to meet the learning needs of a particular class of children; or sequenced according to an individual teacher's professional judgement. Teaching sequences are examined in more detail later in the chapter.

In Mathematics, standards can be deconstructed to form a systematic and cumulative approach to aspects of number and the number system. The Year 1 programme of study contains four standards bearing a clear relationship to one another.

AS1.1 Read, write and interpret mathematical statements involving addition (+), subtraction (-) and equals (=) signs.

AS1.2 Represent and use number bonds and related subtraction facts within 20.

AS1.3 Add and subtract one-digit and two-digit numbers to 20 (9 + 9, 18 - 9), including zero.

NPV1.5 Read and write numbers from 1 to 20 in digits and words.

These grade-level standards can be translated into a structured programme of work with rigorous benchmarks to aid children in achieving mastery of number bonds to twenty by the end of Year 1. The following extract from *Conquering Primary Maths* (CPM), which is a scheme presented and discussed in Chapter Six, shows a cumulative, structured programme involving systematic progression through explicit benchmarks.

CONQUERING PRIMARY MATHS FOR YEAR ONE

When	Alignment to Standards	Order of Topics & Pace Setting
Autumn 1	NVP1.4 NPV1.3 NPV1.5	Comparisons: Ordering- taller, shorter, longer, above, below, to the right, to the left, behind, between
		Comparison of sets: more, less, equal, many, few
		Number pictures: less than, more than, equal to, not equal to < > = ≠
		Identifying, writing and using 0 and 1; number line
		Identifying, writing and using 2; number line (write and use + - and =
		Comparisons: Number pictures and balancing equations and inequalities (2>1 and 1<2)
Autumn 2	AS1.1 AS1.2 AS1.3 AS1.4	Writing and using 3; number line, practise < > + - = (number bonds within)
		Writing and using 4; number line, practise < > + - = (number bonds within)
		Writing and using 5; number line, practise < > + - = (number bonds within)
		Writing and using 6; number line, practise < > + - = (number bonds within)
		Writing and using 7; number line, practise < > + - = (number bonds within)
		Writing and using 8; number line, practise < > + - = (number bonds within)
Spring 1	AS1.1 AS1.2 AS1.3 AS1.4	Revision and Practise: 0, 1, 2, 3, 4, 5 6, 7 and 8
		Writing and using 9 number line, practise < > + - = (number bonds within)
		Writing and using 10 number line, practise < > + - = (number bonds within)
		Revision and Practise: 0 to 10 and mathematical symbols (number bonds within)
Spring 2	NVP1.4 NVP1.3 NVP1.5 AS1.3 AS1.2 AS1.4	Revision and practice: 0 to 10
		Extending the number line 0-20
		Number bonds and sums to 11
		Number bonds and sums to 12
		Number bonds and sums to 13
		Number bonds and sums to 14
Summer 1	NVP1.3 NVP1.4 NVP1.5 AS1.3 AS1.2 AS1.4	Number bonds and sums to 15
		Number bonds and sums to 16 & 17
		Number bonds and sums to 18 & 19
		Number bonds and sums to 20

The sequential progression in acquiring and using number bonds to twenty would therefore dictate teaching, learning and assessment in the classroom. In the complete programme for Year 1, other aspects of the Mathematics programme of study have been taken into account. As noted before, Chapter Eight provides further explanation.

In the context of Science and Mathematics, two examples of unpacking standards and their transference into overviews of what is taught and assessed have been offered in this chapter. At this point, the broad principles for sequencing teaching and learning activities are considered.

Teaching and learning activities are basically the means through which children learn and demonstrate particular skills, knowledge and understanding relative to specific standards. Four main types of teaching and learning activities can be conceived in a standards-based model.

Four Types of Teaching and Learning Activities

Introductory Activities   Introductory activities are intended to generate interest and engagement in a unit of work.

Instructional Activities   These provide opportunities for children to learn skills, knowledge and understanding.

They are logically sequenced, link to specified standards and benchmarks. Instructional activities contain opportunities to assess how well children are achieving expected outcomes.

Assessment Activities   Assessment activities are designed to elicit information on children achieving standards. As far as possible, they should be interesting and stimulating.

Culminating Activities   Culminating activities allow children to demonstrate learning against most or all standards in a unit of work. They are end of unit assessment tasks. A good quality culminating activity is planned to give children opportunities to apply knowledge and skills.

Together, the four main types of activities embody a progression in terms of what children are asked to do; 'they serve as the building blocks to the necessary knowledge, skills [...] needed to attain the standard' (Snow *et al*, 2001, p. 29). There is a need for progression through types of teaching and learning activities and logically ordered and sequenced standards-based skills, knowledge and understanding.

Sequential and Progressive Teaching Sequences Example

In the second half of the Autumn Term Year 3 are taught 'Unit 3B: Add and Subtract Three-Digit Numbers'. The medium term plan, which can be found in Chapter Six, specifies these standards alongside others:

AS3.1 Add and subtract mentally a three-digit number and ones

AS3.2 Add and subtract mentally a three-digit number and tens

First of all, it is possible to see the standards are logically grouped: adding ones, tens and the medium-term plan also includes adding and subtracting hundreds to a three-digit number. These standards are therefore landmarks for the teaching and learning activities, but a finer logical progression in knowledge and understanding needs to be planned.

Standard	Progression in Learning	Commentary
NPV3.2	Revision of place value: recognising the position of digits in a number denotes their worth. Begin with focusing on tens and units then hundreds, tens and units.	AS3.1 and AS3.2 require children to have this conceptual understanding. As a result, it is logical that this prior learning is activated and the children are told how it links to new learning.
AS3.1	Identify that adding ones to a three-digit number only requires the digit in the unit column to be manipulated (not crossing tens boundary). Identify that subtracting ones from a three-digit number only requires the digit in the unit column to be manipulated (not crossing tens boundary).	Adding and subtracting of ones has been broken down to the simplest starting point. At this stage, children manipulate the digit in the unit column and are not required to cross the tens boundary. For example, adding 1 to 347 simply involves increasing the unit column to give 348.
AS3.1	Identify that adding ones to a three-digit number can involve crossing the tens boundary. Identify that subtracting ones from a three-digit number can involve crossing the tens boundary.	The teaching sequence now introduces crossing the tens boundary. So, children learn to work with calculations such as 567 + 4 requiring manipulation of tens and units. In the case of subtraction, children are taught to recognise how to manipulate digits in calculations such as 345 – 6.
AS3.2	Identify that adding ten to a three-digit number requires the digit in the tens column to be manipulated (no crossing of boundary). Identify that subtracting ten from a three-digit number requires the digit in the tens column to be manipulated (no crossing of boundary). Add and subtract tens involving crossing of boundary, for example: 356 + 60.	In regards to AS3.2, the standard has been broken down into logical stages to enable children to secure this grade-level standard. There is progression from manipulation of the digit in the tens column to calculating where crossing the hundred boundary is required.

Template for Planning Teaching and Learning Sequences

Standards	Sequence of Skills, Knowledge and Understanding	Teaching and Learning Activities

Standards are referenced in the first column and benchmarks or components indicated in the second column. When looking down the second column, there should clear progression in how skills, knowledge and understanding are being acquired. The third column can be used to note ideas of teaching activities that will ensure children achieve the standards.

Unpicking standards and establishing a logical sequencing of skills, knowledge and understanding so all children reach grade-level expectations are vital given the nature of the revised National Curriculum for England. In devising progressive teaching sequences, attention also needs to be given to the nature of intended learning opportunities and activities.

Learning opportunities can focus on acquisition of knowledge and skills. Conceptual and procedural understanding is developed. Another element of learning opportunities covers the role of the teacher and children. At times, a teaching sequence may rely more on direct instruction or shift the emphasis to children working collaboratively. Teaching and learning activities will also need to involve children in applying and reflecting on what they know and can do. In a standards-based curriculum, the design of instruction in a teaching sequence will be influenced by what is being learned and the best way of checking children are actually learning it.

Snow *et al* (2001), writing from the Canadian perspective and standards-based curriculum of Vermont, provide some useful suggestions for teaching strategies related to learning opportunities involving content and concepts or skills, processes and procedures. This has been adapted to offer teachers in England a quick reference guide. As part of taking standards apart, classroom teachers should have gained insight into whether they are dealing with content or developing conceptual or procedural understanding through their teaching. The ideas offered by Snow *et al* (2001) can help instruction match the type of learning happening in lessons.

Teaching Strategies for Content and Concept Learning Opportunities

Three Minute Stop

Every ten to fifteen minutes, ask the children to do the following to summarise what they are learning and what they have understood. Identify any difficulties and address these. This is reminiscent of mini-plenaries used in primary schools, but applied more intensively.

KWL Grids

Before a topic or task, ask the children to identify what they already know (K) and what they want to learn and know (W). After teaching and learning activities, the children record what they have actually learned (L).

Examples and Non-Examples

Present the children with clear examples and non-examples of the concept they are learning.

This is an example of a word changing meaning when a prefix is added: unhappy

This is not an example: happy

This is an example: unfriendly

This is not an example: friendly

Several pairs of examples and non-examples can be given so children can make their own statements on the defining characteristics of a concept. Children can go on to produce their own examples and non-examples to demonstrate they have learned and understood a concept.

Graphic Organisers

Create representations of information in a variety of ways.

Facts and characteristics can be grouped using a Venn diagram, for example.

Events can be sequenced into chronological order.

Cause and effect patterns can be represented pictorially.

Mind maps can be generated to show the components involved and their relationships.

For grade-level standards involving skills, processes and procedures, there are several strategies that can be used to promote learning.

Teaching Strategies for Skills, Processes and Procedural Acquisition

Think Aloud

The teacher thinks aloud as a skill or procedure is demonstrated. Children can be asked to think aloud as they work on a task to enable the teacher to ascertain what has been understood.

Written Steps

Steps necessary to complete a task or activity are provided in written form. This could relate to what is needed to read a bar chart successfully in Mathematics and Science. It is applicable to any aspect of learning where several stages are needed.

Mental Rehearsal

Children are taught to mentally rehearse steps involved in a procedure before carrying them out.

Flow Charts

Teaching children to create flow charts can help them to create a visual representation of how steps in a process or procedure are linked

These four strategies promote children starting to internalise the steps needed to engage with specific tasks or procedures.

Critical Questions

The critical questions in this chapter should help guide with planning progressive teaching and learning sequences.

What are the standards that the children need to achieve? How will you know?

Referring to the standards identified in a unit of work, determine what it is expecting children to know, understand and be able to do.

Unpick the standard to form benchmarks to guide a teaching sequence.

Establish the cognitive demands involved.

What are the teaching and learning activities needed for children to learn and demonstrate skills, knowledge and understanding?

Plan the teaching and learning activities that will enable children to acquire skills, knowledge and understanding identified in relation to a standard.

The standards must be kept in mind and teaching and learning activities explicitly linked to these.

Match instructional strategies to the demands of standards: content, concepts, skills and procedural understanding.

How will teaching and learning activities be sequenced?

It is important to check they are sequenced into a logical order so there is a progression in how skills, knowledge and understanding are built.

Are there teaching and learning activities that will be entirely dedicated for assessment?

This involves identifying tasks and activities where more detailed information on children's achievement is elicited.

Essentials

From this chapter, the key points to take away are:

- Unpicking standards enables the complexity and scope of standards to be determined.

- Collaborative unpacking can help promote a common interpretation of standards

- The components of a standard guide teaching and learning activities. Sequencing of teaching and learning activities needs to reflect a logical progression in the acquisition of knowledge, skills and understanding.

- Teaching and learning activities are devised to provide children with opportunities to acquire specific knowledge and understanding in relation to identified standards. The concept of congruency is at the centre of this.

Chapter 4: Assessing Without Levels

*National Curriculum level descriptors have been a profound aspect of monitoring progress, achievement and attainment. The performance of children, reduced to sublevels and corresponding average points scores, have been used to track how well children are progressing within and between year groups. With the revised National Curriculum, level descriptors that reduce a child's learning to abstract notions of 2B, 3A, 4C and so on become obsolete. The Department for Education has made its position clear: 'the current system of 'levels' used to report children's attainment and progress will be removed. It will not be replaced'. Schools are expected to establish their own means of formative assessment to show what children are learning and their achievement against grade-level standards in the programme of study for Mathematics, English and Science. This chapter addresses the issue of how to assess progress and achievement without levels. Assessing without levels involves a shift to a mode of classroom practice where teachers use their professionalism and autonomy to focus assessments on promoting quality learning and teaching. Chapter Four therefore gives intense consideration to **how** grade-level standards are assessed against the background of previous chapters focused on **what** is taught and assessed.*

Outcomes

By the end of this chapter, you should be able to:

- Define what is meant by school-based assessment and understand how this operates on a short-cycle within a unit of work.

- Explain the primary purposes of school-based assessment.

- Define what is meant by reliability and validity, recognising their importance when using school-based assessment.

- Recall the major types of school-based assessment and the ways in which a child's achievement on these can be scored.

- Identify how to construct rubrics to establish what children know and are able to do against grade-level standards.

Standards-based assessment or school-based assessment (two terms for the same practice) determine how children are performing against grade-level expectations. School-based assessment, sometimes abbreviated to SBA or called classroom-based assessment, gives teachers the responsibility for devising their own tasks, activities and the means of scoring children's learning against specified standards. Classroom teachers are expected to exercise professional judgement in selecting appropriate means of assessing learning; using their expertise to measure achievement using a range of tools. In a standards-based curriculum, 'assessment should be viewed as a tool to measure the effectiveness of teaching and learning processes, and should not be interpreted as the objective of [a child's] learning experience' (Mansor *et al*, 2013, p. 102). Effectively, assessment constantly drives teaching and learning and is never a single event occurring at the end of a unit or other fixed points in an academic year. Assessment sharply focuses on facilitating progress as a teaching sequence develops so all children have the opportunity to secure grade-level knowledge and understanding. The child and their learning are at the centre rather than producing data indicating very little about what they know, understand and are able to do.

School-based assessment involves four stages, which form a cycle. This short-cycle of assessment operates regularly in a unit of work.

Assessment planning comes first and should be prioritised by classroom teachers. Multiple assessments are planned and written ahead of a teaching sequence commencing. Following several steps in a teaching sequence, the associated assessment provides evidence of achievement for teachers to determine how well children are acquiring skills, knowledge and understanding. By scrutinising this evidence, a timely response can be made to ensure children are retaught content that they are experiencing difficulties with before moving on. The outcome of analysing evidence of children's learning then leads to decision-making: *Who has mastered the components of a standard taught? Who needs further direct teaching? How will the teaching sequence be adapted to make the necessary provision for all children to achieve what they should? If the vast majority have achieved mastery, what assessments need to be planned for the next stages in the teaching sequence?* (Mansor *et al*, 2013; Snow *et al*, 2001; Brown, 2011). Given the central role of short-cycle assessment driving teaching, Chapter Five is dedicated to assessment planning against grade-level standards and their components.

School-based assessment against nationally determined standards has a relentless focus on learning, progress and mastery of skills, knowledge and understanding. Assessing against specific grade-level standards involves criterion-referenced assessment. As shown in Chapter Three, standards may involve several components that need to be met in order to demonstrate complete achievement of the broader grade-level standard. The components and grade-level standards are therefore the criteria that need to be the focus of assessment. Tasks clearly link to selected benchmarks of achievement or all aspects of a standard. National Curriculum levels were criterion-referenced, but were ultimately reductionist in giving achievement as 2C, 3C and so on. Furthermore, a child may very well be judged as working at 4C but have a very different profile of strengths and weaknesses. The revised National Curriculum specifies standards, the criterion and in the bluntest terms, children will either achieve them or not. It is worth reinforcing and expanding on the primary purpose of assessment in a standards-based model.

For Snow *et al* (2001, p. 42), 'assessment is an integral part of instruction. It is the process of quantifying, describing, gathering data about, or giving feedback about performance'. Assessment is not a single static event. By referring to it as a 'process', Snow *et al* (2001) stress the importance of assessment to monitor the impact of teaching on learning and determining what is taught next and to whom. Another key phrase in the definition by Snow *et al* (2001) is 'giving feedback about performance'. Effective school-based assessment will give specific information to a range of stakeholders. First and foremost, children know what they have learnt and what they need to move forward. Parents and carers have a clear picture of what their child knows and is able to do in relation to grade-level standards as they receive qualitative information on what has been learned. More broadly, school leadership and management teams can identify elements of the curriculum where teaching needs to be strengthened in relation to very specific aspects of a subject. There is a much greater transparency in terms of what is being taught, how well it is taught, and how well it is being learned. The autonomy that teachers assume when assessing without levels makes them no less accountable. In fact, accountability is intensified as the achievement of grade-level standards, within a year group or by the end of a phase, is non-negotiable.

Six desirable features of assessment in a standards-based curriculum have been articulated in the context of the United States of America. These are transferable principles applicable to assessing children within England's renewed National Curriculum.

Six Desirable Features of Standards-Based Assessment

Feature	Explanatory Notes
Authentic tasks and activities	Tasks and activities involve real world problems or situations where skills and knowledge are applied so children see the relevance of learning to everyday life.
Driver of the curriculum	Assessment reflects the body of knowledge and understanding the curriculum requires teachers to teach.
Promote progress of children	Children know what is expected, what will be assessed and how this is going to be done.
Increase quality of teaching	Frequent assessment gives a teacher feedback on what children are learning. Where difficulties arise, classroom teachers are made responsible for seeking out alternative approaches to teaching particular skills, knowledge and understanding.
Continued Professional Development	This feature bears a strong relationship to the point made above.
Increase accountability	There is greater accountability to ensuring coverage of the curriculum with an appropriate depth and breadth of learning and assessment. Classroom teachers should relentlessly focus on moving all children towards grade-level standards.

Adapted from the Education Commission of the States (2002).

School-based assessment is therefore tightly focused on promoting quality of teaching, the professional responsibility of classroom teachers is to develop their practice and a child's learning. Of course, members of school leadership and management teams will be highly conscious of the fact that assessment information is used to judge school effectiveness as part of external inspection. This involves high stakes with inspection judgements of less than 'Outstanding' and 'Good' leading to further scrutiny. In a standards-based curriculum, by ensuring school-based assessment practices are rigorous, a school will be both data rich and information rich on how children are achieving in relation to grade-level standards. Being data rich involves having numerical information showing achievement against grade-level standards within and between year groups. In a standards-based curriculum, being information rich is far more important for classroom teachers. Without diagnosing areas for development, teaching will not address the gaps in a child's knowledge and understanding. As part of the supplementary materials, a means of tracking and summarising achievement and progress year-on-year is suggested.

Traditionally, classroom-based assessment has involved the use of tests that mimic the structure and organisation of those sat at the end of a year or key stage. For example, a series of pitch and expectations materials were produced as part of resources linked to the *Renewed Framework* (2006) with many of the questions taken directly from test papers. Permeation of testing into everyday classroom practice is arguably a natural response to working in a high-stake education system. If testing is how children are ultimately assessed, then it logically follows teaching will reflect this. There are some advantages to test-style assessment in a standards-based curriculum.

Brown (2011) highlights that children and young people can be motivated to make significantly greater effort when they know a test is how they will be assessed. Achievement on tests is socially acceptable and desirable in many countries. However, Brown (2011) is making a generalisation; not all children will perform well on tests and this approach to assessment only provides a snapshot of what children know and are able to do. School-based assessment in a curriculum driven by grade-level standards has moved beyond test-style tasks. Countries stressing the professional and autonomy of teachers to undertake dynamic assessment have promoted the use of multiple measures to capture children's achievement. In the standards-based approach found in New Zealand, 'there is wide spread confidence in the professionalism of teachers and New Zealanders see that there are many routes to life success rather than just [...] high examination scores'. Brown (2011, p. 2) observes: This [has made] it somewhat easier to implement a rich multi-faceted approach to SBA'. Looking towards Malaysia, the Ministry of Education introduced a standards-based curriculum in primary schools and school-based assessment giving teachers the responsibility for assessing achievement and progress towards intended learning outcomes. A small-scale case study by Mansor *et al* (2013) found teachers in their sample responded positively to implementing school-based assessment after receiving continued professional development. It was reported that individual teachers found they were able to use their creativity to develop assessment tasks and the standards-based approach encouraged them to develop teaching strategies to impact more powerfully on children's learning.

From this we can learn that assessing without levels in England requires giving teaching staff autonomy and the professional knowledge and understanding to gather multiple measures of children's learning. The standards-based approach in England requires teachers to have an understanding of different sources of evidence that demonstrate learning and having the capability to develop a range of tasks and appropriate scoring guides for these. Whatever type of assessment is devised, validity and reliability need to be at the forefront of a classroom teacher's mind. If an assessment lacks validity or reliability, the evidence it provides for children achieving grade-level standards will be highly dubious. Given the importance of validity and reliability in assessment, they are considered in more detail before looking at specific types of school-based assessment.

The Importance of Reliability and Validity in School-Based Assessment

Validity and reliability underpin effective assessment in a standards-based curriculum. The two concepts are often discussed independently, but they have a close relationship. Simply defined, reliability is the consistency of measurement. If measurements were repeated over and over again, a reliable assessment would give similar results on each occasion. Validity basically refers to whether what an assessment measures what it claims to measure. However, a reliable assessment may not be valid: it produces consistent results, but does not actually measure what it claims to measure. Equally, a valid assessment may measure what it purports to, yet not provide reliable results each time it is administered. Reliability and validity are key concerns in psychological and psychometric testing (Coaley, 2010) and, in school-based assessment, the need for tools devised by teachers to demonstrate both validity and reliability is no less vital (Bishop *et al*, 2011).

Validity is a key component for ensuring teachers can have confidence in the assessment tools they devise. Later in this chapter, closed response tasks and short answer responses, as evidence of achievement against standards, are discussed. These often have high validity because it is reasonably easy to design them so they tap into specific knowledge and concepts. More authentic assessments, such as products and performances, involve higher-order thinking and involve several variables. The extent to which assessment of products and performances are valid will depend on how effectively the variables have been identified and the different levels of proficiency for each of these defined.

There are two types of validity that have particular relevance to the assessment tools described in this chapter and need to be kept in mind during Chapter Five where assessment planning is the focus.

Type of Validity	Definition	Example(s)/Non-Example(s)
Content	Content validity refers to how the content of a test reflects the standards taught in a unit of work; or by a particular stage of the academic year.	An example is: Children have been taught to calculate unit fractions of number and quantities. The test items all involve children finding fractions of a number or measurements and so on. A non-example is: An end of term assessment in Mathematics that only covers standards taught in the previous two weeks. This would not have content validity and therefore not provide evidence for overall achievement in that term. It is only measuring what has been taught most recently.
Construct	The extent to which the assessment reflects evidence-based theories.	An example is: The rubric for reading comprehension and the observation schedule (given later in the chapter) reflect grade-level standards. They also have foundations in the cognitive model of text comprehension.

Based on Coaley (2010) and Bishop *et al* (2011).

Just as there are different forms of validity, several types of reliability commonly discussed in relation to assessment exist. The two types of reliability of relevance for school-based assessment are inter-rater reliability and test-retest reliability.

Inter-rater reliability refers to whether two individuals presented with the same evidence of learning would arrive at the same judgement on how well a child has achieved grade-level standards. Schools who regularly build in time for moderation of children's work in English, Mathematics or Science are in fact developing inter-rater reliability. This form of reliability can be promoted through training on the use of particular rubrics or observation schedules and collecting exemplars of children's work showing achievement at different levels of proficiency.

Test-retest reliability involves administering an assessment on one occasion followed by a second administration of the same task after a period of time. If the scores on the first administration are close to those achieved the second time the test is taken, then it can be described as reliable. Test-retest reliability tends to be associated with standardised assessments produced by experts in psychological assessment and psychometrics. Statistical analysis is applied to the two sets of results to arrive at a coefficient of how reliable the assessment is (Coaley, 2010). As Bishop *et al* (2011) note, test-retest reliability is not normally done with teacher-devised assessments. It is, however, worth being aware of this form of reliability if schools use standardised, norm-referenced tests. For example, tests determining a reading age and enable the discrepancy between this and chronological age to be established.

Understanding reliability and validity is essential when working in a standards-based curriculum. Teachers must use or devise tools that generate consistent and informative data showing learning taking place against the standards.

There are several sources of evidence that can be analysed to establish what children have learned: closed response tasks; short answer activities; products and performances. Each will be addressed in turn with examples given as necessary. Afterwards, appropriate mark schemes or scoring guides to determine how children have performed against grade-level standards are outlined. The intended source of evidence and how it will be marked or scored are inextricably linked. One cannot exist without the other. In a standards-based curriculum, the task and means by which performance will be assessed are set before a teaching sequence begins. This echoes one of the desirable features given by the Education Commission of the States (2002) and assessment planning for a unit of work is the focus of the next chapter where Assessment Plans are introduced as an enhancement of short-term planning.

Closed Response Tasks

This form of assessment covers tasks where children select an answer from those provided for them. It may involve giving a 'yes' or 'no' response, indicating answers to multiple-choice questions or matching activities. Children do not construct a response or answer; they are simply asked to find the correct one(s) given in the task. Such an assessment is usually easy to mark or score because the answers are non-negotiable.

Caution needs to be exercised when interpreting and reporting the outcomes of closed task response. The task could be scored numerically, recording the number of correct answers. This is appropriate if the task is focused on a narrow body of knowledge. For instance, the multiplication tables for six. In the following example, all items are controlled so only knowledge and understanding of verbs is tapped into. Where more than one standard is being sampled, scoring becomes more complex as an analysis needs to be undertaken to ascertain which of these requires further teaching.

Closed response tasks are only one source of evidence of a child's learning.

In the following example, the first two questions are closed response. The third question is perhaps better described as a short answer item.

Example of Closed Response Items

1. Underline the nouns in red and the verbs in blue. Do this for each sentence.

The child is running to the shop.

The children were sitting on the sofa.

These bikes are broken.

Where are my keys?

This bike is broken.

A child was sitting on the sofa.

The children are running to the shop.

Where is my key?

8 marks

2. Find the verbs in these sentences.

Martin threw the ball to James.

They eat later.

She ate all of her dinner.

The children played in the park.

I am playing with my toys.

5 marks

3. Change these into sentences by adding a verb.

He apples.

_____

They to the shops.

_____

Jason the piano.

_____

3 marks

Example of Closed Response Scoring Guide

1. Both the verb and the noun in each sentence is required for the award of one mark. Do not award half a mark where only the verb or noun has been identified.

2. One mark for each verb identified. Do not award a mark where the verb and other words preceding or following it have been included in the answer.

3. Acceptable responses in order of test items are: 'ate' or 'eats'; 'go' or 'went' and 'plays' ('is playing' can be accepted). Other verbs can be accepted where they make sense.

Short Answer Tasks

Short answer assessments will have pre-determined responses that are required, but the children are required to generate these. Take the third question in the previous example of a test-style grammar task. Children generate the verb and write it therefore it is a short answer item. Short answer tasks could involve a sentence or several sentences, one or two written paragraphs or involve them in constructing a concept map to demonstrate their knowledge and understanding. For example, when children are asked to write down why a mathematical statement is true or false, their explanation can be classed as a short answer response. A series of reading comprehension questions may involve a mixture of closed response and short answer items.

Scoring becomes more complex with short answer items; it will involve professional judgement as to whether a response is sufficiently detailed. The mark scheme, or scoring guide, should be written in advance so classroom teachers are clear about what will or will not be accepted as an answer. Expectations of subject specific terms a child should know and be able to use must be built into the scoring guide to maintain high expectations and ensure these are taught and learned.

Products and Performances

Products and performances are responses constructed by the children. They typically involve them drawing together skills, knowledge and understanding taught in a unit of work. A product can be a piece of extended writing in English or another area of the curriculum, an independent investigation in Mathematics or some other substantial artefact demonstrating their learning. Performances tend to be responses that involve children showing or telling what they can do. This could be carrying out practical work in Science or performing a play in English.

Constructed responses involving products and performances are more cognitively complex than closed response or short answer tasks (Bishop *et al*, 2011). Children are engaged in higher-order thinking and are required to apply knowledge and understanding they have been taught rather than simply reproducing it on-demand. This can be referred to as an authentic assessment. There are varying degrees of authenticity, but this book simply takes authentic assessment as a task where children use and apply what they have learned. The following table summarises the differences in terms of depth, breadth and authenticity of assessment between the constructed responses discussed in this chapter.

Constructed Responses, Authenticity and Cognitive Demand

Products and Performances	Short answer responses		Closed response
Most authentic	←	→	Least authentic
Cognitively most complex	←	→	Cognitively least complex
In-depth coverage	←	→	Coverage of content
Response structured by the child	←	→	Response provided by task

Assessing Using Checklists

Checklists are ideal for assessing procedural knowledge and understanding. These are effectively success criteria, which many primary schools will already be familiar with. They could be used to assess children writing within a particular genre or text-type or stages necessary for correct computation in Mathematics. Checklists must be devised with the grade-level standards in mind or components of a standard. For procedural tasks, the checklist should reflect the logical steps that need to be taken. This means children can use them to guide their independent work and for the purpose of self-assessment. Checklists can be used in conjunction with instructional strategies for procedural knowledge and understanding suggested in Chapter Three.

Example of a Checklist in Mathematics

Let us presume children in Year 3 are being taught to achieve the following grade-level standard:

AS3.4 Add and subtract numbers with up to three-digits using the efficient written method of columnar addition and subtraction.

There are several steps required to use column addition and subtraction successfully assuming children have secured adequate knowledge and understanding of place value. In this checklist, the children are working on column addition where crossing of the tens or hundred barrier is not required. The method has been demonstrated and children are practising the procedure. Children are each given a checklist to stick into their book and refer to as they work.

Column Addition Checklist	How have I done?	
	Me	My teacher
Line digits up so they are in the correct place value column		
Rule a line under the calculation once it is in a column		
Make sure the addition sign has been written at the left-hand side of the numbers to be added		
Begin by adding units followed by tens then hundreds		

At the end of the lesson, children can tick to indicate what they have achieved. The teacher can then confirm this or draw children's attention to elements of column addition they need to pay more attention to in order to be able to do it successfully.

Assessing Achievement with Rubrics

Rubrics are criterion- or standards-referenced scoring guides that define quality performance or products constructed by children. They can be used to discriminate between proficiency in skills and abilities against specific criteria, the grade-level standard(s). There are several types of rubric: holistic, analytic, generalised and task-specific.

It is quite easy to become overwhelmed by trying to identify the distinctions between the four types of rubric. For example, an analytic rubric for reading comprehension may cover several criteria against which children's performance is measured. This can be used across a range of reading tasks also making it a generalised rubric. A holistic rubric focused on assessing one element of children's achievement may also be a generalised rubric. For instance, a rubric focused on sentence structure addresses one element of writing. However, the need for accurate sentence construction is applicable to all written work therefore the boundary between holistic and generalised rubrics becomes blurred.

Given some of the complexities in describing types of rubric, especially given the potential for hybrid forms, this chapter summarises the four types by comparing holistic and analytic then generalised and task-specific rubrics. This is provided for those readers who wish to be more precise about the type of rubrics used in school-based assessment. For the purpose of simplicity, this book will then proceed by making a broad two-way distinction: generalised and task-specific.

Comparing Holistic and Analytic Rubrics

Holistic Rubric	Analytic Rubric
Provide a single score based on an overall impression of a child's performance on a task	Provides detailed information
It only covers one dimension or criterion	This type of rubric covers several dimensions or criteria
It has the advantage of quick scoring and gives an overview of achievement	An advantage of analytic rubrics is that it can give feedback on specific aspects of performance, strengths and areas for development
	An analytic rubric can promote consistency in judgements across children and between assessors
A disadvantage of this type of rubric is that it does not provide detailed information and it is not always possible to give one overall score	It can take longer to score and this can be a disadvantageous aspect of using analytic rubrics

Analytic rubrics are identifiable when several criteria to be assessed are included whereas a holistic rubric will focus on a single grade-level standard or component of this.

Comparing Generalised and Task-Specific Rubrics

Generalised Rubric	Task-Specific Rubric
These are general across tasks	Unique to a task or activity
The same rubric can be used across different tasks	A different rubric would need to be developed for each unique task or activity intended to assess children's performance
Feedback may not always be specific enough	An advantage is that specific assessment of performance can be determined
	It can be difficult to construct a rubric for all specific tasks and activities

Examples of Generalised Rubrics

The generalised rubrics that follow have been devised to aid classroom teachers assess children's reading comprehension at Lower and Upper Key Stage 2. They are generalised rubrics because they can be used to score children's achievement across tasks. The rubrics contain several strands or criteria referenced to standards in the National Curriculum programme of study for English. This means they can be used to build a profile of children's strengths and areas for development across various components of text comprehension. By including several dimensions, the rubric is also analytic. To be precise, we have generalised-analytic rubrics for reading comprehension. Child-friendly versions of the rubrics could be devised to assist children in monitoring their own learning and progress.

Where rows have been shaded in grey, this indicates aspects of comprehension that can be assessed *during* the act of reading. The rubrics are designed to move from activities *before* reading, indicators of achievement to be tapped into *during* reading followed by how understanding of a text is demonstrated *after* reading.

READING COMPREHENSION RUBRIC (LOWER KEY STAGE 2)	Year 3 Exceeding / Year 4 Expected	Year 3 Expected / Year 4 Emerging	Year 3 Emerging / Year 4 Well Below	Year 3 and Year 4 Well Below
Making Connections/ Prior Knowledge	Uses background knowledge to enhance comprehension and interpretation. Makes text-to-text and text-to-self connections; uses author schema with familiar texts to make predictions	Relates background knowledge and experience to text	Talks about what text reminds them of but cannot explain or relate response clearly to the text	Does not make connections with text
Questioning RC3.2 / RC4.2	Asks questions to enhance meaning derived; can easily answer questions; beginning awareness of different types of questions	Asks questions relevant to text; can answer questions	Asks questions about text; may confuse questions and statements	Does not ask questions
Visualisation RC3.4 / RC4.4	Describes own sensory images; images can be elaborated from the literal text and demonstrated using any modality	Describes some sensory images tied directly to text or description of the picture constructed in text	Can describe some simple sensory images, mostly related to text	Does not describe simple sensory images related to the text
Determining Importance RC3.4 / 3.5 RC3.5 / 4.5	Identifies words, characters and/or events as more important to overall meaning; makes some attempt to explain reasoning	Identifies some concepts in text as more important to text meaning (character, plot, main idea or setting)	Inaccurate attempts to identify some concepts (characters, plot, main idea or setting)	Random guessing
Comprehension Monitoring RC3.1 / RC4.1	Identifies location and type of difficulty and articulates need to solve the problem	Identifies difficulties and articulates need to solve problem; does not necessarily articulate what the problem is	Has difficulties with text but sees no need to resolve them	No awareness of own difficulties with text
Inferring RC3.3 / RC4.3	Draws conclusions and makes predictions using examples from text	Draws conclusions and makes predictions that are consistent with text and background knowledge	Attempts prediction or conclusion; inaccurate or unsubstantiated by the text or with the text	Does not attempt prediction or conclusion
Synthesis RC3.4 / RC4.4	Retells elements of the text in logical sequence; may include some extension to overall message or theme	Retells most key elements in sequence	Randomly retells some elements of the text; events may not be in sequence	Does not retell

READING COMPREHENSION UKS2	Year 5 Exceeding / Year 6 Expected	Year 5 Expected / Year 6 Emerging	Year 5 Emerging / Year 6 Well Below	Year 5 and Year 6 Well Below
Making Connections/ Prior Knowledge	Explains how schema enriches interpretation of text and begins to make connections beyond life experience and immediate text	Relates background knowledge an experience to text and expands the interpretations of text using schema; may discuss schema related to author/text structure	Makes simple connections but cannot explain them or the connections are irrelevant to the text	Makes no connections between text and background knowledge
Questioning RC5.2 / RC6.2 RC5.12 / RC6.12	Uses questions to challenge the text (author's purpose, theme or point of view)	Asks questions to deepen meaning of text; may explain how the questions enhance comprehension (metacognition)	Asks questions only to clarify meaning	Asks only literal questions
Visualisation RC5.7 / RC6.7	Creates and describes multi-sensory images that extend and enrich the text and can explain how those images enhance comprehension	Describes own mental images, usually visual; images are somewhat elaborated from literal text	Describes some visual or other sensory images; may be tied directly to text or description of the picture in the text	Cannot describe sensory images
Determining Importance RC5.5 / RC6.5	Identifies at least one key concept, idea or theme in overall text meaning and clearly explains why	Identifies words, characters and/or overall meaning and makes some attempt to explain reasoning	Identifies some elements as more important to text meaning	Guesses randomly or inaccurately attempts to identify important elements
Comprehension Monitoring RC5.1 / RC6.1	Identifies at least one strategy to build meaning when comprehension breaks down; can articulate which strategies are most important for a given text	Identifies problem at word, sentence or schema level; can articulate and use a strategy to fix comprehension breakdown, usually at word or sentence level	Identifies difficulties, comprehension breakdown is often at word level, little or no sense of the need to solve the problem; main strategy is to sound out	Little or no conscious awareness of reading process
Inferring RC5.3 / RC6.3 RC5.4 / RC6.4 RC5.13 / RC6.13	Develops predictions, interpretations and/or conclusions about the text and the reader's background knowledge or ideas and beliefs	Draws conclusions and/or can explain the source of the conclusion or prediction	Draws conclusions or makes predictions that are consistent with the text or schema	Attempts to make predictions or draw conclusions, without using the text or by using the text inappropriately to defend the statement
Synthesis RC5.5 / RC6.5	Stops frequently to reflect on text meaning; relates to the story or genre in a personal way; can identify key theme(s); may articulate how this process has created new meaning upon completion of text	Stops frequently to reflect on text meaning; uses own schema and story elements to enhance meaning; may identify key theme	Stops periodically to identify text events and may incorporate schema into interpretation	Stops occasionally or at the end of a text and identifies some text elements

Example of a Task-Specific Rubric

A task-specific rubric is written for a particular classroom activity. It should contain language that explicitly connects the rubric to the task that children must complete. This example uses child-friendly language for Science task.

The children in Year 5 are learning about reversible and irreversible changes. The teacher has decided to ask the children to find out what happens when some solids are added to water. Some of the solids available are salt, flour and cornflour. Their performance will be assessed in terms of how they work and think scientifically. The following rubric has been developed to determine the quality of how the children perform planning, conducting and recording what they observed.

What happens when some solids are added to water?				
Criteria	**Starting…**	**On the way…**	**Got it!**	**Outstanding!**
Identifying variables ScUK1.1	I identified variables with help	I identified at least three variables with very little help	I identified all variables without help	I identified all variables and was able to find the variables that needed to be controlled
Carrying out a fair test ScUK1.1	I didn't change just one variable so I don't think my test was fair	I knew that I needed to keep one variable the same with help	I changed only one variable and kept all other variables the same to carry out a fair test	I made sure that only one factor was changed and explained how I controlled the other variables to carry out a fair test
Recording results ScUK1.3	I have used adjectives to describe what I observed, but they may not be very scientific	I used some scientific vocabulary I have been taught. I used some language that isn't scientific.	I recorded my observations using scientific vocabulary I have been taught	I recorded my observations using scientific vocabulary I have been taught and suggested how to find out if some of the changes are reversible

The use of rubrics in school-based assessment can be effective when evaluating how children are performing against criteria linked to grade-level standards. Teachers and children (where child-friendly versions of a rubric are appropriate for use) set the expectations for what needs to be achieved and what degrees of success will look like. Rubrics have not escaped criticism. Bishop *et al* (2011) draw attention to how scoring achievement using rubrics may encourage children to focus on how well they are doing rather than what they are doing and supposed to be learning. The objectivity of rubrics is often challenged. For instance, degrees of quality in a child's performance or product are expressed by particular words and phrases in a rubric. These can be open to varying interpretations. There is a need to ensure inter-rater reliability and consistency in scoring through a process of moderation. One further issue with rubrics is that they are not easy to devise and their construction involves a significant commitment of time. Despite this, classroom teachers still need to possess the capacity to construct their own rubrics as part of ensuring multiple measures of achievement are captured. For this reason, we will look at the steps needed to devise a rubric.

Devising Rubrics

The first step in designing a rubric is ensuring the purpose of this assessment tool is clear. Bishop et al (2011) cite two questions that Allen and Tanner (2006) suggest as the starting point of devising a rubric: What do I need the children to know and be able to do? How will I know they have learnt it and have learned it well? Effective rubrics will focus on measuring a clearly identified performance, product or set of behaviours, use a range of proficiencies to rate achievement and contain specific characteristics indicating the degree to which grade-level standards have been met (Bishop et al, 2011; Snow et al, 2001).

Step Two: Identifying criteria	Decide on the success criteria considering any key words in the standards. The critical components of a standard or standards need to be reflected in a rubric.
Step Three: Creating a scale	Write statements for each of the criteria related to the expected quality of a performance or product.
	After writing the descriptions of expected proficiency, write the performance indicators where quality is above or below the expected level.
Step Four: Check the rubric	Identify if there are any design flaws in the descriptors of proficiency at different levels. For example, check whether the differences between them are precise and not too vague.
	Colleagues can be asked to review it and provide feedback on how well it appears to discriminate between individual

	achievements at different levels of proficiency.
Step Five: Pilot the rubric	Use the rubric to assess children's achievement in relation to the aspects of learning it is intended to measure. The rubric can be edited and amended to make it a more informative assessment tool.
Step Six: Finalise the rubric	After a pilot, produce a final version. Collect samples of children's work that act as exemplars for achievement at different levels of proficiency. These are of particular use when the rubric is utilised by another teacher so they can see how the continuum of success contained in the assessment tool relates to actual examples of children's work.

Throughout the process of designing and refining a rubric, classroom teachers need to keep the concept of validity at the forefront of their minds. The rubric should measure what it claims to measure clearly, concisely and consistently.

Annotated Rubric Template

Criteria	Starting...	On the way...	Got it!	Outstanding!
Criteria come from **specific standards** and/or their **components**. Each row deals with a different criterion.	Identify how to describe learning that is **well below** the expected proficiency in positive terms so children get some sense of achievement.	This describes learning that shows some of the expected elements **emerging**, but an individual is not yet fully secure.	The description of performance for the criteria at the **expected** level.	Performance **exceeding** the expected proficiency is described.
Criteria come from **specific standards** and/or their **components**. Each row deals with a different criterion.	Identify how to describe learning that is **well below** the expected proficiency in positive terms so children get some sense of achievement.	This describes learning that shows some of the expected elements **emerging**, but an individual is not yet fully secure.	The description of performance for the criteria at the **expected** level.	Performance **exceeding** the expected proficiency is described.
Criteria come from **specific standards** and/or their **components**. Each row deals with a different criterion.	Identify how to describe learning that is **well below** the expected proficiency in positive terms so children get some sense of achievement.	This describes learning that shows some of the expected elements **emerging**, but an individual is not yet fully secure.	The description of performance for the criteria at the **expected** level.	Performance **exceeding** the expected proficiency is described.

Rubric Template

Standards/Benchmarks Assessed

Overview of Activity (if Task-Specific)

Criteria	Starting...	On the way...	Got it!	Outstanding!

Assessing Using Observation Schedules

Observations provide evidence of what children do rather than what the children say they do (Baker, 2002, cited in Klingner *et al*, 2007). There are several ways of conducting observations and recording these. Regardless of how observations are recorded, they need to be made in relation to criteria dictated by grade-level standards.

Anecdotal observations and records are brief notes on what a child has done, when and in what context. For this information to be useful in evidencing achievement against grade-level standards or their components, a teacher needs to have a sound knowledge of these so anecdotal notes do not become a generalised narrative. An alternative to anecdotal observation is to use ethnographic recording. The focus is on an individual child. Highly detailed notes are made as frequently as possible. An obvious disadvantage of taking ethnographic notes is the time-consuming nature of the approach although a teacher will have a rich source of information about an individual's learning.

Observations can be structured by devising schedules. Observation schedules specify the aspects of learning and performance in relation to elements of grade-level standards. They narrow the focus of what is observed and offer a means of summarising what a child has done for ease of reference later. Consider the following example.

Example Observation Schedule for Reading

At Lower Key Stage 2, the National Curriculum states that children should:

Understand what they read, in books they can read independently, by:

- checking that the text makes sense to them, discussing their understanding and explaining the meaning of words in context

- asking questions to improve their understanding of a text

- drawing inferences such as inferring characters' feelings, thoughts and motives from their actions, and justifying inferences with evidence

- identifying main ideas drawn from more than one paragraph and summarising these

  [...]

- retrieve and record information from non-fiction

(Department for Education, 2013, pp. 36-37)

These five grade-level standards to be met by the end of Year 4 can be translated into the following observation schedule and checklist (after Klingner et al, 2007). As you read the schedule, try and identify how the standards above have been embedded into the assessment tool to ensure alignment and congruency.

Lower Key Stage 2 Standards-Based Reading Comprehension Observation Schedule

Child's Name		Date	
Rating Scale	**EX = always demonstrated**	**E = almost always demonstrated**	**EM = sometimes evident**
Chooses Appropriate Books			
	Chooses between books that are too easy, at instructional level or frustration level accurately and with confidence		
Reads Independently			
	Initiates own reading		
	Spends almost all independent reading time engaging with the text		
Uses Reading Strategies			
	Rereads to solve problems in the event of comprehension breakdown		
	Uses context and knowledge of word structure to determine meaning of unfamiliar words		
	Uses phonics to decode words, including chunking of syllables to tackle longer words		
	Relates reading to own prior experience and background knowledge		
	Relates reading of a text to other books		
	Makes predictions about what will happen next		
	Summarises the important points within a paragraph and across more than one paragraph		
	Generates questions about content		
Participating in Group Discussion			
	Will engage in talk about the text and other books with peers		
	Raises issues and explains problems and confusions encountered when reading		

In this observation schedule, the grade-level standards are reflected in the criteria to be looked for in children's performance during reading comprehension activities. Ratings from the scale can be inserted in the cells forming the left-hand side of the schedule. The observation schedule is criterion-referenced, aligned to the standards and should allow diagnostic information to be collected on aspects of text comprehension children need to develop further. It is clear that the observation schedule is making a valid assessment of children's learning against grade-level standards. In terms of reliability, a degree of subjectivity is required when working with rating scales. Some questions to bear in mind are: *On the basis of evidence observed, would another teacher draw the same conclusion? Is there an opportunity for another member of staff to also observe the child using the schedule as a means of ensuring consistency in scoring achievement?*

The observation schedule shown here (involving elements of a checklist) is appropriate to assessing reading comprehension. Earlier in this chapter, a rubric as an assessment tool for text comprehension was provided. Both involve the need for inter-rater reliability to ensure consistency in judging children's learning against standards.

Critical Questions

The critical questions provided in this chapter relate to the range of considerations that need to be made when devising or selecting types of school-based assessment. Adapted from Snow *et al* (2001), the questions take the form of a checklist that can be used to evaluate assessments intended for use in a standards-based curriculum. Where an assessment does not meet one of the criteria, this does not mean it should be discarded. In this case, the way in which an assessment can be improved and appropriate adaptations made need to be given thought.

Checklist for Evaluating Assessments

Consequences

N/A	Yes	No	Does the assessment encourage good quality teaching?
N/A	Yes	No	Does the assessment have the potential to provide exemplification of the grade-level standard(s) or content being tested?

Equity

N/A	Yes	No	Does the assessment offer adequate time for children to complete so it reflects their capability rather than text-taking skills?
N/A	Yes	No	Does the assessment tap into the knowledge, skills and understanding that children have had adequate time to acquire through classroom teaching?
N/A	Yes	No	Is the assessment free from cultural, ethnic and gender stereotypes?
N/A	Yes	No	To what extent is the assessment culturally and socially fair? For example, does it contain tasks or situations more likely to be familiar to children of particular backgrounds or gender than another?
N/A	Yes	No	Does the scoring of the assessment allow it to be done so without bias?

N/A	Yes	No	Does the assessment avoid unnecessarily difficult language when assessing content from the standards?
N/A	Yes	No	Does the assessment enable all children to demonstrate what they know and can do in the areas being assessed?
N/A	Yes	No	What necessary accommodations can be made?

Reliability and Validity

N/A	Yes	No	Does the assessment describe the National Curriculum standards it intends to assess?
N/A	Yes	No	Does the assessment represent the intended National Curriculum standards? Specifically, does it include a range of important knowledge and skills associated with standards?
N/A	Yes	No	Does the assessment include explicit criteria for scoring and a guide describing the application of these criteria?
N/A	Yes	No	Does the assessment provide evidence that outcomes are consistent across raters or markers across occasions when it is scored?

Cognitive Complexity

N/A	Yes	No	Does the assessment contain tasks for which the children have adequate background knowledge?
N/A	Yes	No	Does the assessment use tasks whose solutions cannot be memorised in advanced? For example, novel situations that require mathematical understanding and application of facts.
N/A	Yes	No	Does the assessment elicit evidence of understanding and problem-solving skills?

Content Quality and Coverage

N/A	Yes	No	Does the assessment assess key concepts and principles in the National Curriculum standards?
N/A	Yes	No	Does the assessment avoid irrelevant tasks and information?
N/A	Yes	No	Does the assessment use tasks consistent with teaching and learning activities that have already taken place or are planned to happen?
N/A	Yes	No	Has the assessment been reviewed by other professionals to ensure quality, accuracy and appropriateness of tasks?
N/A	Yes	No	Does the assessment format reflect typical classroom practice?

Meaningfulness

N/A	Yes	No	Does the assessment provide useful information for children, teachers, parents and carers?
N/A	Yes	No	Is the assessment credible to teachers, children and their parents and carers as a valid indicator of competence and achievement in relation to standards?
N/A	Yes	No	Does the assessment motivate and engage children to do their best?

Cost and Efficiency

N/A	Yes	No	Is the administration of the assessment feasible? Consider this in terms of financial cost as well as use of human resources and time.
N/A	Yes	No	Is the assessment cost-efficient? Consider this in terms of financial cost as well as use of human resources and time.

Essentials

From this chapter, the key points to take away are:

- Assessing without levels in the revised National Curriculum for England requires school-based assessments to be devised. Teachers are given the autonomy and professional trust to link their assessment methods to grade-level standards, obeying the principle of alignment and congruency introduced in Chapter One.

- There are four stages in a short-term assessment cycle that must operate within units of work and teaching sequences. Assessment is planned, evidence of learning collected and interpreted then decisions are made on what is taught next and to whom.

- Four main sources of evidence of children's achievement can be identified in a standards-based curriculum: closed response; short answer; products and performances. These vary in terms of how cognitively demanding they are and their authenticity.

- Multiple measures for assessing learning are necessary in a standards-based curriculum. This chapter has considered means of scoring or describing achievement against grade-level standards: test-style tasks requiring closed and/or short responses accompanied by answer keys; generalised and task-specific rubrics; checklists and observation schedules.

- Professionals in primary schools need to have a firm understanding of reliability and validity if they are to devise assessments that measure what they claim to.

- The workload of teachers should be focused on developing quality assessment tasks and activities aligned to standards. In Chapter Five, this is addressed in further detail when Assessment Plans are introduced and explained.

Chapter 5: Assessment Plans

Assessment assumes a central role in a standards-based curriculum. Assessment Plans are an important document making clear what is going to be assessed and how it is assessed in a unit of work. When classroom teachers engage in assessment planning as part of logical and sequential teaching sequences to demonstrate a child's achievement of standards. An Assessment Plan will influence the design of teaching and learning activities by focusing attention on the standards and their components. It is a document encouraging congruency, a concept introduced in Chapter One and frequently referred to throughout this book. This chapter focuses on the features of a good Assessment Plan and the stages involved in devising these.

Outcomes

By the end of this chapter, you should be able to:

- Describe the importance of assessment planning when developing teaching sequences.

- Recall the essential components of a high quality Assessment Plan.

- Identify how an Assessment Plan offers an alternative means of conceptualising short-term planning.

An Assessment Plan ensures classroom teachers are firmly focused on grade-level standards against which learning is assessed and measured. Shifting attention to Assessment Plans promotes sharper attention being paid to modifying and improving teaching to respond to changing learning needs (Snow *et al*, 2001). Embedding the practice of Assessment Plans ensures multiple opportunities for children to demonstrate learning and achievement during a teaching sequence. As a result, classroom teachers can exercise their professionalism in order to modify pedagogical approaches and adjust the pace of how a teaching sequence progresses. There is a formalisation of assessment for learning, giving it greater rigour than might be found in conventional practice of teaching driven by topic rather than grade-level standards.

Short-term planning typically involves personalising teaching and learning activities to respond to the abilities of different groups and individuals in the classroom. The notion of using an Assessment Plan is an enhancement of this. Very precise assessment tasks and activities are identified and set prior to a teaching sequence commencing, often coinciding with one stage or a couple of stages in teaching specific knowledge and understanding. This is a short-cycle of assessment; discussed in the previous chapter. Smaller steps of learning are assessed and a decision on how this will be done already made before teaching commences. The assessment tools and means of scoring achievement are defined and created before a teaching sequence commences. Classroom teachers are therefore potently aware of what the children need to know, understand or be able to do and assume greater responsibility for ensuring the quality of teaching activities facilitates this. Any school adopting the use of an Assessment Plan must ensure a system is in place for monitoring their construction and implementation. This is essential in ensuring teacher judgements of progress and learning are reliable not to mention vital in establishing whole-school consistency of approach.

The Assessment Plan should evolve according to changes in learning needs as a result of the impact of teaching. In practice, planning for assessment may be more detailed for the first one or two standards (or components of these) taught. Evidence of achievement will then dictate whether teaching needs to be repeated or more detailed assessment planning is required for new content that must be introduced.

An Assessment Plan involves four major components. Each is required to ensure congruency between standards, assessment and teaching. The components are outlined and referred to as part of the critical questions featured in this chapter.

Components of an Assessment Plan

Component	Explanatory Note(s)
Standards	The standards clustered together within a unit of work should be identified: what gets taught is assessed and what is assessed gets taught. If standards have been given an alphanumerical code, these references can be used in an Assessment Plan. Components necessary to meet the broad standard should be stated or included in corresponding Teaching and Learning Activities.
Teaching and Learning Activities	These must be aligned to standards. In devising the teaching sequence, teachers will have already formulated ideas of how classroom activities will introduce knowledge, understanding and skills logically and progressively.
Sources of Evidence	Sources of evidence are ways in which the knowledge and understanding of children is tapped into. Evidence is generated through a range of assessment tasks and strategies.
Assessment Tools and Scoring	This component of an assessment plan focuses on how products and performances are going to be judged against selected standards to show achievement or areas requiring further direct instruction.

An Assessment Plan brings together sequential steps in learning linked to standards, appropriate assessment tasks and activities. These assist in monitoring small increments in children making expected progress towards the broader standards for a unit of work. These are features of a well-designed and robust Assessment Plan.

The format of an Assessment Plan suggested in this chapter involves specific terms and abbreviations to support developing a whole-school approach and a shared language for talking about assessment planning. These have been tabulated and defined for ease of reference.

Defining Terms in Assessment Plans

The following table defines terms associated with Assessment Plans and is derived from a resource by Snow *et al* (2001). It also contains the abbreviations that are used in the Assessment Plan featured in this chapter.

Assessment Plan Terms, Abbreviations and Definitions	What Children Produce			
	Closed Response (CR)	Constructed Responses		
		Short Answer (SA)	Products (PR)	Performances (PER)
Definition	Items where children select a response from those provided to them.	Items where the children must create response or answer.	Documents or artefacts created by the children.	Demonstration and interactions
Example(s)	Multiple Choice True-False Yes-No Matching	Fill in the blank word(s)/phrase(s) Short answer in sentence(s) or paragraph(s) Label diagrams Visual representations (concept map, flow chart, graph or table)	Extended pieces of writing in Literacy and other subjects; piece of artwork, model etc.	Oral presentation, conducing science experiment, dramatic reading or performance, debate, thinking aloud, athletic competition etc.
Use of created assessment	Identifies standards and criteria to be assessed Defines task(s) Creates and uses scoring guide(s)	Identifies standards and criteria to be assessed Defines task(s) Creates and uses scoring guide(s)	Identifies standards and criteria to be assessed Defines task(s) Creates and uses scoring guide(s)	Identifies standards and criteria to be assessed Defines task(s) Creates and uses scoring guide(s)
Assessment and scoring tools	Answer Key Scoring Guide/Mark Scheme Computer-Based Scoring	Answer Key Generalised Rubric Task-Specific Rubric Checklist	Generalised Rubric Task-Specific Rubric Checklist	Generalised Rubric Task-Specific Rubric Checklist Observation Schedule
Reporting, recording and feedback	Numerical: Point Score/Percentages	Letter Grades Checklists Rating Scale	Written Comments Verbal Feedback	Developmental or Proficiency Scale; Generic or Task-Specific Rubric

There is a progression in the nature of constructed responses and what the children produce to show achievement that can be observed by reading the table from left to right. Compared to Closed Response and Short Answers, Products and Performances involve greater application of skills, knowledge and understanding. Authenticity of assessment increases as constructed responses are considered from left to right in the Assessment Plan.

Assessment Plan Template

(Assessment Plan adapted from Snow et al, 2001)

Standards	Teaching & Learning Assessment Activities	CR	Constructed Responses			AK	CL	GR	TSR	OB
			SA	PR	PER					

There are six main steps required when designing an Assessment Plan for a unit of work. These will be summarised and then discussed in relation to examples of Assessment Plans.

Step 1   Identify the standards that need to be achieved. Consider the benchmarks or components these involve.

Step 2   List the Teaching and Learning Activities aligned to standards and their components. The intended teaching sequence should show a logical progression in children's acquisition of skills, knowledge and understanding.

Step 3   For each of the Teaching and Learning Activities, decide what the children will produce in order to demonstrate achievement. There should be multiple opportunities and multiple measures across the teaching sequence.

Step 4   Specify the scoring guide to be used to assess learning against standards and their components. These should be written ahead of the unit being taught, setting high expectations for all children. This also ensures a sense of urgency on the part of classroom teachers to drive children towards grade-level standards.

Step 5   The means by which feedback on achievement is given to children should be decided in the course of devising the assessments and scoring guides.

Step 6   Form a clear idea of who will be scoring assessments and capturing evidence. This is applicable where teaching assistants are involved in supporting individuals or small groups. Where rubrics or observation schedules are used, teachers and teaching assistants could undertake joint assessment of individuals to ensure inter-rater reliability.

Example Assessment Plan for Mathematics

National Curriculum Assessment Plan		What Children Produce				Assessment Scoring				
Standards	Teaching & Learning Assessment Activities	CR	Constructed Responses			AK	CL	GR	TSR	OB
			SA	PR	PER					
NPV 1.4 1.3 1.5	Identifying, writing and using 0 and 1: Spot the error on number lines where 0 and 1 are presented in different fonts and font sizes.	Spot errors				X				
NPV 1.4 1.3 1.5	Identifying, writing and using 2. Correctly write the addition sign and equals sign.	Dictation of digits to be represented					X			
NPV 1.4 1.3 1.5	Balancing equations involving 1 and 2. Show 2>1 and 2<1 and 2 = 2 on balances.				Different objects					X
AS 1.1-1.4	Writing and using 3, practice < > + and =. All possible addition facts for three.		Dot patterns			X				
AS 1.1-1.4	Writing and using 4, practice < > + and =. Using picture, children present true statements. For example, one frog and two spiders equal three animals.				Tell me about...				X	

The example Assessment Plan, the relevant standards are referenced and benchmarks embedded within the teaching and learning activities intended for assessment. The column for teaching and learning activities shows a logical progression that has been derived from the *Conquering Primary Maths* programme for Year 1 (See Chapter Three and Chapter Six). This column can be used to include more details about the short-term plan for children's learning leading up to an assessment point. For example, specifics of individual lessons can be included along with relevant notes on differentiation and lesson structure. This is what would typically feature in a conventional short-term plan.

The constructed responses have been indicated in the plan and identified by the name of the task that will be used. There is no need to include details about the nature of the activity used for assessment in these columns. Time should be spent on the actual construction of them rather than being wasted on duplicating information. It is clear that a range of constructed responses have been planned to generate evidence of achievement when looking across the relevant columns of the Assessment Plan. The expectation is that these tasks will be written as they are planned; they are confirmed before the teaching sequence commences. In the example given here, different means of scoring progress and achievement have been specified. Multiple measures of what the children know and are able to do have been planned. The scoring guides will be written at the same time as the devising of activities resulting in constructed responses.

Note how the Assessment Plan only covers benchmarks for children's learning centred around limited content. This means that future teaching will be responsive and sensitive to ensuring all children achieve mastery. The remainder of the Assessment Plan for the block of work is written with due regard for the outcomes of what has already been taught, assessed and secured by the children. It therefore is a working document that evolves as learning progresses in a unit of work.

Critical Questions

In this chapter, the questions have been structured to assist in teachers producing an Assessment Plan. Major steps in doing so are framed as guiding questions to encourage teachers to reflect on their Assessment Plan as it develops.

Question	Action(s)	Relevant Section of Assessment Plan
What are the standards that need to be met and to which activities must be aligned?	List the standards or alphanumerical references assigned to them.	This should be entered into the first column designated as **Standards** in the Assessment Plan.
What are your teaching and assessment activities for this unit of work?	List the teaching and learning activities linking to standards already identified. Consider whether aspects of more than one standard are covered by a teaching activity.	These should be placed in the second column named **Teaching & Learning Assessment Activities**.
For each of the Teaching & Learning Assessment Activities, what responses will the children produce?	This will involve ensuring a balance between closed response tasks and constructed responses.	Record the intended responses in the appropriate column of the Assessment Plan. **CR = Closed Response** **SA = Short Answer** **PR = Product** **PER = Performance**
Which type of scoring guide is appropriate for each of the planned assessments?	Tick the appropriate box in the Assessment Plan. Devise the scoring guide(s): answer keys, rubric and so on.	**AK = Answer Key** **CL = Checklist** **GR = Generalised Rubric** **TSR = Task Specific Rubric** **OB = Observation Schedule**

How will achievement be reported and feedback given?	Ensure the school procedure for tracking achievement of standards is followed.	This can be annotated on the Assessment Plan.
	Identify how children can be involved in developing rubrics, checklists of observation schedules if this is appropriate.	
	Take steps to produce child-friendly versions of scoring guides where necessary.	
Who will undertake the assessments?	Determine whether support staff will be assigned to assessing a specific child or group.	Annotations may be placed on the Assessment Plan to indicate this.
	Identify opportunities for self-assessment and peer assessment.	

Essentials

From this chapter, the key points to take away are:

- Assessment Plans need to be at the centre of classroom planning; they focus teaching and learning on grade-level standards. This places a sharp focus on assessing what is taught and teaching what is assessed.

- Through the process of producing Assessment Plans, classroom teachers must consider how they assess so teaching can rapidly respond to emerging learning needs during a unit of work.

- Teaching and learning activities must provide multiple opportunities for children to demonstrate achievement of standards. A strong plan for assessment will show evidence of a variety of opportunities.

- An Assessment Plan of a high quality will indicate the variety of responses produced by the children and the scoring guides. This ensures multiple measures of achievement are being used to build a complete picture of what children know, understand and are able to do.

Chapter 6: A Standards-Based Model for Mathematics

This chapter is the first of three focusing on standards-based units of work, or medium-term planning. Unit plans frame the opportunities for learning in greater detail than curriculum and assessment maps. It is at the level of medium-term planning that classroom teachers are able to create teaching sequences, exercising professional judgement in how to move children towards identified standards and evidence their achievement against these. Unit plans for Mathematics must be viewed as working documents to be interacted with and adapted to meet the learning needs of children within a cohort.

There are several aspects of medium-term planning that should be carefully considered as the unit plan is reconstructed into a working document focusing on children's learning and progress. First of all, curriculum and assessment maps, the long-term plan, will have specified what is taught and when this occurs. It is imperative the unit plans are taught in the sequence dictated by the curriculum and assessment mapping. The long-term plan encodes broader dimensions of progression through standards across an academic year. Secondly, unit plans should include annotations related to decoding standards and unpicking the components where medium-term planning does not have this built in or sparse indictors of achievement are provided. A third expectation for using unit plans as a working document relates to creating sequential and logical progression in teaching and learning activities. This was examined in Chapter Three. An Assessment Plan aligns to the standards in a unit of work and indicative teaching and learning activities established at the level of medium-term planning. The principles of a good Assessment Plan and the significance of such a document in a standards-based curriculum were encountered in Chapter Five. As you read the medium-term planning for Mathematics, keep in mind how they can be utilised as working documents in the classroom.

The unit plans in this chapter cover Year 1 through to Year 6, forming a programme called *Conquering Primary Maths* (CPM). Each medium-term plan provides a section for **Key Vocabulary** that must form part of teaching and learning. Unit 1A and Unit 1B includes examples of vocabulary. The remainder of CPM requires teachers to actively seek out and plan mathematical language to include in units of work. Unit plans feature a space for classroom teachers entitled **Mastered Content: Rehearse, Recall, Refresh, Refine, Read & Reason**. This is intended to encourage teachers to ensure that knowledge and understanding secured previously is regularly revisited. The six Rs, associated with oral and mental work in the *Renewed Framework for Mathematics and Literacy* (2006), offer a reminder that no new teaching points are being introduced. The focus is firmly on ensuring mastered mathematical content remains active in the children's minds.

Suggested Order & Pace Setting in the unit plans provides a summary of key learning that must take place. At Year 1, these benchmarks are used for formative assessment with overall performance assessed against the grade-level standards undertaken at the end of an academic year. For all other year groups, the standards in each medium-term plan should be at the forefront of teaching and assessment from unit to unit. Example tracking grids can be found in the supplementary materials in this book.

At Year 1, CPM offers a highly structured approach to children acquiring knowledge of number bonds to twenty, a sense of number and a firm understanding of addition and subtraction. As a result, there is a column for teachers to annotate as they develop a pathway through the unit of work. It is entitled **Indicative T & L Activities**. Beyond Year 1, CPM unit plans might include reference to statements in *Assessing Pupils' Progress in Mathematics* criteria using grey as the font colour. The purpose of this is two-fold. Inclusion of selected statements can help experienced classroom teachers to recognise how pitch and expectations within year groups have been raised in the revised programme of study. In addition, the statements from *Assessing Pupils' Progress in Mathematics* may help to prompt thinking about further unpicking standards. The previous National Curriculum level associated with a statement is included parenthetically for information. All unit plans in CPM provide space for teachers to incorporate any significant information from the whole-school calculation policy as a means of guiding their classroom practice.

It was previously mentioned that CPM for Year 1 has a systematic and cumulative design and before presenting an overview of CPM and the unit plans for Autumn Term, Spring Term and Summer Term, an explanation of the rationale and underlying principles of CPM for Year 1 is given.

Year 1 Conquering Primary Maths Rationale and Principles

The *Conquering Primary Maths* overview and unit plans for Year 1, to a certain extent, draw on previous work by the Centre for Innovation in Mathematics Teaching (CIMT, 1995) based at the University of Plymouth. Their original programme, *Mathematics Enhancement Programme* (MEP), was derived from a Hungarian model for structuring content with an emphasis on number and the number system. This was adapted for England's primary schools. A major feature of the MEP is the systematic and cumulative approach taken to introducing number bonds in Year 1. In other year groups, expectations of what children know and are able to do are raised and reminiscent of the revised National Curriculum. CPM is a hybridisation of the MEP and Mathematics programme of study.

A systematic and cumulative approach to teaching number bonds, involving addition and subtraction within twenty, may appear restrictive. However, a structured approach can ensure classroom teaching acts as a preventative measure in children acquiring difficulties in learning Mathematics. Difficulties in Mathematics can be attributed to ABC: it is abstract (A) involving symbols representing concepts; requires building blocks (B) to be established to give the foundations for later learning and the subject has many complexities (C) (Emerson and Babtie, 2010; Das and Janzen, 2004). The CPM materials in this book seek to enable classroom teachers to gradually expand knowledge and understanding of number in Year 1. It allows time for children to work with concrete objects and pictorial representations of number, gradually building their knowledge of number bonds to ten and then twenty.

Through using CPM for Year 1, classroom teachers can ensure the following:

- Children acquiring a sound **sense of number.** A certain number represents a specific value or quantity; numbers are part of a sequence and can be compared with one another.
- Children can **distinguish between –teen and –ty numbers** presented orally because they are introduced in a systematic way.
- Children develop **automaticity in writing numbers and using number bonds** because this knowledge is built up gradually. Reversals and transpositions of digits can be addressed as each number is introduced one-by-one and explicit practice in forming them expected.
- Children experience **growth in confidence** because learning always starts from what they have secured previously.
- The knowledge of all children in relation to number is subject to **frequent assessment** so early difficulties are addressed as soon as possible so individual's do not fall behind their peers.

Year 1 Conquering Primary Maths Programme Overview

When	Alignment to Standards	Order of Topics & Pace Setting	
		CONQUERING PRIMARY MATHS FOR YEAR ONE	
Autumn 1	NVP1.4 NPV1.3 NPV1.5 GPS1.1 GPD1.1	Comparisons: Ordering- taller, shorter, longer, above, below, to the right, to the left, behind, between	
		Comparison of sets: more, less, equal, many, few	
		Number pictures: less than, more than, equal to, not equal to < > = ≠	
		Identifying, writing and using 0 and 1; number line	
		Identifying, writing and using 2; number line (write and use + - and =	
		Comparisons: Number pictures and balancing equations and inequalities (2>1 and 1<2)	
		2D Shapes: Square, Rectangle, Triangle and Circle Ordering and arranging objects and shapes in patterns	
	HALF TERM		
Autumn 2	AS1.1 AS1.2 AS1.3 AS1.4	Writing and using 3; number line, practise < > + - = (number bonds within)	
		Writing and using 4; number line, practise < > + - = (number bonds within)	
		Writing and using 5; number line, practise < > + - = (number bonds within)	
		Writing and using 6; number line, practise < > + - = (number bonds within)	
		Writing and using 7; number line, practise < > + - = (number bonds within)	
		Writing and using 8; number line, practise < > + - = (number bonds within)	
	END OF TERM		
Spring 1	AS1.1 AS1.2 AS1.3 AS1.4 M1.10 M1.11 M1.12 M1.8 M1.4	Revision and Practise: 0, 1, 2, 3, 4, 5 6, 7 and 8	
		Writing and using 9 number line, practise < > + - = (number bonds within)	
		Writing and using 10 number line, practise < > + - = (number bonds within)	
		Revision and Practise: 0 to 10 and mathematical symbols (number bonds within)	
		Sequence events in chronological order	
		Days, weeks, months and years	
		Measure and record time	
		Tell the time (hour and half past hour)	
	HALF TERM		
Spring 2	NVP1.4 NVP1.3 NVP1.5 AS1.3 AS1.2 AS1.4 M1.1-M1.7	Revision and practice: 0 to 10	Compare and describe length/height
		Extending the number line 0-20	Compare and describe mass/weight
		Number bonds and sums to 11	Compare and describe capacity/volume
		Number bonds and sums to 12	Measure and record lengths/heights
		Number bonds and sums to 13	Measure and record mass/weight
		Number bonds and sums to 14	Measure and record capacity/volume
	END OF TERM		
Summer 1	NVP1.3 NVP1.4 NVP1.5 AS1.3 AS1.2 AS1.4 M1.9 GPD1.2	Number bonds and sums to 15	
		Number bonds and sums to 16 & 17	
		Number bonds and sums to 18 & 19	
		Number bonds and sums to 20	
		Counting, read and write numbers to 100 in numerals	
		Money- denominations	
		Turns	
	HALF TERM		
Summer 2	NVP1.2 MD1.1 F1.1 F1.2	Count, read and write numbers to 100 in numerals	
		Count in multiples of one, two, fives and tens	
		Solve multiplication and divisions using objects and arrays	
		Fractions: Halves and Quarters	

Year 1 Unit Overviews

Year 1 Conquering Primary Maths Autumn 1	Unit 1A Number to 10, Add, Subtract and Shape

In all units of work:
- Provision for solving problems and puzzles
- Concrete and pictorial representations of number and mathematical concepts before and alongside the abstract

In this unit of work:

Standards for Teaching and Assessment in Mathematics	Suggested Order & Pace Setting	Indicative Teaching & Learning Activities
NVP1.4 identify and represent numbers using concrete objects and pictorial representations including the number line, and use the language of: equal to, more than, less than (fewer), most, least NPV1.3 Given a number, identify one more and one less NPV1.5 read and write numbers from 1 to 20 in digits and words GPS1.1 2-D shapes (e.g. rectangles (including squares), circles and triangles) GPD1.1 Order and arrange combinations of objects and shapes in patterns	Comparisons: Ordering-taller, shorter, longer, above, below, to the right, to the left, behind, between	
	Comparison of sets: more, less, equal, many, few	
	Number pictures: less than, more than, equal to, not equal to < > = ≠	
	Identifying, writing and using 0 and 1; number line	
	Identifying, writing and using 2; number line (write and use + - and =	
	Comparisons: Number pictures and balancing equations and inequalities (2>1 and 1<2)	
	2D Shapes: Square, Rectangle, Triangle and Circle Ordering and arranging objects and shapes in patterns	
Key Vocabulary	*add, more, plus make, sum, total, altogether , score, double, near double, one more, two more... ten more, how many more to make...? how many more is... than...? how much more is...?=, equals, sign, is the same as how many more is... than...? take (away) leave, how many are left/left over? how many have gone? one less, two less... ten less... how many fewer is... than...? difference between*	

Working To Whole-School School Calculation Policy

Subtraction	Addition

133

Year 1 Conquering Primary Maths Autumn 2	Unit 1B Extending The Number Line to 20

In all units of work:

- Provision for solving problems and puzzles
- Concrete and pictorial representations of number and mathematical concepts before and alongside the abstract

Content from Unit 1A not yet mastered	Mastered Content: Rehearse, Recall, Refresh, Refine, Read & Reason

In this unit of work:

Standards for Teaching and Assessment in Mathematics	Suggested Order & Pace Setting	Indicative Teaching & Learning Activities
AS1.3 Add and subtract one-digit and two-digit numbers to 20 (9 + 9, 18 - 9), including zero AS1.1 Read, write and interpret mathematical statements involving addition (+), subtraction (-) and equals (=) signs AS1.2 Represent and use number bonds and related subtraction facts within 20 AS1.4 Solve simple one-step problems that involve addition and subtraction, using concrete objects and pictorial representations, and missing number problems	Writing and using 3; number line, practise < > + - = (number bonds within) Writing and using 4; number line, practise < > + - = (number bonds within) Writing and using 5; number line, practise < > + - = (number bonds within) Writing and using 6; number line, practise < > + - = (number bonds within) Writing and using 7; number line, practise < > + - = (number bonds within) Writing and using 8; number line, practise < > + - = (number bonds within)	
Key Vocabulary	*add, more, plus make, sum, total, altogether , score, double, near double, one more, two more... ten more, how many more to make...? how many more is... than...? how much more is...?=, equals, sign, is the same as how many more is... than...? take (away) leave, how many are left/left over? how many have gone? one less, two less... ten less... how many fewer is... than...? difference between*	

Working In-Line Whole-School School Calculation Policy

Year 1 Conquering Primary Maths Spring 1	Unit 1C Extending The Number Line to 20 & Time

In all units of work:

- Provision for solving problems and puzzles
- Concrete and pictorial representations of number and mathematical concepts before and alongside the abstract

Content from Unit 1B not yet mastered	Mastered Content: Rehearse, Recall, Refresh, Refine, Read & Reason

In this unit of work:

Standards for Teaching and Assessment in Mathematics	Suggested Order & Pace Setting	Indicative Teaching & Learning Activities
M1.10 Sequence events in chronological order using language such as: before and after, next, first, today, yesterday, tomorrow, morning, afternoon and evening M1.11 Recognise and use language relating to dates, including days of the week, weeks, months and years M1.12 Tell the time to the hour and half past the hour and draw the hands on a clock face to show these times M1.8 Measure and begin to record time (hours, minutes, seconds) M1.14 Compare, describe and solve practical problems for time (quicker, slower, earlier, later	Revision and Practise: 0, 1, 2, 3, 4, 5 6, 7 and 8	
	Writing and using 9 number line, practise < > + - = (number bonds within)	
	Writing and using 10 number line, practise < > + - = (number bonds within)	
	Revision and Practise: 0 to 10 and mathematical symbols (number bonds within)	
	Sequence events in chronological order	
	Days, weeks, months and years	
	Measure and record time	
	Tell the time (hour and half past hour)	

Key Vocabulary	

Working In-Line Whole-School School Calculation Policy

Year 1 Conquering Primary Maths Spring 2	Unit 1D Extending The Number Line & Measures

In all units of work:
- Provision for solving problems and puzzles
- Concrete and pictorial representations of number and mathematical concepts before and alongside the abstract

Content from Unit 1C not yet mastered	Mastered Content: Rehearse, Recall, Refresh, Refine, Read & Reason

In this unit of work:

Standards for Teaching and Assessment in Mathematics	Suggested Order & Pace Setting	Indicative Teaching & Learning Activities
M1.5 Measure and begin to record lengths and heights	Revision and practice: 0 to 10	
	Extending the number line 0-20	
M1.6 Measure and begin to record mass/weight	Number bonds and sums to 11	
	Number bonds and sums to 12	
M1.7 Measure and begin to record capacity and volume	Number bonds and sums to 13	
M1.1 I Compare, describe and solve practical problems for lengths and heights (e.g. long/short, longer/shorter, tall/short, double/half)	Number bonds and sums to 14	
	Compare and describe length/height	
	Compare and describe mass/weight	
M1.2 Compare, describe and solve practical problems for mass or weight (e.g. heavy/light, heavier than, lighter than)	Compare and describe capacity/volume	
	Measure and record lengths/heights	
M1.3 Compare, describe and solve practical problems for capacity/volume (full/empty, more than, less than, quarter)	Measure and record mass/weight	
	Measure and record capacity/volume	

Key Vocabulary	

Working In-Line Whole-School School Calculation Policy

Year 1 Conquering Primary Maths Summer 1	Unit 1E Number, Money and Turns

In all units of work:
- Provision for solving problems and puzzles
- Concrete and pictorial representations of number and mathematical concepts before and alongside the abstract

Content from Unit 1D not yet mastered	Mastered Content: Rehearse, Recall, Refresh, Refine, Read & Reason

In this unit of work:

Standards for Teaching and Assessment in Mathematics	Suggested Order & Pace Setting	Indicative Teaching & Learning Activities
NPV1.1 Count to and across 100, forwards and backwards, beginning with 0 or 1, or from any given number M1.9 Recognise and know the value of different denominations of coins and notes GPD1.2 Describe position, directions and movements, including half, quarter and three-quarter turns.	Number bonds and sums to 15	
	Number bonds and sums to 16 & 17	
	Number bonds and sums to 18 & 19	
	Number bonds and sums to 20	
	Counting, read and write numbers to 100 in numerals	
	Money- denominations	
	Turns	

Key Vocabulary	

Working In-Line Whole-School School Calculation Policy

Year 1 Conquering Primary Maths Summer 2	Unit 1F Number, Multiply, Divide & Fractions

In all units of work:
- Provision for solving problems and puzzles
- Concrete and pictorial representations of number and mathematical concepts before and alongside the abstract

Content from Unit 1E not yet mastered	Mastered Content: Rehearse, Recall, Refresh, Refine, Read & Reason

In this unit of work:

Standards for Teaching and Assessment in Mathematics	Suggested Order & Pace Setting	Indicative Teaching & Learning Activities
NPV1.2 Count, read and write numbers to 100 in numerals, count in different multiples including ones, twos, fives and tens MD1.1 Solve simple one-step problems involving multiplication and division, calculating the answer using concrete objects, pictorial representations and arrays with the support of the teacher. F1.1 Recognise, find and name a half as one of two equal parts of an object, shape or quantity F1.2 Recognise, find and name a quarter as one of four equal parts of an object, shape or quantity	Count, read and write numbers to 100 in numerals Count in multiples of one, two, fives and tens Solve multiplication and divisions using objects and arrays Fractions: Halves and Quarters	
Key Vocabulary		

Working In-Line Whole-School School Calculation Policy

Year 2 to Year 6 Conquering Primary Maths Overview

CONQUERING PRIMARY MATHS FOR YEAR TWO		
When	**Alignment to Standards**	**Order of Topics & Pace Setting**
Autumn 1	AS2.3 AS2.4 AS2.8 AS2.9 GPS2.1 GPD2.1 PV2.2 PV2.6 AS2 AS2. 1&2.5 AS2.6 AS2.7	Revision: Numbers to 20 (Addition and Subtraction from Year 1)
		Properties of 2D shape: number of sides and symmetry
		Objects and patterns
		Ordering two-digit numbers; creating two-digit numbers from three or four digits & place value in two-digit numbers
		Addition and subtraction; TU +/- T and TU +/- U
		Addition and subtraction: TU/U and TU/TU without tens crossing
		Addition and subtraction: TU/U and TU/TU with tens crossing
	HALF TERM	
Autumn 2	AS2.3 PV2.1 MD2.2 MD2.3 MD2.4	Number 0 to 100
		Counting by 10s, 5s and 2s
		Multiplication and division facts for 2
		Multiplication and division facts for 5
		Multiplication and division facts for 10
	END OF TERM	
Spring 1	PV2.3 PV2.4 PV2.5 M2.6 M2.7	Revision of multiplication and division facts 2, 5 and 10
		Compare and order numbers 0 to 100 < > = ≠
		Compare and sequence time intervals
		Telling the time to five minutes, quarter past and to hour
	HALF TERM	
Spring 2	M2.1 M2.2 M2.3 AS2.1&2 GPS2.2 GPS2.3 GPS2.4	Standard units of measure
		Compare and order measures
		Solve addition and subtraction involving measures
		3D shape (vertices, edges and faces)
		2D shapes on surface of 3D shapes
		Compare and sort 2D and 3D shapes
	END OF TERM	
Summer 1	M2.4 M2.5 D2.1 D2.2 D2.3	Money £ and p
		Add and subtract money in same unit
		Add and subtract money, giving change
		Data: pictograms, tally charts and simple tables
		Data: total and compare categorical data
	HALF TERM	
Summer 2	F2.1 F2.2 GPD2.2	Fractions of length, shape and objects (halves, quarters and a third)
		Rotation
		Revision
		Revision

CONQUERING PRIMARY MATHS FOR YEAR THREE		
When	**Alignment to Standards**	**Order of Topics & Pace Setting**
Autumn 1	NPV3.2	Revision: Number to 100, addition and subtraction
	NPV3.3	Revision: Multiplication
	NPV3.5	Revision: Division
	NPV3.1	Compare, order and know place value in number up to 100
	NPV3.4	Count in steps of 4, 8, 50 and 100
	NPV3.6	Draw 2D shape and make 3D shapes
	GPS3.1 M3.2	Measure perimeter
HALF TERM		
Autumn 2	AS3.1	Extending numbers to 200
	AS3.2	Addition and subtraction involving three-digit number and units
	AS3.3	Addition and subtraction involving three-digit number and tens
	NPV3.2	Addition and subtraction involving three-digit numbers and hundreds
	NPV3.3	Extending number line to 1000
	NPV3.5	Add and subtract three-digit numbers using columnar method without crossing tens extending to crossing tens
	AS3.4 AS3.5	
	AS3.6	Add and subtract money to give change
	M3.3	
END OF TERM		
Spring 1	NPV3.2	Extending the number line 0 to 1000
	NPV3.3	Multiplication and division facts for 3, 4 and 8
	NPV3.5	TU x U
	MD3.1 MD3.2	Data: bar charts, pictograms and tables
	MD3.3	
	D3.1 D3.2	One- and two-step questions on scaled bar charts, pictograms and tables
HALF TERM		
Spring 2	F3.1 F3.2	Calculate unit fractions
	F3.3 F3.4	Use diagrams to identify equivalent fractions
	F3.5 F3.6	Compare and order unit fractions (same denominator)
	F3.7	Add and subtract fractions with same denominator within a whole
		Count in tenths
END OF TERM		
Summer 1		Angles as property of shapes
	GPS3.2	Right angles and angles in half and three-quarter turns
	GPS3.3	Compare angles as < or > right angle
	GPS3.4	Identify types of lines (parallel, perpendicular, horizontal and vertical)
HALF TERM		
Summer 2	M3.1	Measures: compare and order
	M3.4 M3.5	Measures: addition and subtraction
	M3.6 M3.7	Reading time
		Facts about time
		Calculate durations

CONQUERING PRIMARY MATHS FOR YEAR FOUR

When	Alignment to Standards	Order of Topics & Pace Setting
Autumn 1	NPV4.2	Revision: Numbers to 1000 (Write, order, compare, round and sequence)
	NPV4.4	
	NPV4.5	Revision: Operations with numbers up to 1000 (Addition and Subtraction)
	NPV4.6	
	NPV4.7	Revision: Operations (Multiplication and Division)
	NPV4.8	Numbers up to 2000
		Number and calculation up to 2000
	AS4.1 AS4.2	Extending number line and calculations o 10 000
	AS4.3	Columnar addition and subtraction
	HALF TERM	
Autumn 2	NPV4.1	Multiples of 6, 7, 9, 25 and 1000
	NPV4.3	Multiplication and division facts for multiplication tables up to 12x12
	MD4.1 MD4.2	Multiply and divide mentally using place value
	MD4.3 MD4.5	TU x U and HTU x U
	GPS4.1	Compare and classify 2D shapes & lines of symmetry
	GPS4.2	Angles
	GPS4.3	
	GPS4.4	
	END OF TERM	
Spring 1	MD4.4 MD4.6	Factor pairs
		Multiplying and adding problems
	F4.2 F4.3	Equivalent fractions
	F4.4	Add and subtract fractions
		Solve problems involving fractions
	M4.2 M4.3	Perimeter and area
	HALF TERM	
Spring 2	F4.1	Fractions and decimals
	DF4.1	Place value in decimals
	DF4.2	Multiply and divide by 10 and 100
	DF4.3	Convert units of measure
	DF4.4	Compare measures
	DF4.5	Solve problems with decimals to two decimal places
	DF4.6	
	M4.1 M4.5	
	END OF TERM	
Summer 1	M4.6 M4.7	Analogue and digital time: twelve and twenty-four hour clock
		Converting time and solving time problems
	D4.1	Bar charts and continuous data in line graphs
	D4.2	Sum and difference problems using bar charts, pictograms, tables and simple line graphs
	HALF TERM	
Summer 2	NPV4.9	Roman numerals to 100 (I to C)
	GPD4.1	Coordinates and translating shape
	GPD4.2	
	GPD4.3	

When	Alignment to Standards	Order of Topics & Pace Setting
	**CONQUERING PRIMARY MATHS FOR YEAR FIVE**	

When	Alignment to Standards	Order of Topics & Pace Setting
Autumn 1	NPV5.1 NPV5.2 NPV5.3 AS5.1 AS5.2 AS5.3 AS5.4 NPV5.4 GPS5.1 GPS5.8 GPS5.9	Extending number to 1,000,000
		Round to nearest 10, 100, 1000, 10 000 and 10, 000, 000
		Mental calculation with larger numbers
		Columnar addition and subtraction with more than four-digits
		Solving addition and subtraction problems
		3D shapes from 2D representations
		Properties of a rectangle
		Regular and irregular polygons
HALF TERM		
Autumn 2	F5.1 F5.2 F5.3 F5.4 DF5.1 DF5.2 DF5.3 DF5.4 DF5.5 M5.1	Compare and order fractions
		Converting improper fractions and mixed numbers
		Fractions to decimals
		Rounding decimals
		Multiply and divide by 10, 100 and 1000
		Convert units of measure
END OF TERM		
Spring 1	MD5.1 MD5.3 MD5.4 MD5.9 MD5.6 M5.3 M5.4 M5.5	Multiples and factors
		Prime and composite numbers
		Square and cubed numbers
		Perimeter and area
		Volume and capacity
HALF TERM		
Spring 2	MD5.5 MD5.7 MD5.2 MD5.11 MD5.10	Th H T U x U or TU
		Divide Th H T U by U
		Solving multiplication and division problems
		Use all four operations to solve problems
END OF TERM		
Summer 1	PDF5.1 PDF5.2 GPS5.2 GPS5.3 GPS5.4 GPS5.5 GPS5.6 GPD5.1	Per cent as parts per 100
		Percentage, decimal and fraction equivalents
		Angles
		Reflection and translation
		Probability experiments, predictions; fair and unfair games
HALF TERM		
Summer 2	M5.2 M5.6 M5.7 D5.1 D5.1	Metric and imperial units
		Problems involving converting time
		Addition and subtraction of units of measure
		Line graph comparisons, sums and differences
		Complete, read and interpret tabulated information

CONQUERING PRIMARY MATHS FOR YEAR SIX

When	Alignment to Standards	Order of Topics & Pace Setting
Autumn 1	NPV6.1	Revision of numbers to 1, 000, 000; read, write, place value order and round
	DF6.1	
	NPV6.2	Multiply and divide by 10, 100 and 1000
	NPV6.3	Mental calculation strategies review (brackets and order of operations)
	NPV6.4	
	ASMD6.4	Written calculation review
	ASMD6.5	Miscellaneous problems involving whole numbers and decimals
	ASMD6.3	Calculate unknown angles in 2D shape
	ASMD6.6	Area and perimeter (same area, different perimeter)
	GPS6.2	Area of parallelograms and triangles
	M6.4 M6.5	
	HALF TERM	
Autumn 2	ASMD6.8	Th H T U x TU
	ASMD6.1	Divide Th H T U by TU
	ASMD6.2	Problems involving all four operations
	ASMD6.7	Nets and 3D shape construction
	GPS6.1	Formula for area and volume of shapes
	M6.6 M6.7	Calculate volume of cubes and cuboids
	END OF TERM	
Spring 1	ASMD6.4	Common factors, common multiples and prime numbers
	F6.1 F6.2	Simplify fractions
	F6.3 F6.4	Compare and order fractions, decimal and fraction equivalents
	F6.5 F6.6	Add and subtract fractions
	DF6.2 DF6.3	
	DF6.4	Multiply pairs of proper fractions and divide proper fractions by whole number
	GPS6.4	
		Multiply and divide numbers with two decimal places
		Finding unknown angles: straight line and vertically opposite
	HALF TERM	
Spring 2	PDF6.1	Percentages of whole numbers and measures and using FDP equivalences
	PDF6.2	
	AL6.1 AL6.2	Ratio and proportion
	AL6.3 AL6.4	Probability
	RP6.1 RP6.2	Algebra
	END OF TERM	
Summer 1	M6.2	Read, write and convert standard units of measure
	M6.1	Solve problems involving conversion of units of measure
		Review: Diagnostic tests and practice
		KEY STAGE 2 TESTS
	HALF TERM	
Summer 2	D6.1 D6.2	Pie charts and line graphs
	GPS6.3	Miles to kilometres conversion
	GPD6.1	Parts of a circle
	GPD6.2	Coordinates in all four quadrants
		Translate shape and reflect in axes

Year 2 to Year 6 Unit Plans for Conquering Primary Maths

Year 2 Conquering Primary Maths Autumn 1	Unit 2A Addition, Subtraction, Place Value and Shape

In all units of work:
- Provision for solving problems and puzzles
- Concrete and pictorial representations of number and mathematical concepts before and alongside the abstract

Content from Year 1 not yet mastered	Mastered Content: Rehearse, Recall, Refresh, Refine, Read & Reason

In this unit of work:

Standards for Teaching and Assessment in Mathematics	Suggested Order & Pace Setting	Indicative Teaching & Learning Activities
AS2.3 Recall and use addition and subtraction facts to 20 fluently, and derive and use related facts up to 100 AS2.8 Show that addition of two numbers can be done in any order (commutative) and subtraction of one number from another cannot AS2.4 Add and subtract numbers using concrete objects, pictorial representations, and mentally, including a two-digit number and ones PV2.2 Recognise the place value of each digit in a two-digit number PV2.6 Use place value and number facts to solve problems. AS2.5 Add and subtract numbers using concrete objects, pictorial representations, and mentally, including a two-digit number and tens AS2.6 Add and subtract numbers using concrete objects, pictorial representations, and mentally, including two two-digit numbers AS2.7 Add and subtract numbers using concrete objects, pictorial representations, and mentally, including adding three one-digit numbers AS2.9 Recognise and use the inverse relationship between addition and subtraction and use this to check calculations and missing number problems. AS2.1&2 Solve simple one-step problems with addition and subtraction applying their increasing knowledge of mental and written methods GPS2.1 Identify and describe the properties of 2-D shapes, including the number of sides and symmetry in a vertical line GPD2.1 Order and arrange combinations of mathematical objects in patterns	Revision: Numbers to 20 (Addition and Subtraction from Year 1) Properties of 2D shape: number of sides and symmetry Objects and patterns Ordering two-digit numbers; creating two-digit numbers from three or four digits & place value in two-digit numbers Addition and subtraction; TU +/- T and TU +/- U Addition and subtraction: TU/U and TU/TU without tens crossing Addition and subtraction: TU/U and TU/TU with tens crossing	Add and subtract 2-digit numbers mentally -Calculate 36 + 19, 63 – 26, and complements to 100 such as 100 – 24 (L3) Begin to understand the place value of each digit, use this to order numbers up to 100 (L2) Use mental recall of addition and subtraction facts to 20 in solving problems involving larger numbers (L3)
Key Vocabulary		

Working In-Line Whole-School School Calculation Policy

Year 2 Conquering Primary Maths Autumn 2	Unit 2B Count in 2s, 3s and 5s & Multiply and Divide by 2, 3 and 5

In all units of work:
- Provision for solving problems and puzzles
- Concrete and pictorial representations of number and mathematical concepts before and alongside the abstract

Content from Unit 2A not yet mastered	Mastered Content: Rehearse, Recall, Refresh, Refine, Read & Reason

In this unit of work:

Standards for Teaching and Assessment in Mathematics	Suggested Order & Pace Setting	Indicative Teaching & Learning Activities
PV2.1 Count in steps of 2, 3, and 5 from 0, and count in tens from any number, forward or backward MD2.1 Recall and use multiplication and division facts for the 2, 5 and 10 multiplication tables, including recognising odd and even numbers MD2.2 Calculate mathematical statements for multiplication and division within the multiplication tables and write them using the multiplication (×), division (÷) and equals (=) signs MD2.3 Recognise and use the inverse relationship between multiplication and division in calculations MD2.4 Show that multiplication of two numbers can be done in any order (commutative) and division of one number by another cannot MD2.5 Solve one-step problems involving multiplication and division, using materials, arrays, repeated addition, mental methods, and multiplication and division facts including problems in contexts.	Number 0 to 100	Count sets of objects reliably, e.g. *group objects in twos, fives and tens* (L2 & L3)
	Counting by 10s, 5s and 2s	Recognise sequences of numbers, including odd and even numbers, e.g.
	Multiplication and division facts for 2	- *Continue a sequence that increases or decreases in regular steps & recognise numbers from counting in tens or twos* (L2)
	Multiplication and division facts for 5	Recognise a wider range of sequences
	Multiplication and division facts for 10	-*Recognise sequences of multiples of 2, 5 and 10* (L3)
		Use mental recall of the 2, 5 and 10 multiplication tables (L3)
		Derive associated division facts from known multiplication facts (L3)
Key Vocabulary		

Working In-Line Whole-School School Calculation Policy

145

Year 2 Conquering Primary Maths Spring 1	Unit 2C Number to 100 and Time

In all units of work:
- Provision for solving problems and puzzles
- Concrete and pictorial representations of number and mathematical concepts before and alongside the abstract

Content from Unit 2B not yet mastered	Mastered Content: Rehearse, Recall, Refresh, Refine, Read & Reason

In this unit of work:

Standards for Teaching and Assessment in Mathematics	Suggested Order & Pace Setting	Indicative Teaching & Learning Activities
PV2.3 Identify, represent and estimate numbers using different representations, including the number line PV2.4 Compare and order numbers from 0 up to 100; use <, > and = signs PV2.5 Read and write numbers to at least 100 in numerals and in words M2.6 Compare and sequence intervals of time M2.7 Tell and write the time to five minutes, including quarter past/to the hour and draw the hands on a clock face to show these times.	Revision of multiplication and division facts 2, 5 and 10 Compare and order numbers 0 to 100 < > = ≠ Compare and sequence time intervals Telling the time to five minutes, quarter past and to hour	Begin to understand the place value of each digit, use this to order numbers up to 100 -Know the relative size of numbers to 100 (L2)
Key Vocabulary		

Working In-Line Whole-School School Calculation Policy

Year 2 Conquering Primary Maths Spring 2	Unit 2D Measures & 2D and 3D Shape

In all units of work:
- Provision for solving problems and puzzles
- Concrete and pictorial representations of number and mathematical concepts before and alongside the abstract

Content from Unit 2C not yet mastered	Mastered Content: Rehearse, Recall, Refresh, Refine, Read & Reason

In this unit of work:

Standards for Teaching and Assessment in Mathematics	Suggested Order & Pace Setting	Indicative Teaching & Learning Activities
M2.1 Choose and use appropriate standard units to estimate and measure length/height in any direction (m/cm); mass (kg/g); temperature (°C); capacity (litres/ml) to the nearest appropriate unit, using rulers, scales, thermometers and measuring vessels M2.2 Compare and order lengths, mass, volume/capacity and record the results using >, < and = M2.3 Read relevant scales to the nearest numbered unit AS2.1&2 solve simple one-step problems with addition and subtraction including those involving numbers, quantities and measures GPS2.2 identify and describe the properties of 3-D shapes, including the number of edges, vertices and faces GPS2.3 Identify 2-D shapes on the surface of 3-D shapes, for example a circle on a cylinder and a triangle on a pyramid GPS2.4 Compare and sort common 2-D and 3-D shapes and everyday objects.	Standard units of measure Compare and order measures Solve addition and subtraction involving measures 3D shape (vertices, edges and faces) 2D shapes on surface of 3D shapes Compare and sort 2D and 3D shapes	-

Key Vocabulary	

Working In-Line Whole-School School Calculation Policy

Year 2 Conquering Primary Maths Summer 1	Unit 2E Money and Data

In all units of work:

- Provision for solving problems and puzzles
- Concrete and pictorial representations of number and mathematical concepts before and alongside the abstract

Content from Unit 2D not yet mastered	Mastered Content: Rehearse, Recall, Refresh, Refine, Read & Reason

In this unit of work:

Standards for Teaching and Assessment in Mathematics	Suggested Order & Pace Setting	Indicative Teaching & Learning Activities
M2.4 Recognise and use symbols for pounds (£) and pence (p); combine amounts to make a particular value and match different combinations of coins to equal the same amounts of money; add and subtract money of the same unit, including giving change	Money £ and p	Solve number problems involving money and measures
	Add and subtract money in same unit	-Add/subtract two-digit and one-digit numbers, bridging tens where necessary in contexts using units such as pence, pounds (L2)
	Add and subtract money, giving change	Extract and interpret information presented in simple tables lists, bar charts and pictograms (L3)
M2.5 Solve simple problems in a practical context involving addition and subtraction of money	Data: pictograms, tally charts and simple tables	Use a key to interpret represented data
D2.1 Interpret and construct simple pictograms, tally charts, block diagrams and simple tables	Data: total and compare categorical data	Read scales labelled in twos, fives and tens, including reading between labelled divisions such as a point halfway between 40 and 50 or 8 and 10
D2.2 Ask and answer simple questions by counting the number of objects in each category and sorting the categories by quantity		- Compare data e.g. say how many more... than...
D2.3 Ask and answer questions about totalling and compare categorical data		

Key Vocabulary	

Working In-Line Whole-School School Calculation Policy

Year 2 Conquering Primary Maths Summer 2	Unit 2F Fractions, Shape & Turns

In all units of work:
- Provision for solving problems and puzzles
- Concrete and pictorial representations of number and mathematical concepts before and alongside the abstract

Content from Unit 2E not yet mastered	Mastered Content: Rehearse, Recall, Refresh, Refine, Read & Reason

In this unit of work:

Standards for Teaching and Assessment in Mathematics	Suggested Order & Pace Setting	Indicative Teaching & Learning Activities
F2.1 Recognise, find, name and write fractions $\frac{1}{3}$, $\frac{1}{4}$, $\frac{2}{4}$ and $\frac{3}{4}$ of length, shape, set of objects or quantity F2.2 Write simple fractions e.g. $\frac{1}{2}$ of 6 = 3 and recognise the equivalence of two quarters and one half GPD2.2 Use mathematical vocabulary to describe position, direction and movement, including distinguishing between rotation as a turn and in terms of right angles for quarter, half and three- quarter turns (clockwise and anti-clockwise), and movement in a straight line.	Fractions of length, shape and objects (halves, quarters and a third) Rotation Revision	Use simple fractions that are several parts of a whole and recognise when two simple fractions are equivalent -Understand and use unit fractions such as $\frac{1}{2}$, $\frac{1}{4}$, $\frac{3}{4}$, $\frac{2}{4}$ and find those fractions of shapes and sets of objects (L3) -Recognise and record fractions that are several parts of the whole such as $\frac{3}{4}$ (L3) Recognise some fractions that are equivalent to ½ (L3)

Key Vocabulary	

Working In-Line Whole-School School Calculation Policy

Year 3 Conquering Primary Maths Autumn 1	Unit 3A Number, Place Value and Shape

In all units of work:
- Provision for solving problems and puzzles
- Concrete and pictorial representations of number and mathematical concepts before and alongside the abstract

Content from Year 2 not yet mastered	Mastered Content: Rehearse, Recall, Refresh, Refine, Read & Reason

In this unit of work:

Standards for Teaching and Assessment in Mathematics	Suggested Order & Pace Setting	Indicative Teaching & Learning Activities
NPV3.2 Recognise the place value of each digit in a three-digit number (hundreds, tens, ones) NPV3.3 Compare and order numbers up to 1000 NPV3.5 Read and write numbers to at least 1000 in numerals and in words NPV3.1 Count from 0 in multiples of 4, 8, 50 and 100; finding 10 or 100 more or less than a given number NPV3.6 Solve number problems and practical problems involving these ideas. NPV3.4 Identify, represent and estimate numbers using different representations GPS3.1 Draw 2-D shapes and make 3-D shapes using modelling materials; recognise 3-D shapes in different orientations; and describe them with increasing accuracy M3.2 Measure the perimeter of simple 2-D shapes	Revision: Number to 100, addition and subtraction	Begin to understand the place value of each digit, use this to order numbers up to 100 (L2)
	Revision: Multiplication	- Know the relative size of numbers to 100 (L2)
	Revision: Division	Understand place value in numbers to 1000 (L3)
	Compare, order and know place value in number up to 100	Begin to know multiplication facts for 4 and 8 multiplication tables (L3)
	Count in steps of 4, 8, 50 and 100	Use mental recall of the multiplication table for 4 (L3)
	Draw 2D shape and make 3D shapes	Recognise a wider range of sequences (L3)
	Measure perimeter	

Key Vocabulary	

Working In-Line Whole-School School Calculation Policy

Year 3 Conquering Primary Maths Autumn 2		Unit 3B Add and Subtract Three-Digit Numbers

In all units of work:
- Provision for solving problems and puzzles
- Concrete and pictorial representations of number and mathematical concepts before and alongside the abstract

Content from Unit 3A not yet mastered	Mastered Content: Rehearse, Recall, Refresh, Refine, Read & Reason

In this unit of work:

Standards for Teaching and Assessment in Mathematics	Suggested Order & Pace Setting	Indicative Teaching & Learning Activities
AS3.1 Add and subtract mentally a three-digit number and ones	Extending numbers to 200	Add and subtract 3-digit numbers using written method
AS3.2 Add and subtract mentally a three-digit number and tens	Addition and subtraction involving three-digit number and units	*Use written methods that involve bridging 10 or 100* (L3)
AS3.3 Add and subtract a three-digit number and hundreds	Addition and subtraction involving three-digit number and tens	
AS3.4 Add and subtract numbers with up to three digits, using the efficient written methods of columnar addition and subtraction	Addition and subtraction involving three-digit numbers and hundreds	
AS3.5 Estimate the answer to a calculation and use inverse operations to check answers	Extending number line to 1000	
AS3.6 Solve problems, including missing number problems, using number facts, place value, and more complex addition and subtraction.	Add and subtract three-digit numbers using columnar method without crossing tens extending to crossing tens	
M3.3 Add and subtract amounts of money to give change, using both £ and p in practical contexts	Add and subtract money to give change	

Key Vocabulary	

Working In-Line Whole-School School Calculation Policy

Year 3 Conquering Primary Maths Spring 1	Unit 3C Count in 4s, 8s, Multiplication and Division & Data

In all units of work:
- Provision for solving problems and puzzles
- Concrete and pictorial representations of number and mathematical concepts before and alongside the abstract

Content from Unit 3B not yet mastered	Mastered Content: Rehearse, Recall, Refresh, Refine, Read & Reason

In this unit of work:

Standards for Teaching and Assessment in Mathematics	Suggested Order & Pace Setting	Indicative Teaching & Learning Activities
MD3.1 Recall and use multiplication and division facts for the 3, 4 and 8 multiplication tables	Extending the number line 0 to 1000	Understand place value in numbers to 1000 (L3)
MD3.2 Write and calculate mathematical statements for multiplication and division using the multiplication tables that they know, including for two-digit numbers times one-digit numbers, using mental and progressing to efficient written methods	Multiplication and division facts for 3, 4 and 8	Begin to know multiplication facts for 4 and 8 multiplication tables (L3)
MD3.3 Solve problems, including missing number problems, involving multiplication and division, including integer scaling problems and correspondence problems in which n objects are connected to m objects.	TU x U	
D3.1 Interpret and present data using bar charts, pictograms and tables	Data: bar charts, pictograms and tables	
D3.1 Solve one-step and two-step questions such as 'How many more?' and 'How many fewer?' using information presented in scaled bar charts and pictograms and tables.	One- and two-step questions on scaled bar charts, pictograms and tables	

Key Vocabulary	

Working In-Line Whole-School School Calculation Policy

Year 3 Conquering Primary Maths Spring 2	Unit 3D Fractions

In all units of work:
- Provision for solving problems and puzzles
- Concrete and pictorial representations of number and mathematical concepts before and alongside the abstract

Content from Unit 3C not yet mastered	Mastered Content: Rehearse, Recall, Refresh, Refine, Read & Reason

In this unit of work:

Standards for Teaching and Assessment in Mathematics	Suggested Order & Pace Setting	Indicative Teaching & Learning Activities
F3.1 Count up and down in tenths; recognise that tenths arise from dividing an object into 10 equal parts and in dividing one-digit numbers or quantities by 10 F3.2 Recognise, find and write fractions of a discrete set of objects: unit fractions and non-unit fractions with small denominators F3.3 Recognise and use fractions as numbers: unit fractions and non-unit fractions with small denominators F3.4 Recognise and show, using diagrams, equivalent fractions with small denominators F3.5 Add and subtract fractions with the same denominator within one whole (e.g. $\frac{5}{7} + \frac{1}{7} = \frac{6}{7}$) F.3.6 Compare and order unit fractions with the same denominator F3.7 Solve problems that involve all of the above.	Calculate unit fractions	Use understanding of place value to multiply and divide whole numbers and decimals by 10 (L4)
	Use diagrams to identify equivalent fractions	Recognise simple equivalence between fractions, decimals (L4)
	Compare and order unit fractions (same denominator)	Order decimals with one decimal place (L3)
	Add and subtract fractions with same denominator within a whole	Convert fractions into tenths (L5)
	Count in tenths	

Key Vocabulary

Working In-Line Whole-School School Calculation Policy

In all units of work:
- Provision for solving problems and puzzles
- Concrete and pictorial representations of number and mathematical concepts before and alongside the abstract

Content from Unit 3D not yet mastered	Mastered Content: Rehearse, Recall, Refresh, Refine, Read & Reason

In this unit of work:

Standards for Teaching and Assessment in Mathematics	Suggested Order & Pace Setting	Indicative Teaching & Learning Activities
GPS3.2 Recognise angles as a property of shape and associate angles with turning GPS3.3 Identify right angles, recognise that two right angles make a half-turn, three make three quarters of a turn and four a complete turn; identify whether angles are greater than or less than a right angle GPS3.4 Identify horizontal, vertical, perpendicular and parallel lines in relation to other lines.	Angles as property of shapes	Recognise angles as a measure of turn and know that one whole turn is 360 degrees (L3)
	Right angles and angles in half and three-quarter turns	Use terms such as left/right, clockwise/anticlockwise, quarter turn/90° to give directions along a route (L3)
	Compare angles as < or > right angle	Recognise right angles in shapes in different orientations (L3)
	Identify types of lines (parallel, perpendicular, horizontal and vertical)	Recognise angles which are bigger/smaller than 90° and begin to know the terms 'obtuse' and 'acute' (L3)
		Understand 'parallel' and begin to understand 'perpendicular' in relation to edges or faces (L5)

Key Vocabulary	

Working In-Line Whole-School School Calculation Policy

In all units of work:

- Provision for solving problems and puzzles
- Concrete and pictorial representations of number and mathematical concepts before and alongside the abstract

Content from Unit 3E not yet mastered	Mastered Content: Rehearse, Recall, Refresh, Refine, Read & Reason

In this unit of work:

Standards for Teaching and Assessment in Mathematics	Suggested Order & Pace Setting	Indicative Teaching & Learning Activities
M3.1 Measure, compare, add and subtract: lengths (m/cm/mm); mass (kg/g); volume/capacity (l/ml) M3.4 Tell and write the time from an analogue clock, including using Roman numerals from I to XII, and 12-hour and 24- hour clocks M3.5 Estimate and read time with increasing accuracy to the nearest minute; record and compare time in terms of seconds, minutes, hours and o'clock; use vocabulary such as a.m./p.m., morning, afternoon, noon and midnight M3.6 Know the number of seconds in a minute and the number of days in each month, year and leap year M3.7 Compare durations of events, for example to calculate the time taken by particular events or tasks	Measures: compare and order	Use units of time
	Measures: addition and subtraction	*Calculate time durations that go over the hour (L4)*
	Reading time	
	Facts about time	
	Calculate durations	

Key Vocabulary	

Working In-Line Whole-School School Calculation Policy

In all units of work:
- Provision for solving problems and puzzles
- Concrete and pictorial representations of number and mathematical concepts before and alongside the abstract

Content from Year 3 not yet mastered	Mastered Content: Rehearse, Recall, Refresh, Refine, Read & Reason

In this unit of work:

Standards for Teaching and Assessment in Mathematics	Suggested Order & Pace Setting	Indicative Teaching & Learning Activities
NPV4.4 Recognise the place value of each digit in a four-digit number (thousands, hundreds, tens, and ones) NPV4.5 Order and compare numbers beyond 1000 NPV4.6 Identify, represent and estimate numbers using different representations NPV4.2 Find 1000 more or less than a given number NPV4.7 Round any number to the nearest 10, 100 or 1000 NPV4.8 Solve number and practical problems that involve all of the above and with increasingly large positive numbers AS4.1 Add and subtract numbers with up to 4 digits using the efficient written methods of columnar addition and subtraction where appropriate AS4.2 Estimate and use inverse operations to check answers to a calculation AS5.3 Solve addition and subtraction two-step problems in contexts, deciding which operations and methods to use and why	Revision: Numbers to 1000 (Write, order, compare, round and sequence) Revision: Operations with numbers up to 1000 (Addition and Subtraction) Revision: Operations (Multiplication and Division) Numbers up to 2000 Number and calculation up to 2000 Extending number line and calculations to 10 000 Columnar addition and subtraction	Understand place value in numbers to 1000 (L3) Use place value to make approximations (L3) Use efficient written methods of addition and subtraction (L4) Calculate complements to 1000 (L4)
Key Vocabulary		

Working In-Line Whole-School School Calculation Policy

Year 4 Conquering Primary Maths Autumn 2	Unit 4B Count in 6s, 7s and 9s & Multiplication and Division

In all units of work:
- Provision for solving problems and puzzles
- Concrete and pictorial representations of number and mathematical concepts before and alongside the abstract

Content from Unit 4A not yet mastered	Mastered Content: Rehearse, Recall, Refresh, Refine, Read & Reason

In this unit of work:

Standards for Teaching and Assessment in Mathematics	Suggested Order & Pace Setting	Indicative Teaching & Learning Activities
NPV4.1 Count in multiples of 6, 7, 9, 25 and 1000	Multiples of 6, 7, 9, 25 and 1000	Begin to know multiplication facts for 6, 9 and 7 tables (L3)
NPV4.3 Count backwards through zero to include negative numbers	Multiplication and division facts for multiplication tables up to 12x12	Recall multiplication facts up to 10 and quickly derive corresponding division facts (L4)
MD4.1 Recall multiplication and division facts for multiplication tables up to 12 × 12		
MD4.2 Use place value, known and derived facts to multiply and divide mentally, multiplying by 0 and 1; dividing by 1	Multiply and divide mentally using place value	
MD4.3 Use place value, known and derived facts to multiply and divide mentally, multiplying together three numbers	TU x U and HTU x U	
MD4.5 Multiply two-digit and three-digit numbers by a one-digit number using formal written layout	Compare and classify 2D shapes & lines of symmetry	
GPS4.1 Compare and classify geometric shapes, including quadrilaterals and triangles, based on their properties and sizes	Angles	
GPS4.2 Identify acute and obtuse angles and compare and order angles up to two right angles by size		
GPS4.3 Identify lines of symmetry in 2-D shapes presented in different orientations		
GPS4.4 Complete a simple symmetric figure with respect to a specific line of symmetry		

Key Vocabulary	

Working In-Line Whole-School School Calculation Policy

Year 4 Conquering Primary Maths Spring 1	Unit 4C Multiplication, Fractions and Shape

In all units of work:
- Provision for solving problems and puzzles
- Concrete and pictorial representations of number and mathematical concepts before and alongside the abstract

Content from Unit 4B not yet mastered	Mastered Content: Rehearse, Recall, Refresh, Refine, Read & Reason

In this unit of work:

Standards for Teaching and Assessment in Mathematics	Suggested Order & Pace Setting	Indicative Teaching & Learning Activities
MD4.4 Recognise and use factor pairs and commutativity in mental calculations	Factor pairs	Recognise and describe number relationships including multiple, factor and square (L4)
MD4.6 Solve problems involving multiplying and adding, including using the distributive law and harder multiplication problems such as which n objects are connected to m objects.	Multiplying and adding problems	Convert mixed numbers to improper fractions and vice versa (L4)
F4.2 Solve problems involving increasingly harder fractions to calculate quantities, and fractions to divide quantities, including non-unit fractions where the answer is a whole number	Equivalent fractions	Use equivalence between fractions, converting fractions such as $^2/_5$ into tenths or hundredths (L4 & L5)
	Add and subtract fractions	Understand and use the formula for the area of a rectangle and distinguish area from perimeter (L5)
	Solve problems involving fractions	*Find the length of a rectangle given its perimeter and width & find the area or perimeter of simple L shapes, given some edge lengths (L5)*
F4.3 Identify, name and write equivalent fractions of a given fraction, including tenths and hundredths	Perimeter and area	
F4.4 Add and subtract fractions with the same denominator.		
M4.2 Measure and calculate the perimeter of a rectilinear figure (including squares) in centimetres and metres		
M4.3 Find the area of rectilinear shapes by counting		

Key Vocabulary	

Working In-Line Whole-School School Calculation Policy

Year 4 Conquering Primary Maths Spring 2	Unit 4D Decimals and Fractions & Measure

In all units of work:
- Provision for solving problems and puzzles
- Concrete and pictorial representations of number and mathematical concepts before and alongside the abstract

Content from Unit 4C not yet mastered	Mastered Content: Rehearse, Recall, Refresh, Refine, Read & Reason

In this unit of work:

Standards for Teaching and Assessment in Mathematics	Suggested Order & Pace Setting	Indicative Teaching & Learning Activities
F4.1 Count up and down in hundredths; recognise that hundredths arise when dividing an object by a hundred and dividing tenths by ten DF4.1 Recognise and write decimal equivalents of any number of tenths or hundredths DF4.2 Recognise and write decimal equivalents to $\frac{1}{4}$; $\frac{1}{2}$; $\frac{3}{4}$ DF4.3 Find the effect of dividing a one- or two-digit number by 10 and 100, identifying the value of the digits in the answer as units, tenths and hundredths DF4.4 Round decimals with one decimal place to the nearest whole number DF4.5 Compare numbers with the same number of decimal places up to two decimal places DF4.6 Solve simple measure and money problems involving fractions and decimals to two decimal places M4.1 Convert between different units of measure (e.g. kilometre to metre; hour to minute) M4.5 Estimate, compare and calculate different measures, including money in pounds and pence	Fractions and decimals Place value in decimals Multiply and divide by 10 and 100 Convert units of measure Compare measures Solve problems with decimals to two decimal places	Use equivalence between fractions, e.g. convert fractions such as $\frac{2}{5}$ into tenths or hundredths and express them as decimals (L4 & L5) Use place value to multiply and divide whole numbers by 10 or 100 (L4) *Order decimals with one decimal place, or two decimal places in context of money (L3)*

Key Vocabulary	

Working In-Line Whole-School School Calculation Policy

In all units of work:

- Provision for solving problems and puzzles
- Concrete and pictorial representations of number and mathematical concepts before and alongside the abstract

Content from Unit 4D not yet mastered	Mastered Content: Rehearse, Recall, Refresh, Refine, Read & Reason

In this unit of work:

Standards for Teaching and Assessment in Mathematics	Suggested Order & Pace Setting	Indicative Teaching & Learning Activities
M4.6 Read, write and convert time between analogue and digital 12 and 24-hour clocks M4.7 Solve problems involving converting from hours to minutes; minutes to seconds; years to months; weeks to days. D4.1 Interpret and present discrete data using bar charts and continuous data using line graphs D4.2 Solve comparison, sum and difference problems using information presented in bar charts, pictograms, tables and simple line graphs	Analogue and digital time: twelve and twenty-four hour clock Converting time and solving time problems Bar charts and continuous data in line graphs Sum and difference problems using bar charts, pictograms, tables and simple line graphs	
Key Vocabulary		

Working In-Line Whole-School School Calculation Policy

In all units of work:
- Provision for solving problems and puzzles
- Concrete and pictorial representations of number and mathematical concepts before and alongside the abstract

Content from Unit 4E not yet mastered	Mastered Content: Rehearse, Recall, Refresh, Refine, Read & Reason

In this unit of work:

Standards for Teaching and Assessment in Mathematics	Suggested Order & Pace Setting	Indicative Teaching & Learning Activities
NPV4.9 Read Roman numerals to 100 (I to C) and understand how, over time, the numeral system changed to include the concept of zero and place value GPD4.1 Describe positions on a 2-D grid as coordinates in the first quadrant GPD4.2 Describe movements between positions as translations of a given unit to the left/right and up/down GPD4.3 Plot specified points and draw sides to complete a given polygon	Roman numerals to 100 (I to C) Coordinates and translating shape	

Key Vocabulary	

Working In-Line Whole-School School Calculation Policy

Year 5 Conquering Primary Maths Autumn 1	Unit 5A Number, Place Value, Add and Subtract & Shape

In all units of work:
- Provision for solving problems and puzzles
- Concrete and pictorial representations of number and mathematical concepts before and alongside the abstract

Content from Year 4 not yet mastered	Mastered Content: Rehearse, Recall, Refresh, Refine, Read & Reason

In this unit of work:

Standards for Teaching and Assessment in Mathematics	Suggested Order & Pace Setting	Indicative Teaching & Learning Activities
NPV5.1 Read, write, order and compare numbers to at least 1 000 000 and determine the value of each digit NPV5.2 Count forwards or backwards in steps of powers of 10 for any given number up to 1 000 000 NPV5.3 Round any number up to 1 000 000 to the nearest 10, 100,1000, 10 000 and 100 000 AS5.1 Add and subtract whole numbers with more than 4 digits, including using efficient written methods (columnar addition and subtraction) AS5.2 Add and subtract numbers mentally with increasingly large numbers AS5.3 Use rounding to check answers to calculations and determine, in the context of a problem, levels of accuracy AS5.4 Solve addition and subtraction multi-step problems in contexts, deciding which operations and methods to use and why. NPV5.4 Solve number problems and practical problems that involve all of the above GPS5.1 Identify 3-D shapes, including cubes and cuboids, from 2-D representations GPS5.8 State and use the properties of a rectangle (including squares) to deduce related facts GPS5.9 Distinguish between regular and irregular polygons based on reasoning about equal sides and angles	Extending number to 1,000,000 Round to nearest 10, 100, 1000, 10 000 and 10, 000, 000 Mental calculation with larger numbers Columnar addition and subtraction with more than four-digits Solving addition and subtraction problems 3D shapes from 2D representations Properties of a rectangle Regular and irregular polygons	-
Key Vocabulary		

Working In-Line Whole-School School Calculation Policy

Year 5 Conquering Primary Maths Autumn 2	Unit 5B Fractions, Decimals and Measures

In all units of work:

- Provision for solving problems and puzzles
- Concrete and pictorial representations of number and mathematical concepts before and alongside the abstract

Content from Unit 5A not yet mastered	Mastered Content: Rehearse, Recall, Refresh, Refine, Read & Reason

In this unit of work:

Standards for Teaching and Assessment in Mathematics	Suggested Order & Pace Setting	Indicative Teaching & Learning Activities
F5.1 Compare and order fractions whose denominators are all multiples of the same number	Compare and order fractions	Convert mixed numbers to improper fractions and vice versa (L4)
F5.2 Recognise mixed numbers and improper fractions and convert from one form to the other	Converting improper fractions and mixed numbers	Use equivalence between fractions, e.g. convert fractions such as $^2/_5$ into tenths or hundredths and express them as decimals (L4 & L5)
F5.3 Add and subtract fractions with the same denominator and related fractions; write mathematical statements >1 as a mixed number (e.g. $^2/_5 + ^4/_5 = ^6/_5 = 1\,^1/_5$)	Fractions to decimals	Use understanding of place value to multiply and divide whole numbers and decimals by 10, 100 and 1000 and explain the effect (L5)
F5.4 Multiply proper fractions and mixed numbers by whole numbers, supported by materials and diagrams.	Rounding decimals	Round decimals to the nearest decimal place (L5)
DF5.1 Read and write decimal numbers as fractions (e.g. $0.71 = ^{71}/_{100}$)	Multiply and divide by 10, 100 and 1000	Order decimals to three decimal places (L4)
DF5.2 Recognise and use thousandths and relate them to tenths, hundredths and decimal equivalents	Convert units of measure	Order decimals that have a mixture of 1, 2 or 3 decimal places (L5)
DF5.3 Round decimals with two decimal places to the nearest whole number and to one decimal place		
DF5.4 Read, write, order and compare numbers with up to three decimal places		
DF5.5 Solve problems involving number up to three decimal places		
MD5.8 Multiply and divide whole numbers and those involving decimals by 10, 100 and 1000		
M5.1 Convert between different units of measure (e.g. kilometre and metre; metre and centimetre; centimetre and millimetre; kilogram and gram; litre and millilitre)		

Key Vocabulary

Working In-Line Whole-School School Calculation Policy

In all units of work:
- Provision for solving problems and puzzles
- Concrete and pictorial representations of number and mathematical concepts before and alongside the abstract

Content from Unit 5B not yet mastered	Mastered Content: Rehearse, Recall, Refresh, Refine, Read & Reason

In this unit of work:

Standards for Teaching and Assessment in Mathematics	Suggested Order & Pace Setting	Indicative Teaching & Learning Activities
MD5.1 Identify multiples and factors, including finding all factor pairs	Multiples and factors	Recognise and use number patterns and relationships
MD5.3 Know and use the vocabulary of prime numbers, prime factors and composite (non-prime) numbers	Prime and composite numbers	*Find two-digit prime numbers* (L5)
MD5.4 Establish whether a number up to 100 is prime and recall prime numbers up to 19	Square and cubed numbers	Recognise and describe number relationships including multiple, factor and square (L4)
MD5.9 Recognise and use square numbers and cube numbers, and the notation for squared and cubed	Perimeter and area	
MD5.6 Multiply and divide numbers mentally drawing upon known facts		
M5.3 Measure and calculate the perimeter of composite rectilinear shapes in centimetres and metres	Volume and capacity	
M5.4 Calculate and compare the area of squares and rectangles including using standard units, square centimetres (cm^2) and square metres (m^2) and estimate the area of irregular shapes		
M5.5 Recognise and estimate volume (e.g. using 1 cm^3 blocks to build cubes and cuboids) and capacity (e.g. using water)		

Key Vocabulary	

Working In-Line Whole-School School Calculation Policy

Year 5 Conquering Primary Maths Spring 2	Unit 5D Multiplication and Division

In all units of work:
- Provision for solving problems and puzzles
- Concrete and pictorial representations of number and mathematical concepts before and alongside the abstract

Content from Unit 5C not yet mastered	Mastered Content: Rehearse, Recall, Refresh, Refine, Read & Reason

In this unit of work:

Standards for Teaching and Assessment in Mathematics	Suggested Order & Pace Setting	Indicative Teaching & Learning Activities
MD5.5 Multiply numbers up to 4 digits by a one- or two-digit number using an efficient written method, including long multiplication for two-digit numbers	Th H T U x U or TU	Use efficient written methods of addition and subtraction and of short multiplication and division (L4)
MD5.7 Divide numbers up to 4 digits by a one-digit number using the efficient written method of short division and interpret remainders appropriately for the context	Divide Th H T U by U	
	Solving multiplication and division problems	
MD5.2 Solve problems involving multiplication and division where larger numbers are used by decomposing them into their factors	Use all four operations to solve problems	
MD5.11 Solve problems involving multiplication and division, including scaling by simple fractions and problems involving simple rates.		
MD5.10 Solve problems involving addition, subtraction, multiplication and division and a combination of these, including understanding the meaning of the equals sign		

Key Vocabulary	

Working In-Line Whole-School School Calculation Policy

In all units of work:
- Provision for solving problems and puzzles
- Concrete and pictorial representations of number and mathematical concepts before and alongside the abstract

Content from Unit 5D not yet mastered	Mastered Content: Rehearse, Recall, Refresh, Refine, Read & Reason

In this unit of work:

Standards for Teaching and Assessment in Mathematics	Suggested Order & Pace Setting	Indicative Teaching & Learning Activities
PDF5.1 Recognise the per cent symbol (%) and understand that per cent relates to "number of parts per hundred", and write percentages as a fraction with denominator hundred, and as a decimal fraction PDF5.2 Solve problems which require knowing percentage and decimal equivalents of 1/2, 1/4, 1/5, 2/5, 4/5 and those with a denominator of a multiple of 10 or 25. GPS5.2 Know angles are measured in degrees; estimate and measure them and draw a given angle, writing its size in degrees (o) GPS5.3 Identify multiples of 90 degrees GPS5.4 Identify angles at a point on a straight line and ½ a turn (total 180 degrees) GPS5.5 identify angles at a point and one whole turn (total 360 degrees) GPS5.6 Identify reflex angles, and compare different angles GPS5.7 Draw shapes using given dimensions and angles GPD5.1 Identify, describe and represent the position of a shape following a reflection or translation, using the appropriate language, and know that the shape has not changed.	Per cent as parts per 100 Percentage, decimal and fraction equivalents Angles Reflection and translation Probability experiments, predictions; fair and unfair games	Use equivalence between fractions *Convert fractions such as $^2/_5$ into tenths or hundredths and express them as decimals or percentages and vice versa (L5)* Calculate simple fractions or percentages of a number/quantity e.g. ¾ of 400g or 60% of £300 (L5)

Key Vocabulary	

Working In-Line Whole-School School Calculation Policy

Year 5 Conquering Primary Maths Summer 2	Unit 5F Measure, Time & Data

In all units of work:
- Provision for solving problems and puzzles
- Concrete and pictorial representations of number and mathematical concepts before and alongside the abstract

Content from Unit 5E not yet mastered	Mastered Content: Rehearse, Recall, Refresh, Refine, Read & Reason

In this unit of work:

Standards for Teaching and Assessment in Mathematics	Suggested Order & Pace Setting	Indicative Teaching & Learning Activities
M5.2 Understand and use basic equivalences between metric and common imperial units and express them in approximate terms M5.6 Solve problems involving converting between units of time M5.7 Solve problems involving addition and subtraction of units of measure (e.g. length, mass, volume, money) using decimal notation. D5.1 Solve comparison, sum and difference problems using information presented in line graphs D5.1 Complete, read and interpret information in tables, including timetables.	Metric and imperial units	Read and interpret timetables (L4)
	Problems involving converting time	
	Addition and subtraction of units of measure	
	Line graph comparisons, sums and differences	
	Complete, read and interpret tabulated information	

Key Vocabulary	

Working In-Line Whole-School School Calculation Policy

In all units of work:
- Provision for solving problems and puzzles
- Concrete and pictorial representations of number and mathematical concepts before and alongside the abstract

Content from Year 5 not yet mastered	Mastered Content: Rehearse, Recall, Refresh, Refine, Read & Reason

In this unit of work:

Standards for Teaching and Assessment in Mathematics	Suggested Order & Pace Setting	Indicative Teaching & Learning Activities
NPV6.1 Read, write, order and compare numbers up to 10 000 000 and determine the value of each digit	Revision of numbers to 1, 000, 000; read, write, place value order and round	Use understanding of place value to multiply and divide whole numbers and decimals by 10, 100 and 1000 and explain the effect (L5)
DF6.1 Identify the value of each digit to three decimal places and multiply and divide numbers by 10, 100 and 1000 where the answers are up to three decimal places	Multiply and divide by 10, 100 and 1000	Add and subtract negative numbers in context (L5)

Use brackets appropriately, e.g. *know and use the order of operations, including brackets* (L5) |
| NPV6.2 Round any whole number to a required degree of accuracy | Mental calculation strategies review (brackets and order of operations) | Understand that the angle sum of a triangle is 180° and of a quadrilateral is 360° (L6) |
| NPV6.3 Use negative numbers in context, and calculate intervals across zero | Written calculation review | Use the formula for the area of a triangle and parallelogram (L6) |
| NPV6.4 Solve number problems and practical problems that involve all of the above. | Miscellaneous problems involving whole numbers and decimals | Know and use the angle sum of a triangle and that of angles at a point, e.g.

- *Calculate 'missing angles' in triangles, including isosceles triangles or right angled triangles, when only one/one other angle is given (L5)* |
ASMD6.5 Use their knowledge of the order of operations to carry out calculations involving the four operations	Calculate unknown angles in 2D shape	*- Calculate angles on a straight line or at a point such as the angle between the hands of a clock, or intersecting diagonals at the centre of a regular hexagon (L5)*
ASMD6.3 Perform mental calculations, including with mixed operations and large numbers	Area and perimeter (same area, different perimeter)	
ASMD6.6 Solve addition and subtraction multi-step problems in contexts, deciding which operations and methods to use and why	Area of parallelograms and triangles	
GPS6.2 Compare and classify geometric shapes based on their properties and sizes and find unknown angles in any triangles, quadrilaterals, and regular polygons		
M6.4 Recognise that shapes with the same areas can have different perimeters and vice versa		
M6.5 Calculate the area of parallelograms and triangles		

Key Vocabulary

Working In-Line Whole-School School Calculation Policy

In all units of work:

- Provision for solving problems and puzzles
- Concrete and pictorial representations of number and mathematical concepts before and alongside the abstract

Content from Unit 6A not yet mastered	Mastered Content: Rehearse, Recall, Refresh, Refine, Read & Reason

In this unit of work:

Standards for Teaching and Assessment in Mathematics	Suggested Order & Pace Setting	Indicative Teaching & Learning Activities
ASMD6.8 Use estimation to check answers to calculations and determine, in the context of a problem, levels of accuracy	Th H T U x TU	Use the formula for volume of a cuboid calculate volumes and surface areas of cuboids (L6)
ASMD6.1 Multiply multi-digit numbers up to 4 digits by a two-digit whole number using the efficient written method of long multiplication	Divide Th H T U by TU	
ASMD6.2 Divide numbers up to 4 digits by a two-digit whole number using the efficient written method of long division, and interpret remainders as whole number remainders, fractions, or by rounding, as appropriate for the context	Problems involving all four operations	
	Nets and 3D shape construction	
ASMD6.7 Solve problems involving addition, subtraction, multiplication and division	Formula for area and volume of shapes	
GPS6.1 Recognise, describe and build simple 3-D shapes, including making nets	Calculate volume of cubes and cuboids	
M6.6 Recognise when it is necessary to use the formulae for area and volume of shapes		
M6.7 Calculate, estimate and compare volume of cubes and cuboids using standard units including cm cubed, cubic metres and extend to other units (mm/km)		

Key Vocabulary	

Working In-Line Whole-School School Calculation Policy

In all units of work:
- Provision for solving problems and puzzles
- Concrete and pictorial representations of number and mathematical concepts before and alongside the abstract

Content from Unit 6B not yet mastered	Mastered Content: Rehearse, Recall, Refresh, Refine, Read & Reason

In this unit of work:

Standards for Teaching and Assessment in Mathematics	Suggested Order & Pace Setting	Indicative Teaching & Learning Activities
ASMD6.4 Identify common factors, common multiples and prime numbers F6.1 Use common factors to simplify fractions; use common multiples to express fractions in the same denomination F6.2 Compare and order fractions, including fractions >1 F6.3 Associate a fraction with division to calculate decimal fraction equivalents (e.g. 0.375) for a simple fraction F6.4 Add and subtract fractions with different denominators and mixed numbers, using the concept of equivalent fractions F6.5 Multiply simple pairs of proper fractions, writing the answer in its simplest form F6.6 Divide proper fractions by whole numbers (e.g. $\frac{1}{3} \div 2 = \frac{1}{6}$). DF6.2 Multiply one-digit numbers with up to two decimal places by whole numbers DF6.3 Use written division methods in cases where the answer has up to two decimal places DF6.4 Solve problems requiring answers to be rounded to specified degrees of accuracy. GPS6.4 Find unknown angles where they meet at a point, are on a straight line, and are vertically opposite	Common factors, common multiples and prime numbers Simplify fractions Compare and order fractions, decimal and fraction equivalents Add and subtract fractions Multiply pairs of proper fractions and divide proper fractions by whole number Multiply and divide numbers with two decimal places Finding unknown angles: straight line and vertically opposite	Add and subtract fractions by writing them with a common denominator (L6)

Key Vocabulary	

Working In-Line Whole-School School Calculation Policy

Year 6 Conquering Primary Maths Spring 2	Unit 6D Percentages, Decimals and Fractions & Algebra

In all units of work:
- Provision for solving problems and puzzles
- Concrete and pictorial representations of number and mathematical concepts before and alongside the abstract

Content from Unit 6C not yet mastered	Mastered Content: Rehearse, Recall, Refresh, Refine, Read & Reason

In this unit of work:

Standards for Teaching and Assessment in Mathematics	Suggested Order & Pace Setting	Indicative Teaching & Learning Activities
PDF6.1 Solve problems involving the calculation of percentages of whole numbers or measures such as 15% of 360 and the use of percentages for comparison	Percentages of whole numbers and measures and using FDP equivalences	Construct, express in symbolic form, and use simple formulae involving one or two operations, e.g.
PDF6.2 Recall and use equivalences between simple fractions, decimals and percentages, including in different contexts.	Ratio and proportion	-Understand simple expressions using symbols e.g. '2 less than n' can be written as 'n - 2'
AL6.1 Express missing number problems algebraically	Probability	-Evaluate expressions by substituting numbers into them
AL6.2 Use simple formulae expressed in words	Algebra	-Use symbols to represent an unknown number or a variable (L5)
AL6.3 Generate and describe linear number sequences		Generate terms of a sequence using term to term and position to term definitions of the sequence (L6)
AL6.4 Find pairs of numbers that satisfy number sentences involving two unknowns.		Find the nth term of a linear sequence (L6)
RP6.1 Solve problems involving the relative sizes of two quantities, including similarity		Use systematic trial and improvement to find solutions to equations (L6)
RP6.2 Solve problems involving unequal sharing and grouping.		Solve simple inequalities, e.g. $3x + 1 < 16$ (L7)

Key Vocabulary	

Working In-Line Whole-School School Calculation Policy

In all units of work:
- Provision for solving problems and puzzles
- Concrete and pictorial representations of number and mathematical concepts before and alongside the abstract

Content from Unit 6D not yet mastered	Mastered Content: Rehearse, Recall, Refresh, Refine, Read & Reason

In this unit of work:

Standards for Teaching and Assessment in Mathematics	Suggested Order & Pace Setting	Indicative Teaching & Learning Activities
M6.2 Use, read, write and convert between standard units, converting measurements of length, mass, volume and time from a smaller unit of measure to a larger unit, and vice versa, using decimal notation to three decimal places M6.1 Solve problems involving the calculation and conversion of units of measure, using decimal notation to three decimal places where appropriate	Read, write and convert standard units of measure Solve problems involving conversion of units of measure Review: Diagnostic tests and practice **KEY STAGE 2 TESTS**	

Key Vocabulary	

Working In-Line Whole-School School Calculation Policy

Year 6 Conquering Primary Maths Summer 2	Unit 6F Data and Shape

In all units of work:
- Provision for solving problems and puzzles
- Concrete and pictorial representations of number and mathematical concepts before and alongside the abstract

Content from Unit 6E not yet mastered	Mastered Content: Rehearse, Recall, Refresh, Refine, Read & Reason

In this unit of work:

Standards for Teaching and Assessment in Mathematics	Suggested Order & Pace Setting	Indicative Teaching & Learning Activities
D6.1 Interpret and construct pie charts and line graphs and use these to solve problems M6.3 Convert between miles and kilometres D6.2 Calculate and interpret the mean as an average. GPS6.3 Illustrate and name parts of circles, including radius, diameter and circumference GPD6.1 Describe positions on the full coordinate grid (all four quadrants) GPD6.2 Draw and translate simple shapes on the coordinate plane, and reflect them in the axes.	Pie charts and line graphs Miles to kilometres conversion Parts of a circle Coordinates in all four quadrants Translate shape and reflect in axes	Interpret frequency diagrams and simple line graphs (L4) Interpret simple pie charts (L4) Interpret graphs and diagrams, including pie charts, and draw conclusions (L5) - *Interpret and compare pie charts where it is not necessary to measure angles (L5)* - *Recognise when information is presented in a misleading way, for example compare two pie charts where the sample sizes are different (L5)* Know and use the formulae for the circumference and area of a circle (L6) Use and interpret coordinates in all four quadrants (L5) - *Translate shapes along an oblique line (L5)* *Given the coordinates of three vertices of a parallelogram, find the fourth (L5)*

Key Vocabulary	

Working In-Line Whole-School School Calculation Policy

Chapter 7: A Standards-Based Model for English

In this chapter, unit plans for English are provided. Grade-level standards to be achieved by the end of an academic year are specified. Classroom teachers will need to establish teaching sequences to move children towards end of year expectations. Chapter Three and Chapter Five contain information on how to ensure logical progression in learning is built into a teaching sequence and a short-cycle of assessment is planned to closely monitor the learning that is taking place.

The medium-term plans assume Year 1 and Year 2 will undertake seven blocks of work covering a variety of texts spanning poetry narrative and non-fiction. Grade-level standards for word structure have been set by each half term. Systematic synthetic phonics is conspicuous by its absence in the unit plans. This omission is deliberate. Schools use a variety of schemes and programmes introducing grapheme-phoneme correspondences and irregular words in slightly different orders. Classroom teachers are therefore best placed to set the expectation for which correspondences and exception words children transcribe correctly as an academic year progresses.

For Key Stage 2, the unit plans specify the word structure standards children need in either a half term block or within a term. Each medium-term plan is labelled with the half term or term it corresponds to. The word structure standards that need to be taught at that point in the year appear in black type. Those rendered in grey are grade-level standards that require teaching in the future or have been covered previously. This should become clearer as you survey the unit plans.

Text-types and genres have not been specified on the medium-term plans. The standards will remain the same regardless of what text is being used to stimulate children and offer a context for reading and writing activities in English.

Key Stage 1 Standards-Based English Unit Plans

YEAR 1 Genre/Text-Type: Title(s): Autumn Term & Approximate Date Span:		STANDARDS-BASED ENGLISH UNIT PLAN 1
Embedded Standards for ALL units of work		
Reading Comprehension		**Composition**
(a) Listen to and discuss wide range of poems, stories and non-fiction at a level beyond that at which they can read independently (b) Link what they read or hear to own experiences (c) Become familiar with key stories, fairy tales and traditional tales, retelling these and considering their characteristics (d) Recognise and join in with predictable phrases (e) Appreciate rhymes and poems, and to recite some by heart		(a) Saying aloud what they are going to write about (b) Composing a sentence orally before writing it (c) Re-reading what they have written to check that it makes sense (d) Discuss what they have written with the teacher or other children (e) Read aloud their writing clearly enough to be heard by peers and the teacher
Year 1 Standards		**Year 1 Word Structure Standard Introduced**
SS1.1 How words can combine to make sentences SS1.2 Joining words and joining sentences using *and*	P1.1 Separation of words with spaces P1.2 Introduction to capital letters, full stops, question marks and exclamation marks to demarcate sentences P1.3 Capital letters for names and for the personal pronoun *I*	WS1.1 Regular plural noun suffixes –*s* or –*es* (e.g. *dog, dogs; wish, wishes*)
TS1.1 Sequencing sentences to form short narratives		
Key Vocabulary for Teaching and Learning		word, sentence, letter, capital letter, full stop, punctuation, singular, plural, question mark, exclamation mark
Reading Comprehension & Immersion → Gathering & Capturing Content → Composing Text		

YEAR 1 Genre/Text-Type: Title(s): Autumn Term & Approximate Date Span:	STANDARDS-BASED ENGLISH UNIT PLAN 2

Embedded Standards for ALL units of work

Reading Comprehension	Composition
(a) Listen to and discuss wide range of poems, stories and non-fiction at a level beyond that at which they can read independently **(b)** Link what they read or hear to own experiences **(c)** Become familiar with key stories, fairy tales and traditional tales, retelling these and considering their characteristics **(d)** Recognise and join in with predictable phrases **(e)** Appreciate rhymes and poems, and to recite some by heart	**(a)** Saying aloud what they are going to write about **(b)** Composing a sentence orally before writing it **(c)** Re-reading what they have written to check that it makes sense **(d)** Discuss what they have written with the teacher or other children **(e)** Read aloud their writing clearly enough to be heard by peers and the teacher

Year 1 Standards		Year 1 Word Structure Continued
SS1.1 How words can combine to make sentences **SS1.2 Joining words and joining sentences using** *and*	**P1.1 Separation of words with spaces** **P1.2 Introduction to capital letters, full stops, question marks and exclamation marks to demarcate sentences** **P1.3 Capital letters for names and for the personal pronoun** *I*	**WS1.1 Regular plural noun suffixes** *–s* or *–es* (e.g. *dog, dogs; wish, wishes*)
TS1.1 Sequencing sentences to form short narratives		
Key Vocabulary for Teaching and Learning	word, sentence, letter, capital letter, full stop, punctuation, singular, plural, question mark, exclamation mark	

Reading Comprehension & Immersion → Gathering & Capturing Content → Composing Text

YEAR 1 Genre/Text-Type: Title(s): Spring Term & Approximate Date Span:	STANDARDS-BASED ENGLISH UNIT PLAN 3

Embedded Standards for ALL units of work

Reading Comprehension	Composition
(a) Listen to and discuss wide range of poems, stories and non-fiction at a level beyond that at which they can read independently (b) Link what they read or hear to own experiences (c) Become familiar with key stories, fairy tales and traditional tales, retelling these and considering their characteristics (d) Recognise and join in with predictable phrases (e) Appreciate rhymes and poems, and to recite some by heart	(a) Saying aloud what they are going to write about (b) Composing a sentence orally before writing it (c) Re-reading what they have written to check that it makes sense (d) Discuss what they have written with the teacher or other children (e) Read aloud their writing clearly enough to be heard by peers and the teacher

Year 1 Standards		Year 1 Word Structure Standard Introduced
SS1.1 How words can combine to make sentences SS1.2 Joining words and joining sentences using *and*	P1.1 Separation of words with spaces P1.2 Introduction to capital letters, full stops, question marks and exclamation marks to demarcate sentences P1.3 Capital letters for names and for the personal pronoun *I*	WS1.1 Regular plural noun suffixes *–s* or *–es* (e.g. *dog*, *dogs; wish, wishes*)
TS1.1 Sequencing sentences to form short narratives		
Key Vocabulary for Teaching and Learning	word, sentence, letter, capital letter, full stop, punctuation, singular, plural, question mark, exclamation mark	

Reading Comprehension & Immersion → Gathering & Capturing Content → Composing Text

YEAR 1 Genre/Text-Type: Title(s): Spring Term & Approximate Date Span:	STANDARDS-BASED ENGLISH UNIT PLAN 4

Embedded Standards for ALL units of work

Reading Comprehension	Composition
(a) Listen to and discuss wide range of poems, stories and non-fiction at a level beyond that at which they can read independently

(b) Link what they read or hear to own experiences

(c) Become familiar with key stories, fairy tales and traditional tales, retelling these and considering their characteristics

(d) Recognise and join in with predictable phrases

(e) Appreciate rhymes and poems, and to recite some by heart | (a) Saying aloud what they are going to write about

(b) Composing a sentence orally before writing it

(c) Re-reading what they have written to check that it makes sense

(d) Discuss what they have written with the teacher or other children

(e) Read aloud their writing clearly enough to be heard by peers and the teacher |

Year 1 Standards		Year 1 Word Structure Continued
SS1.1 How words can combine to make sentences

SS1.2 Joining words and joining sentences using *and* | P1.1 Separation of words with spaces

P1.2 Introduction to capital letters, full stops, question marks and exclamation marks to demarcate sentences

P1.3 Capital letters for names and for the personal pronoun *I* | WS1.2 Suffixes that can be added to verbs (e.g. *helping, helped, helper*) |
| TS1.1 Sequencing sentences to form short narratives | | |
| **Key Vocabulary for Teaching and Learning** | | word, sentence, letter, capital letter, full stop, punctuation, singular, plural, question mark, exclamation mark |

Reading Comprehension & Immersion → Gathering & Capturing Content → Composing Text

YEAR 1 Genre/Text-Type: Title(s): Summer Term & Approximate Date Span:	STANDARDS-BASED ENGLISH UNIT PLAN 5

Embedded Standards for ALL units of work

Reading Comprehension	Composition
(a) Listen to and discuss wide range of poems, stories and non-fiction at a level beyond that at which they can read independently	(a) Saying aloud what they are going to write about
(b) Link what they read or hear to own experiences	(b) Composing a sentence orally before writing it
(c) Become familiar with key stories, fairy tales and traditional tales, retelling these and considering their characteristics	(c) Re-reading what they have written to check that it makes sense
(d) Recognise and join in with predictable phrases	(d) Discuss what they have written with the teacher or other children
(e) Appreciate rhymes and poems, and to recite some by heart	(e) Read aloud their writing clearly enough to be heard by peers and the teacher

Year 1 Standards		Year 1 Word Structure Standard Introduced
SS1.1 How words can combine to make sentences SS1.2 Joining words and joining sentences using *and*	P1.1 Separation of words with spaces P1.2 Introduction to capital letters, full stops, question marks and exclamation marks to demarcate sentences P1.3 Capital letters for names and for the personal pronoun *I*	WS1.3 How the prefix *un–* changes the meaning of verbs and adjectives (negation, *e.g. unkind*, or undoing, *e.g. untie the boat*)
TS1.1 Sequencing sentences to form short narratives		
Key Vocabulary for Teaching and Learning		word, sentence, letter, capital letter, full stop, punctuation, singular, plural, question mark, exclamation mark

Reading Comprehension & Immersion → Gathering & Capturing Content → Composing Text

YEAR 1	STANDARDS-BASED ENGLISH UNIT PLAN 6
Genre/Text-Type:	
Title(s):	
Summer Term & Approximate Date Span:	

Embedded Standards for ALL units of work

Reading Comprehension	Composition
(a) Listen to and discuss wide range of poems, stories and non-fiction at a level beyond that at which they can read independently	**(a)** Saying aloud what they are going to write about
	(b) Composing a sentence orally before writing it
(b) Link what they read or hear to own experiences	**(c)** Re-reading what they have written to check that it makes sense
(c) Become familiar with key stories, fairy tales and traditional tales, retelling these and considering their characteristics	**(d)** Discuss what they have written with the teacher or other children
(d) Recognise and join in with predictable phrases	**(e)** Read aloud their writing clearly enough to be heard by peers and the teacher
(e) Appreciate rhymes and poems, and to recite some by heart	

Year 1 Standards		Year 1 Word Structure Continued
SS1.1 How words can combine to make sentences **SS1.2 Joining words and joining sentences using _and_**	**P1.1 Separation of words with spaces** **P1.2 Introduction to capital letters, full stops, question marks and exclamation marks to demarcate sentences** **P1.3 Capital letters for names and for the personal pronoun _I_**	**WS1.3 How the prefix _un–_ changes the meaning of verbs and adjectives (negation, _e.g. unkind_, or undoing, _e.g. untie the boat_)**
TS1.1 Sequencing sentences to form short narratives		
Key Vocabulary for Teaching and Learning		word, sentence, letter, capital letter, full stop, punctuation, singular, plural, question mark, exclamation mark

Reading Comprehension & Immersion → Gathering & Capturing Content → Composing Text

YEAR 1 Genre/Text-Type: Title(s): Summer Term & Approximate Date Span:	STANDARDS-BASED ENGLISH UNIT PLAN 7

Embedded Standards for ALL units of work

Reading Comprehension	Composition
(a) Listen to and discuss wide range of poems, stories and non-fiction at a level beyond that at which they can read independently **(b) Link what they read or hear to own experiences** **(c) Become familiar with key stories, fairy tales and traditional tales, retelling these and considering their characteristics** **(d) Recognise and join in with predictable phrases** **(e) Appreciate rhymes and poems, and to recite some by heart**	**(a) Saying aloud what they are going to write about** **(b) Composing a sentence orally before writing it** **(c) Re-reading what they have written to check that it makes sense** **(d) Discuss what they have written with the teacher or other children** **(e) Read aloud their writing clearly enough to be heard by peers and the teacher**

Year 1 Standards		Year 1 Word Structure Standards to Secure
SS1.1 How words can combine to make sentences **SS1.2 Joining words and joining sentences using *and***	**P1.1 Separation of words with spaces** **P1.2 Introduction to capital letters, full stops, question marks and exclamation marks to demarcate sentences** **P1.3 Capital letters for names and for the personal pronoun *I***	**WS1.1 Regular plural noun suffixes *–s* or *–es* (e.g. *dog, dogs; wish, wishes*)** **WS1.2 Suffixes that can be added to verbs (e.g. *helping, helped, helper*)** **WS1.3 How the prefix *un–* changes the meaning of verbs and adjectives (negation, *e.g. unkind*, or undoing, *e.g. untie the boat*)**
TS1.1 Sequencing sentences to form short narratives		
Key Vocabulary for Teaching and Learning	word, sentence, letter, capital letter, full stop, punctuation, singular, plural, question mark, exclamation mark	

Reading Comprehension & Immersion → Gathering & Capturing Content → Composing Text

YEAR 2	STANDARDS-BASED ENGLISH UNIT PLAN 1
Genre/Text-Type:	
Title(s):	
Autumn Term (1) & Approximate Date Span:	

Embedded Standards for ALL units of work

Reading Comprehension	Composition
(a) Listening to, discussing and expressing views about a wide range of poetry (including contemporary and classic), stories and non-fiction at a level beyond that at which they can read independently	(a) Planning or saying out loud what they are going to write about
	(b) Writing down ideas and/or key words, including new vocabulary
(b) Discussing sequence of events in books and how items of information are related	(c) Encapsulating what they want to say, sentence by sentence
(c) Become familiar with and retelling a wider range of stories, fairy stories and traditional tales	(d) Make simple additions, revisions and corrections to their work
	(e) Evaluate their writing with the teacher and other children
(d) Introduced to non-fiction books structured in different ways	(f) Re-reading to check that their writing makes sense and that verbs used to indicate time are used correctly, including verbs in the continuous form
(e) Recognise simple recurring literary language	
(f) Discuss favourite words and phrases	(g) Proof-reading to check for errors in spelling, grammar and punctuation (e.g. ends of sentences punctuated correctly)
(g) Build up repertoire of poems learnt by heart	(h) Read aloud what they have written with appropriate intonation to make meaning clear

Year 2 Standards	Year 2 Word Structure Standards Introduced
SS2.1 Subordination (using when, if, that, or because) and co-ordination (using or, and, or but)	WS2.1 Formation of nouns using suffixes such as –ness, –er
SS2.2 Expanded noun phrases for description and specification (e.g. the blue butterfly, plain flour, the man in the moon)	
SS2.3 Sentences with different forms: statement, question, exclamation, command	
TS2.1 Correct choice and consistent use of present tense and past tense throughout writing	
TS2.2 Use of the continuous form of verbs in the present and past tense to mark actions in progress (e.g. she is drumming, he was shouting)	

Key Vocabulary for Teaching and Learning	verb, tense (past, present), adjective, noun, suffix, apostrophe, comma

Reading Comprehension & Immersion → Gathering & Capturing Content → Composing Text

YEAR 2 Genre/Text-Type: Title(s): Autumn Term (2) & Approximate Date Span:	STANDARDS-BASED ENGLISH UNIT PLAN 2

Embedded Standards for ALL units of work

Reading Comprehension	Composition
(a) Listening to, discussing and expressing views about a wide range of poetry (including contemporary and classic), stories and non-fiction at a level beyond that at which they can read independently	(a) Planning or saying out loud what they are going to write about
	(b) Writing down ideas and/or key words, including new vocabulary
(b) Discussing sequence of events in books and how items of information are related	(c) Encapsulating what they want to say, sentence by sentence
(c) Become familiar with and retelling a wider range of stories, fairy stories and traditional tales	(d) Make simple additions, revisions and corrections to their work
(d) Introduced to non-fiction books structured in different ways	(e) Evaluate their writing with the teacher and other children
(e) Recognise simple recurring literary language	(f) Re-reading to check that their writing makes sense and that verbs used to indicate time are used correctly, including verbs in the continuous form
(f) Discuss favourite words and phrases	(g) Proof-reading to check for errors in spelling, grammar and punctuation (e.g. ends of sentences punctuated correctly)
(g) Build up repertoire of poems learnt by heart	(h) Read aloud what they have written with appropriate intonation to make meaning clear

Year 2 Standards	Year 2 Word Structure Continued
SS2.1 Subordination (using when, if, that, or because) and co-ordination (using or, and, or but)	
SS2.2 Expanded noun phrases for description and specification (e.g. the blue butterfly, plain flour, the man in the moon)	WS2.1 Formation of nouns using suffixes such as –ness, –er
SS2.3 Sentences with different forms: statement, question, exclamation, command	
TS2.1 Correct choice and consistent use of present tense and past tense throughout writing	
TS2.2 Use of the continuous form of verbs in the present and past tense to mark actions in progress (e.g. she is drumming, he was shouting)	
Key Vocabulary for Teaching and Learning	verb, tense (past, present), adjective, noun, suffix, apostrophe, comma

Reading Comprehension & Immersion → Gathering & Capturing Content → Composing Text

YEAR 2 Genre/Text-Type: Title(s): Spring Term (1) & Approximate Date Span:	STANDARDS-BASED ENGLISH UNIT PLAN 3

Embedded Standards for ALL units of work

Reading Comprehension	Composition
(a) Listening to, discussing and expressing views about a wide range of poetry (including contemporary and classic), stories and non-fiction at a level beyond that at which they can read independently	(a) Planning or saying out loud what they are going to write about
	(b) Writing down ideas and/or key words, including new vocabulary
(b) Discussing sequence of events in books and how items of information are related	(c) Encapsulating what they want to say, sentence by sentence
(c) Become familiar with and retelling a wider range of stories, fairy stories and traditional tales	(d) Make simple additions, revisions and corrections to their work
(d) Introduced to non-fiction books structured in different ways	(e) Evaluate their writing with the teacher and other children
(e) Recognise simple recurring literary language	(f) Re-reading to check that their writing makes sense and that verbs used to indicate time are used correctly, including verbs in the continuous form
(f) Discuss favourite words and phrases	(g) Proof-reading to check for errors in spelling, grammar and punctuation (e.g. ends of sentences punctuated correctly)
(g) Build up repertoire of poems learnt by heart	(h) Read aloud what they have written with appropriate intonation to make meaning clear

Year 2 Standards	Year 2 Word Structure Standard Introduced
SS2.1 Subordination (using when, if, that, or because) and co-ordination (using or, and, or but)	
SS2.2 Expanded noun phrases for description and specification (e.g. the blue butterfly, plain flour, the man in the moon)	WS2.2 Formation of adjectives using suffixes such as –ful, –less
SS2.3 Sentences with different forms: statement, question, exclamation, command	
TS2.1 Correct choice and consistent use of present tense and past tense throughout writing	
TS2.2 Use of the continuous form of verbs in the present and past tense to mark actions in progress (e.g. she is drumming, he was shouting)	

Key Vocabulary for Teaching and Learning	verb, tense (past, present), adjective, noun, suffix, apostrophe, comma

Reading Comprehension & Immersion → Gathering & Capturing Content → Composing Text

YEAR 2	STANDARDS-BASED ENGLISH UNIT PLAN 4
Genre/Text-Type:	
Title(s):	
Spring Term (2) & Approximate Date Span:	

Embedded Standards for ALL units of work

Reading Comprehension	Composition
(a) Listening to, discussing and expressing views about a wide range of poetry (including contemporary and classic), stories and non-fiction at a level beyond that at which they can read independently	**(a)** Planning or saying out loud what they are going to write about
	(b) Writing down ideas and/or key words, including new vocabulary
(b) Discussing sequence of events in books and how items of information are related	**(c)** Encapsulating what they want to say, sentence by sentence
(c) Become familiar with and retelling a wider range of stories, fairy stories and traditional tales	**(d)** Make simple additions, revisions and corrections to their work
(d) Introduced to non-fiction books structured in different ways	**(e)** Evaluate their writing with the teacher and other children
(e) Recognise simple recurring literary language	**(f)** Re-reading to check that their writing makes sense and that verbs used to indicate time are used correctly, including verbs in the continuous form
(f) Discuss favourite words and phrases	**(g)** Proof-reading to check for errors in spelling, grammar and punctuation (e.g. ends of sentences punctuated correctly)
(g) Build up repertoire of poems learnt by heart	**(h)** Read aloud what they have written with appropriate intonation to make meaning clear

Year 2 Standards	Year 2 Word Structure Continued
SS2.1 Subordination (using when, if, that, or because) and co-ordination (using or, and, or but)	
SS2.2 Expanded noun phrases for description and specification (e.g. the blue butterfly, plain flour, the man in the moon)	**WS2.2 Formation of adjectives using suffixes such as *–ful, –less***
SS2.3 Sentences with different forms: statement, question, exclamation, command	
TS2.1 Correct choice and consistent use of present tense and past tense throughout writing	
TS2.2 Use of the continuous form of verbs in the present and past tense to mark actions in progress (e.g. she is drumming, he was shouting)	
Key Vocabulary for Teaching and Learning	verb, tense (past, present), adjective, noun, suffix, apostrophe, comma

Reading Comprehension & Immersion → Gathering & Capturing Content → Composing Text

YEAR 2 Genre/Text-Type: Title(s): Summer Term (1) & Approximate Date Span:	STANDARDS-BASED ENGLISH UNIT PLAN 5

Embedded Standards for ALL units of work

Reading Comprehension	Composition
(a) Listening to, discussing and expressing views about a wide range of poetry (including contemporary and classic), stories and non-fiction at a level beyond that at which they can read independently (b) Discussing sequence of events in books and how items of information are related (c) Become familiar with and retelling a wider range of stories, fairy stories and traditional tales (d) Introduced to non-fiction books structured in different ways (e) Recognise simple recurring literary language (f) Discuss favourite words and phrases (g) Build up repertoire of poems learnt by heart	(a) Planning or saying out loud what they are going to write about (b) Writing down ideas and/or key words, including new vocabulary (c) Encapsulating what they want to say, sentence by sentence (d) Make simple additions, revisions and corrections to their work (e) Evaluate their writing with the teacher and other children (f) Re-reading to check that their writing makes sense and that verbs used to indicate time are used correctly, including verbs in the continuous form (g) Proof-reading to check for errors in spelling, grammar and punctuation (e.g. ends of sentences punctuated correctly) (h) Read aloud what they have written with appropriate intonation to make meaning clear
Year 2 Standards	Year 2 Word Structure Standard Introduced
SS2.1 Subordination (using when, if, that, or because) and co-ordination (using or, and, or but) SS2.2 Expanded noun phrases for description and specification (e.g. the blue butterfly, plain flour, the man in the moon) SS2.3 Sentences with different forms: statement, question, exclamation, command TS2.1 Correct choice and consistent use of present tense and past tense throughout writing TS2.2 Use of the continuous form of verbs in the present and past tense to mark actions in progress (e.g. she is drumming, he was shouting)	WS2.3 Use of the suffixes *–er* and *–est* to form comparisons of adjectives and adverbs
Key Vocabulary for Teaching and Learning	verb, tense (past, present), adjective, noun, suffix, apostrophe, comma

Reading Comprehension & Immersion → Gathering & Capturing Content → Composing Text

YEAR 2 Genre/Text-Type: Title(s): Summer Term (2) & Approximate Date Span:	STANDARDS-BASED ENGLISH UNIT PLAN 6

Embedded Standards for ALL units of work

Reading Comprehension	Composition
(a) Listening to, discussing and expressing views about a wide range of poetry (including contemporary and classic), stories and non-fiction at a level beyond that at which they can read independently	(a) Planning or saying out loud what they are going to write about
	(b) Writing down ideas and/or key words, including new vocabulary
(b) Discussing sequence of events in books and how items of information are related	(c) Encapsulating what they want to say, sentence by sentence
(c) Become familiar with and retelling a wider range of stories, fairy stories and traditional tales	(d) Make simple additions, revisions and corrections to their work
(d) Introduced to non-fiction books structured in different ways	(e) Evaluate their writing with the teacher and other children
(e) Recognise simple recurring literary language	(f) Re-reading to check that their writing makes sense and that verbs used to indicate time are used correctly, including verbs in the continuous form
(f) Discuss favourite words and phrases	(g) Proof-reading to check for errors in spelling, grammar and punctuation (e.g. ends of sentences punctuated correctly)
(g) Build up repertoire of poems learnt by heart	(h) Read aloud what they have written with appropriate intonation to make meaning clear

Year 2 Standards	Year 2 Word Structure Continued
SS2.1 Subordination (using when, if, that, or because) and co-ordination (using or, and, or but)	
SS2.2 Expanded noun phrases for description and specification (e.g. the blue butterfly, plain flour, the man in the moon)	WS2.3 Use of the suffixes –er and –est to form comparisons of adjectives and adverbs
SS2.3 Sentences with different forms: statement, question, exclamation, command	
TS2.1 Correct choice and consistent use of present tense and past tense throughout writing	
TS2.2 Use of the continuous form of verbs in the present and past tense to mark actions in progress (e.g. she is drumming, he was shouting)	
Key Vocabulary for Teaching and Learning	verb, tense (past, present), adjective, noun, suffix, apostrophe, comma

Reading Comprehension & Immersion → Gathering & Capturing Content → Composing Text

YEAR 2	STANDARDS-BASED ENGLISH UNIT PLAN 7
Genre/Text-Type:	
Title(s):	
Summer Term (2) & Approximate Date Span:	

Embedded Standards for ALL units of work

Reading Comprehension	Composition
(a) Listening to, discussing and expressing views about a wide range of poetry (including contemporary and classic), stories and non-fiction at a level beyond that at which they can read independently	(a) Planning or saying out loud what they are going to write about
	(b) Writing down ideas and/or key words, including new vocabulary
(b) Discussing sequence of events in books and how items of information are related	(c) Encapsulating what they want to say, sentence by sentence
(c) Become familiar with and retelling a wider range of stories, fairy stories and traditional tales	(d) Make simple additions, revisions and corrections to their work
	(e) Evaluate their writing with the teacher and other children
(d) Introduced to non-fiction books structured in different ways	(f) Re-reading to check that their writing makes sense and that verbs used to indicate time are used correctly, including verbs in the continuous form
(e) Recognise simple recurring literary language	
(f) Discuss favourite words and phrases	(g) Proof-reading to check for errors in spelling, grammar and punctuation (e.g. ends of sentences punctuated correctly)
(g) Build up repertoire of poems learnt by heart	(h) Read aloud what they have written with appropriate intonation to make meaning clear

Year 2 Standards	Year 2 Word Structure Standards to Secure
SS2.1 Subordination (using when, if, that, or because) and co-ordination (using or, and, or but)	
SS2.2 Expanded noun phrases for description and specification (e.g. the blue butterfly, plain flour, the man in the moon)	WS2.1 Formation of nouns using suffixes such as –ness, –er
SS2.3 Sentences with different forms: statement, question, exclamation, command	WS2.2 Formation of adjectives using suffixes such as –ful, –less
TS2.1 Correct choice and consistent use of present tense and past tense throughout writing	WS2.3 Use of the suffixes –er and –est to form comparisons of adjectives and adverbs
TS2.2 Use of the continuous form of verbs in the present and past tense to mark actions in progress (e.g. she is drumming, he was shouting)	
Key Vocabulary for Teaching and Learning	verb, tense (past, present), adjective, noun, suffix, apostrophe, comma

Reading Comprehension & Immersion → Gathering & Capturing Content → Composing Text

Lower Key Stage 2 and Year 5 Standards-Based Unit Plans

YEAR 3	STANDARDS-BASED ENGLISH UNIT OF WORK
Genre/Text-Type:	
Title(s):	
Autumn Term (1) & Approximate Date Span:	

Embedded Standards for ALL units of work

Reading Comprehension	Composition
(a) Listening to and discussing a wide range of fiction, poetry, plays, non-fiction and reference books or textbooks	(a) Discuss writing similar to that which they are planning to write in order to understand and learn from its structure, grammar and vocabulary
(b) Reading books structured in different ways and reading for a range of purposes	(b) Compose and rehearse sentences orally (including dialogue), progressively building a rich and varied vocabulary and increasing range of sentence structures
(c) Use dictionaries to check the meaning of words that they have read	
(d) Increase familiarity with wide range of books, including fairy stories, myths and legends and retelling some of these orally	(c) Organise paragraphs around a theme
	(d) Assessing effectiveness of own and others' writing and suggest improvements
(e) Prepare poems and play scripts to read aloud showing understanding of intonation, tone, volume and action	(e) Propose changes to grammar and vocabulary to improve consistency, e.g. accurate use of pronouns in sentences
(f) Discuss words and phrases that capture reader's interest and imagination	(f) Proof-read for spelling and punctuation errors
(g) Recognise some different forms of poetry (free verse, narrative poetry)	(g) Read aloud own writing, to group or whole class, using appropriate intonation and controlling tone and volume so meaning is clear

Year 3 Standards

SS4.1 Expressing time and cause using conjunctions (e.g. *when, so, before, after, while, because*), adverbs (e.g. *then, next, soon, therefore,* or prepositions (e.g. *before, after, during, in, because of*)	TS3.1 Introduction to paragraphs as a way to group related material TS3.2 Headings and sub-headings to aid presentation TS3.3 Use of the perfect form of verbs to mark relationships of time and cause (e.g. *I have written it down so we can check what he said*)	P3.1 Introduction to inverted commas to punctuate direct speech

Year 3 Word Structure Standard(s) Introduced

SP3.1 Adding suffixes beginning with vowel letters to words of more than one syllable	forgetting, forgotten, beginning, beginner, prefer, preferred
SP3.2 Sound /i/ is 'y' elsewhere than at end of words	myth, gym, Egypt, pyramid, mystery
SP3.3 Spelling 'ou'	young, touch, double, trouble, country
SP3.4 Prefixes	un- dis- and mis- for negative meaning / re- for 'again' or 'back' / sub- for 'under', inter- for 'between' or 'among' / super- for 'above', anti- as 'against' and auto- meaning 'self' or 'own'
SP3.5 The suffix –ation	information, adoration, sensation, preparation, admiration
SP3.6 Suffix –ly	Added to adjectives to form adverbs (y changes to i) and exceptions –le changes to –ly and –ic to –ally and 'truly', 'duly' and 'wholly'
SP3.7 Words with endings –sure and –ture	measure, treasure, pleasure, enclosure creature, furniture, picture, nature, adventure
SP3.8 Ending –sion	division, invasion, confusion, decision, collision, television

WS3.2 Use of the determiner 'a' or 'an'

Key Vocabulary for Teaching and Learning	word family, conjunction, adverb, preposition, direct speech, inverted commas (or "speech marks"), prefix, consonant, vowel, consonant letter, vowel letter, clause, subordinate clause

Reading Comprehension & Immersion → Gathering & Capturing Content → Composing Text

YEAR 3	STANDARDS-BASED ENGLISH UNIT OF WORK
Genre/Text-Type:	
Title(s):	
Autumn Term (2) & Approximate Date Span:	

Embedded Standards for ALL units of work

Reading Comprehension	Composition
(a) Listening to and discussing a wide range of fiction, poetry, plays, non-fiction and reference books or textbooks	(a) Discuss writing similar to that which they are planning to write in order to understand and learn from its structure, grammar and vocabulary
(b) Reading books structured in different ways and reading for a range of purposes	(b) Compose and rehearse sentences orally (including dialogue), progressively building a rich and varied vocabulary and increasing range of sentence structures
(c) Use dictionaries to check the meaning of words that they have read	(c) Organise paragraphs around a theme
(d) Increase familiarity with wide range of books, including fairy stories, myths and legends and retelling some of these orally	(d) Assessing effectiveness of own and others' writing and suggest improvements
(e) Prepare poems and play scripts to read aloud showing understanding of intonation, tone, volume and action	(e) Propose changes to grammar and vocabulary to improve consistency, e.g. accurate use of pronouns in sentences
(f) Discuss words and phrases that capture reader's interest and imagination	(f) Proof-read for spelling and punctuation errors
(g) Recognise some different forms of poetry (free verse, narrative poetry)	(g) Read aloud own writing, to group or whole class, using appropriate intonation and controlling tone and volume so meaning is clear

Year 3 Standards

SS4.1 Expressing time and cause using conjunctions (e.g. *when, so, before, after, while, because*), adverbs (e.g. *then, next, soon, therefore*, or prepositions (e.g. *before, after, during, in, because of*)	TS3.1 Introduction to paragraphs as a way to group related material TS3.2 Headings and sub-headings to aid presentation TS3.3 Use of the perfect form of verbs to mark relationships of time and cause (e.g. *I have written it down so we can check what he said*)	P3.1 Introduction to inverted commas to punctuate direct speech

Year 3 Word Structure Standard(s) Introduced

SP3.1 Adding suffixes beginning with vowel letters to words of more than one syllable	forgetting, forgotten, beginning, beginner, prefer, preferred
SP3.2 Sound /i/ is 'y' elsewhere than at end of words	myth, gym, Egypt, pyramid, mystery
SP3.3 Spelling 'ou'	young, touch, double, trouble, country
SP3.4 Prefixes	un- dis- and mis- for negative meaning / re- for 'again' or 'back' / sub- for 'under', inter- for 'between' or 'among' / super- for 'above', anti- as 'against' and auto- meaning 'self' or 'own'
SP3.5 The suffix –ation	information, adoration, sensation, preparation, admiration
SP3.6 Suffix –ly	Added to adjectives to form adverbs (y changes to i) and exceptions –le changes to –ly and –ic to –ally and 'truly', 'duly' and 'wholly'
SP3.7 Words with endings –sure and –ture	measure, treasure, pleasure, enclosure creature, furniture, picture, nature, adventure
SP3.8 Ending –sion	division, invasion, confusion, decision, collision, television

WS3.2 Use of the determiner 'a' or 'an'

Key Vocabulary for Teaching and Learning	word family, conjunction, adverb, preposition, direct speech, inverted commas (or "speech marks"), prefix, consonant, vowel, consonant letter, vowel letter, clause, subordinate clause

Reading Comprehension & Immersion → Gathering & Capturing Content → Composing Text

YEAR 3	STANDARDS-BASED ENGLISH UNIT OF WORK
Genre/Text-Type:	
Title(s):	
Spring Term (1) & Approximate Date Span:	

Embedded Standards for ALL units of work

Reading Comprehension	Composition
(a) Listening to and discussing a wide range of fiction, poetry, plays, non-fiction and reference books or textbooks	(a) Discuss writing similar to that which they are planning to write in order to understand and learn from its structure, grammar and vocabulary
(b) Reading books structured in different ways and reading for a range of purposes	(b) Compose and rehearse sentences orally (including dialogue), progressively building a rich and varied vocabulary and increasing range of sentence structures
(c) Use dictionaries to check the meaning of words that they have read	
(d) Increase familiarity with wide range of books, including fairy stories, myths and legends and retelling some of these orally	(c) Organise paragraphs around a theme
	(d) Assessing effectiveness of own and others' writing and suggest improvements
(e) Prepare poems and play scripts to read aloud showing understanding of intonation, tone, volume and action	(e) Propose changes to grammar and vocabulary to improve consistency, e.g. accurate use of pronouns in sentences
(f) Discuss words and phrases that capture reader's interest and imagination	(f) Proof-read for spelling and punctuation errors
(g) Recognise some different forms of poetry (free verse, narrative poetry)	(g) Read aloud own writing, to group or whole class, using appropriate intonation and controlling tone and volume so meaning is clear

Year 3 Standards

SS4.1 Expressing time and cause using conjunctions (e.g. *when, so, before, after, while, because*), adverbs (e.g. *then, next, soon, therefore,* or prepositions (e.g. *before, after, during, in, because of*)	TS3.1 Introduction to paragraphs as a way to group related material TS3.2 Headings and sub-headings to aid presentation TS3.3 Use of the perfect form of verbs to mark relationships of time and cause (e.g. *I have written it down so we can check what he said*)	P3.1 Introduction to inverted commas to punctuate direct speech

Year 3 Word Structure Standard(s) Introduced

SP3.1 Adding suffixes beginning with vowel letters to words of more than one syllable	forgetting, forgotten, beginning, beginner, prefer, preferred
SP3.2 Sound /i/ is 'y' elsewhere than at end of words	myth, gym, Egypt, pyramid, mystery
SP3.3 Spelling 'ou'	young, touch, double, trouble, country
SP3.4 Prefixes	un- dis- and mis- for negative meaning / re- for 'again' or 'back' / sub- for 'under', inter- for 'between' or 'among' / super- for 'above', anti- as 'against' and auto- meaning 'self' or 'own'
SP3.5 The suffix –ation	information, adoration, sensation, preparation, admiration
SP3.6 Suffix –ly	Added to adjectives to form adverbs (y changes to i) and exceptions –le changes to –ly and –ic to –ally and 'truly', 'duly' and 'wholly'
SP3.7 Words with endings –sure and –ture	measure, treasure, pleasure, enclosure creature, furniture, picture, nature, adventure
SP3.8 Ending –sion	division, invasion, confusion, decision, collision, television

WS3.2 Use of the determiner 'a' or 'an'

Key Vocabulary for Teaching and Learning	word family, conjunction, adverb, preposition, direct speech, inverted commas (or "speech marks"), prefix, consonant, vowel, consonant letter, vowel letter, clause, subordinate clause

Reading Comprehension & Immersion → Gathering & Capturing Content → Composing Text

YEAR 3	STANDARDS-BASED ENGLISH UNIT OF WORK
Genre/Text-Type:	
Title(s):	
Spring Term (2) & Approximate Date Span:	

Embedded Standards for ALL units of work

Reading Comprehension	Composition
(a) Listening to and discussing a wide range of fiction, poetry, plays, non-fiction and reference books or textbooks	**(a)** Discuss writing similar to that which they are planning to write in order to understand and learn from its structure, grammar and vocabulary
(b) Reading books structured in different ways and reading for a range of purposes	**(b)** Compose and rehearse sentences orally (including dialogue), progressively building a rich and varied vocabulary and increasing range of sentence structures
(c) Use dictionaries to check the meaning of words that they have read	**(c)** Organise paragraphs around a theme
(d) Increase familiarity with wide range of books, including fairy stories, myths and legends and retelling some of these orally	**(d)** Assessing effectiveness of own and others' writing and suggest improvements
(e) Prepare poems and play scripts to read aloud showing understanding of intonation, tone, volume and action	**(e)** Propose changes to grammar and vocabulary to improve consistency, e.g. accurate use of pronouns in sentences
(f) Discuss words and phrases that capture reader's interest and imagination	**(f)** Proof-read for spelling and punctuation errors
(g) Recognise some different forms of poetry (free verse, narrative poetry)	**(g)** Read aloud own writing, to group or whole class, using appropriate intonation and controlling tone and volume so meaning is clear

Year 3 Standards

SS4.1 Expressing time and cause using conjunctions (e.g. *when, so, before, after, while, because*), adverbs (e.g. *then, next, soon, therefore,* or prepositions (e.g. *before, after, during, in, because of*)	TS3.1 Introduction to paragraphs as a way to group related material TS3.2 Headings and sub-headings to aid presentation TS3.3 Use of the perfect form of verbs to mark relationships of time and cause (e.g. *I have written it down so we can check what he said*)	P3.1 Introduction to inverted commas to punctuate direct speech

Year 3 Word Structure Standard(s) Introduced

SP3.1 Adding suffixes beginning with vowel letters to words of more than one syllable	forgetting, forgotten, beginning, beginner, prefer, preferred
SP3.2 Sound /i/ is 'y' elsewhere than at end of words	myth, gym, Egypt, pyramid, mystery
SP3.3 Spelling 'ou'	young, touch, double, trouble, country
SP3.4 Prefixes	un- dis- and mis- for negative meaning / re- for 'again' or 'back' / sub- for 'under', inter- for 'between' or 'among' / super- for 'above', anti- as 'against' and auto- meaning 'self' or 'own'
SP3.5 The suffix –ation	information, adoration, sensation, preparation, admiration
SP3.6 Suffix –ly	Added to adjectives to form adverbs (y changes to i) and exceptions –le changes to –ly and –ic to –ally and 'truly', 'duly' and 'wholly'
SP3.7 Words with endings –sure and –ture	measure, treasure, pleasure, enclosure creature, furniture, picture, nature, adventure
SP3.8 Ending –sion	division, invasion, confusion, decision, collision, television

WS3.2 Use of the determiner 'a' or 'an'

Key Vocabulary for Teaching and Learning	word family, conjunction, adverb, preposition, direct speech, inverted commas (or "speech marks"), prefix, consonant, vowel, consonant letter, vowel letter, clause, subordinate clause

Reading Comprehension & Immersion → Gathering & Capturing Content → Composing Text

YEAR 3	STANDARDS-BASED ENGLISH UNIT OF WORK
Genre/Text-Type:	
Title(s):	
Summer Term (1) & Approximate Date Span:	

Embedded Standards for ALL units of work

Reading Comprehension	Composition
(a) Listening to and discussing a wide range of fiction, poetry, plays, non-fiction and reference books or textbooks	(a) Discuss writing similar to that which they are planning to write in order to understand and learn from its structure, grammar and vocabulary
(b) Reading books structured in different ways and reading for a range of purposes	(b) Compose and rehearse sentences orally (including dialogue), progressively building a rich and varied vocabulary and increasing range of sentence structures
(c) Use dictionaries to check the meaning of words that they have read	
(d) Increase familiarity with wide range of books, including fairy stories, myths and legends and retelling some of these orally	(c) Organise paragraphs around a theme
	(d) Assessing effectiveness of own and others' writing and suggest improvements
(e) Prepare poems and play scripts to read aloud showing understanding of intonation, tone, volume and action	(e) Propose changes to grammar and vocabulary to improve consistency, e.g. accurate use of pronouns in sentences
(f) Discuss words and phrases that capture reader's interest and imagination	(f) Proof-read for spelling and punctuation errors
(g) Recognise some different forms of poetry (free verse, narrative poetry)	(g) Read aloud own writing, to group or whole class, using appropriate intonation and controlling tone and volume so meaning is clear

Year 3 Standards

SS4.1 Expressing time and cause using conjunctions (e.g. *when, so, before, after, while, because*), adverbs (e.g. *then, next, soon, therefore*, or prepositions (e.g. *before, after, during, in, because of*)	TS3.1 Introduction to paragraphs as a way to group related material TS3.2 Headings and sub-headings to aid presentation TS3.3 Use of the perfect form of verbs to mark relationships of time and cause (e.g. *I have written it down so we can check what he said*)	P3.1 Introduction to inverted commas to punctuate direct speech

Year 3 Word Structure Standard(s) Introduced

SP3.1 Adding suffixes beginning with vowel letters to words of more than one syllable	forgetting, forgotten, beginning, beginner, prefer, preferred
SP3.2 Sound /i/ is 'y' elsewhere than at end of words	myth, gym, Egypt, pyramid, mystery
SP3.3 Spelling 'ou'	young, touch, double, trouble, country
SP3.4 Prefixes	un- dis- and mis- for negative meaning / re- for 'again' or 'back' / sub- for 'under', inter- for 'between' or 'among' / super- for 'above', anti- as 'against' and auto- meaning 'self' or 'own'
SP3.5 The suffix –ation	information, adoration, sensation, preparation, admiration
SP3.6 Suffix –ly	Added to adjectives to form adverbs (y changes to i) and exceptions –le changes to –ly and –ic to –ally and 'truly', 'duly' and 'wholly'
SP3.7 Words with endings –sure and –ture	measure, treasure, pleasure, enclosure creature, furniture, picture, nature, adventure
SP3.8 Ending –sion	division, invasion, confusion, decision, collision, television

WS3.2 Use of the determiner 'a' or 'an'

Key Vocabulary for Teaching and Learning	word family, conjunction, adverb, preposition, direct speech, inverted commas (or "speech marks"), prefix, consonant, vowel, consonant letter, vowel letter, clause, subordinate clause

Reading Comprehension & Immersion → Gathering & Capturing Content → Composing Text

YEAR 3	STANDARDS-BASED ENGLISH UNIT OF WORK
Genre/Text-Type:	
Title(s):	
Summer Term (2) & Approximate Date Span:	

Embedded Standards for ALL units of work

Reading Comprehension	Composition
(a) Listening to and discussing a wide range of fiction, poetry, plays, non-fiction and reference books or textbooks	(a) Discuss writing similar to that which they are planning to write in order to understand and learn from its structure, grammar and vocabulary
(b) Reading books structured in different ways and reading for a range of purposes	(b) Compose and rehearse sentences orally (including dialogue), progressively building a rich and varied vocabulary and increasing range of sentence structures
(c) Use dictionaries to check the meaning of words that they have read	(c) Organise paragraphs around a theme
(d) Increase familiarity with wide range of books, including fairy stories, myths and legends and retelling some of these orally	(d) Assessing effectiveness of own and others' writing and suggest improvements
(e) Prepare poems and play scripts to read aloud showing understanding of intonation, tone, volume and action	(e) Propose changes to grammar and vocabulary to improve consistency, e.g. accurate use of pronouns in sentences
(f) Discuss words and phrases that capture reader's interest and imagination	(f) Proof-read for spelling and punctuation errors
(g) Recognise some different forms of poetry (free verse, narrative poetry)	(g) Read aloud own writing, to group or whole class, using appropriate intonation and controlling tone and volume so meaning is clear

Year 3 Standards

SS4.1 Expressing time and cause using conjunctions (e.g. *when, so, before, after, while, because*), adverbs (e.g. *then, next, soon, therefore,* or prepositions (e.g. *before, after, during, in, because of*)	TS3.1 Introduction to paragraphs as a way to group related material TS3.2 Headings and sub-headings to aid presentation TS3.3 Use of the perfect form of verbs to mark relationships of time and cause (e.g. *I have written it down so we can check what he said*)	P3.1 Introduction to inverted commas to punctuate direct speech

Year 3 Word Structure Standard(s) Introduced

SP3.1 Adding suffixes beginning with vowel letters to words of more than one syllable	forgetting, forgotten, beginning, beginner, prefer, preferred
SP3.2 Sound /i/ is 'y' elsewhere than at end of words	myth, gym, Egypt, pyramid, mystery
SP3.3 Spelling 'ou'	young, touch, double, trouble, country
SP3.4 Prefixes	un- dis- and mis- for negative meaning / re- for 'again' or 'back' / sub- for 'under', inter- for 'between' or 'among' / super- for 'above', anti- as 'against' and auto- meaning 'self' or 'own'
SP3.5 The suffix –ation	information, adoration, sensation, preparation, admiration
SP3.6 Suffix –ly	Added to adjectives to form adverbs (y changes to i) and exceptions –le changes to –ly and –ic to –ally and 'truly', 'duly' and 'wholly'
SP3.7 Words with endings –sure and –ture	measure, treasure, pleasure, enclosure creature, furniture, picture, nature, adventure
SP3.8 Ending –sion	division, invasion, confusion, decision, collision, television

WS3.2 Use of the determiner 'a' or 'an'

Key Vocabulary for Teaching and Learning	word family, conjunction, adverb, preposition, direct speech, inverted commas (or "speech marks"), prefix, consonant, vowel, consonant letter, vowel letter, clause, subordinate clause

Reading Comprehension & Immersion → Gathering & Capturing Content → Composing Text

YEAR 4	STANDARDS-BASED ENGLISH UNIT OF WORK
Genre/Text-Type:	
Title(s):	
Autumn Term & Approximate Date Span:	

Embedded Standards for ALL units of work

Reading Comprehension	Composition
(a) Listening to and discussing a wide range of fiction, poetry, plays, non-fiction and reference books or textbooks	**(a)** Discuss writing similar to that which they are planning to write in order to understand and learn from its structure, grammar and vocabulary
(b) Reading books structured in different ways and reading for a range of purposes	**(b)** Compose and rehearse sentences orally (including dialogue), progressively building a rich and varied vocabulary and increasing range of sentence structures
(c) Use dictionaries to check the meaning of words that they have read	
(d) Increase familiarity with wide range of books, including fairy stories, myths and legends and retelling some of these orally	**(c)** Organise paragraphs around a theme
	(d) Assessing effectiveness of own and others' writing and suggest improvements
(e) Prepare poems and play scripts to read aloud showing understanding of intonation, tone, volume and action	**(e)** Propose changes to grammar and vocabulary to improve consistency, e.g. accurate use of pronouns in sentences
(f) Discuss words and phrases that capture reader's interest and imagination	**(f)** Proof-read for spelling and punctuation errors
(g) Recognise some different forms of poetry (free verse, narrative poetry)	**(g)** Read aloud own writing, to group or whole class, using appropriate intonation and controlling tone and volume so meaning is clear

Year 4 Standards

SS4.1 Appropriate choice of pronoun or noun within a sentence to avoid ambiguity and repetition SS4.2 Fronted adverbials (e.g. _Later that day, I heard the bad news._)	TS4.1 Use of paragraphs to organise ideas around a theme TS4.2 Appropriate choice of pronoun or noun across sentences to aid cohesion and avoid repetition	P4.1 Use of inverted commas to punctuate direct speech P4.2 Apostrophes to mark singular and plural possession (e.g. _the girl's name, the boys' boots_) P4.3 Use of commas after fronted adverbials

Year 4 Word Structure Standard(s) Introduced

SP4.1 Suffix –ous	poisonous, dangerous, tremendous, famous, various, serious
SP4.2 Endings –tion, -sion, -ssion, -cian	invention, injection, action, expression, confession, admission, musician, mathematician
SP4.3 Words with /k/ written as 'ch' and Greek origin	chorus ,scheme, chemistry, chemist, echo and character
SP4.4 /ch/ as /sh/ French origin	chef, chalet, machine, brochure
SP4.5 Words ending /g/ sound spelt –gue and /k/ as –que (French origin)	league, tongue, antique and unique
SP4.6 Words with /s/ spely 'sc' (Latin origin)	science, scene, discipline, fascinate, crescent
SP4.7 Words with 'ei', 'eigh' or 'ey'	

SP4.8 Possessive apostrophe with plural words

SP4.9 Homophones or near-homophones

Key Vocabulary for Teaching and Learning	pronoun, possessive

Reading Comprehension & Immersion → Gathering & Capturing Content → Composing Text

YEAR 4	STANDARDS-BASED ENGLISH UNIT OF WORK
Genre/Text-Type:	
Title(s):	
Spring Term & Approximate Date Span:	

Embedded Standards for ALL units of work

Reading Comprehension	Composition
(a) Listening to and discussing a wide range of fiction, poetry, plays, non-fiction and reference books or textbooks	(a) Discuss writing similar to that which they are planning to write in order to understand and learn from its structure, grammar and vocabulary
(b) Reading books structured in different ways and reading for a range of purposes	(b) Compose and rehearse sentences orally (including dialogue), progressively building a rich and varied vocabulary and increasing range of sentence structures
(c) Use dictionaries to check the meaning of words that they have read	
	(c) Organise paragraphs around a theme
(d) Increase familiarity with wide range of books, including fairy stories, myths and legends and retelling some of these orally	(d) Assessing effectiveness of own and others' writing and suggest improvements
(e) Prepare poems and play scripts to read aloud showing understanding of intonation, tone, volume and action	(e) Propose changes to grammar and vocabulary to improve consistency, e.g. accurate use of pronouns in sentences
(f) Discuss words and phrases that capture reader's interest and imagination	(f) Proof-read for spelling and punctuation errors
(g) Recognise some different forms of poetry (free verse, narrative poetry)	(g) Read aloud own writing, to group or whole class, using appropriate intonation and controlling tone and volume so meaning is clear

Year 4 Standards

SS4.1 Appropriate choice of pronoun or noun within a sentence to avoid ambiguity and repetition SS4.2 Fronted adverbials (e.g. *Later that day, I heard the bad news.*)	TS4.1 Use of paragraphs to organise ideas around a theme TS4.2 Appropriate choice of pronoun or noun across sentences to aid cohesion and avoid repetition	P4.1 Use of inverted commas to punctuate direct speech P4.2 Apostrophes to mark singular and plural possession (e.g. *the girl's name, the boys' boots*) P4.3 Use of commas after fronted adverbials

Year 4 Word Structure Standard(s) Introduced

SP4.1 Suffix –ous	poisonous, dangerous, tremendous, famous, various, serious
SP4.2 Endings –tion, -sion, -ssion, -cian	invention, injection, action, expression, confession, admission, musician, mathematician
SP4.3 Words with /k/ written as 'ch' and Greek origin	chorus ,scheme, chemistry, chemist, echo and character
SP4.4 /ch/ as /sh/ French origin	chef, chalet, machine, brochure
SP4.5 Words ending /g/ sound spelt –gue and /k/ as –que (French origin)	league, tongue, antique and unique
SP4.6 Words with /s/ spely 'sc' (Latin origin)	science, scene, discipline, fascinate, crescent
SP4.7 Words with 'ei', 'eigh' or 'ey'	

SP4.8 Possessive apostrophe with plural words

SP4.9 Homophones or near-homophones

Key Vocabulary for Teaching and Learning	pronoun, possessive

Reading Comprehension & Immersion → Gathering & Capturing Content → Composing Text

YEAR 4	STANDARDS-BASED ENGLISH UNIT OF WORK
Genre/Text-Type:	
Title(s):	
Summer Term & Approximate Date Span:	

Embedded Standards for ALL units of work

Reading Comprehension	Composition
(a) Listening to and discussing a wide range of fiction, poetry, plays, non-fiction and reference books or textbooks	**(a)** Discuss writing similar to that which they are planning to write in order to understand and learn from its structure, grammar and vocabulary
(b) Reading books structured in different ways and reading for a range of purposes	**(b)** Compose and rehearse sentences orally (including dialogue), progressively building a rich and varied vocabulary and increasing range of sentence structures
(c) Use dictionaries to check the meaning of words that they have read	
(d) Increase familiarity with wide range of books, including fairy stories, myths and legends and retelling some of these orally	**(c)** Organise paragraphs around a theme
	(d) Assessing effectiveness of own and others' writing and suggest improvements
(e) Prepare poems and play scripts to read aloud showing understanding of intonation, tone, volume and action	**(e)** Propose changes to grammar and vocabulary to improve consistency, e.g. accurate use of pronouns in sentences
(f) Discuss words and phrases that capture reader's interest and imagination	**(f)** Proof-read for spelling and punctuation errors
(g) Recognise some different forms of poetry (free verse, narrative poetry)	**(g)** Read aloud own writing, to group or whole class, using appropriate intonation and controlling tone and volume so meaning is clear

Year 4 Standards

SS4.1 Appropriate choice of pronoun or noun within a sentence to avoid ambiguity and repetition SS4.2 Fronted adverbials (e.g. *Later that day, I heard the bad news.*)	TS4.1 Use of paragraphs to organise ideas around a theme TS4.2 Appropriate choice of pronoun or noun across sentences to aid cohesion and avoid repetition	P4.1 Use of inverted commas to punctuate direct speech P4.2 Apostrophes to mark singular and plural possession (e.g. *the girl's name, the boys' boots*) P4.3 Use of commas after fronted adverbials

Year 4 Word Structure Standard(s) Introduced

SP4.1 Suffix –ous	poisonous, dangerous, tremendous, famous, various, serious
SP4.2 Endings –tion, -sion, -ssion, -cian	invention, injection, action, expression, confession, admission, musician, mathematician
SP4.3 Words with /k/ written as 'ch' and Greek origin	chorus ,scheme, chemistry, chemist, echo and character
SP4.4 /ch/ as /sh/ French origin	chef, chalet, machine, brochure
SP4.5 Words ending /g/ sound spelt –gue and /k/ as –que (French origin)	league, tongue, antique and unique
SP4.6 Words with /s/ spely 'sc' (Latin origin)	science, scene, discipline, fascinate, crescent
SP4.7 Words with 'ei', 'eigh' or 'ey'	

SP4.8 Possessive apostrophe with plural words
SP4.9 Homophones or near-homophones

Key Vocabulary for Teaching and Learning	pronoun, possessive

Reading Comprehension & Immersion → Gathering & Capturing Content → Composing Text

YEAR 5	STANDARDS-BASED ENGLISH UNIT OF WORK
Genre/Text-Type:	
Title(s):	
Autumn Term & Approximate Date Span:	

Embedded Standards for ALL units of work

Reading Comprehension	Composition
(a) Continue to read and discuss an increasingly wide range of fiction, poetry, plays and non-fiction and reference books or textbooks	(a) Use dictionaries to check spelling and meaning of words
(b) Reading books that are structured in different ways and reading for a range of purposes	(b) Use the first three or four letters of a word to check spelling, meaning or both of these in a dictionary
(c) Increasing familiarity with a wide range of books, including myths, legends and traditional tales, modern fiction, fiction from our literary heritage, and books from other cultures and traditions	(c) Use a thesaurus
	(d) Noting and developing initial ideas, drawing on reading and research where necessary
(d) Recommending books that they have read to their peers, giving reason for their choices	(e) Draft and write selecting appropriate grammar and vocabulary, understanding how such choices can change and enhance meaning
(e) Identifying and discussing themes and conventions in and across a wide range of writing	(f) Précising longer passages
(f) Learning a wider range of poetry by heart	(g) Assessing effectiveness of own writing and others'
(g) Preparing poems and plays to read aloud and to perform, showing understanding through intonation, tone and volume so that meaning is clear to the audience	(h) Proposing changes to grammar, vocabulary and punctuation to enhance effects and clarify meaning
	(i) Proof-read for spelling and punctuation errors
(h) Explain and discuss their understanding of what they have read, including through formal presentations and debates, maintaining a focus on topic and using notes where necessary	(j) Perform their own compositions, using appropriate intonation, volume and movement so meaning is clear

Year 5 Standards

SS5.1 Relative clauses beginning with *who, which, where, why, whose, that,* or an omitted relative pronoun SS5.2 Indicating degrees of possibility using modal verbs (e.g. *might, should, will, must*) or adverbs (e.g. *perhaps, surely*)	TS5.1 Devices to build cohesion within a paragraph (e.g. *then, after that, this, firstly*) TS5.2 Linking ideas across paragraphs using adverbials of time (e.g. *later*), place (e.g. *nearby*) and number (e.g. *secondly*)	P5.1 Brackets, dashes or commas to indicate parenthesis P5.2 Use of commas to clarify meaning or avoid ambiguity

Year 5 Word Structure Standard(s) Introduced

SP5.1 –cious or –tious	vicious, precious, infectious, nutritious
SP5.2 Endings –cial and –tial	official, confidential, essential
SP5.3 Word ending –ant, -ance, -ancy, -ent, -ence/-ency	observant, observance, expectant, innocent, decent, assistant, obedient
SP5.4 Words ending –able and –ible	adorable, applicable, considerable, changeable, possible
SP5.5 Adding suffixes beginning with vowel letters to words ending –fer	transferred, reference, transference
SP5.7 Words with 'ei' after 'c'	deceive, conceive, ceiling

SP5.6 Use of hyphen

Key Vocabulary for Teaching and Learning	relative clause, modal verb, relative pronoun, parenthesis, bracket, dash, determiner, cohesion, ambiguity

Reading Comprehension & Immersion → Gathering & Capturing Content → Composing Text

YEAR 5	STANDARDS-BASED ENGLISH UNIT OF WORK
Genre/Text-Type:	
Title(s):	
Spring Term & Approximate Date Span:	

Embedded Standards for ALL units of work

Reading Comprehension	Composition
(a) Continue to read and discuss an increasingly wide range of fiction, poetry, plays and non-fiction and reference books or textbooks	(a) Use dictionaries to check spelling and meaning of words
(b) Reading books that are structured in different ways and reading for a range of purposes	(b) Use the first three or four letters of a word to check spelling, meaning or both of these in a dictionary
(c) Increasing familiarity with a wide range of books, including myths, legends and traditional tales, modern fiction, fiction from our literary heritage, and books from other cultures and traditions	(c) Use a thesaurus
	(d) Noting and developing initial ideas, drawing on reading and research where necessary
(d) Recommending books that they have read to their peers, giving reason for their choices	(e) Draft and write selecting appropriate grammar and vocabulary, understanding how such choices can change and enhance meaning
(e) Identifying and discussing themes and conventions in and across a wide range of writing	(f) Précising longer passages
(f) Learning a wider range of poetry by heart	(g) Assessing effectiveness of own writing and others'
(g) Preparing poems and plays to read aloud and to perform, showing understanding through intonation, tone and volume so that meaning is clear to the audience	(h) Proposing changes to grammar, vocabulary and punctuation to enhance effects and clarify meaning
	(i) Proof-read for spelling and punctuation errors
(h) Explain and discuss their understanding of what they have read, including through formal presentations and debates, maintaining a focus on topic and using notes where necessary	(j) Perform their own compositions, using appropriate intonation, volume and movement so meaning is clear

Year 5 Standards

SS5.1 Relative clauses beginning with *who, which, where, why, whose, that*, or an omitted relative pronoun	TS5.1 Devices to build cohesion within a paragraph (e.g. *then, after that, this, firstly*)	P5.1 Brackets, dashes or commas to indicate parenthesis
SS5.2 Indicating degrees of possibility using modal verbs (e.g. *might, should, will, must*) or adverbs (e.g. *perhaps, surely*)	TS5.2 Linking ideas across paragraphs using adverbials of time (e.g. *later*), place (e.g. *nearby*) and number (e.g. *secondly*)	P5.2 Use of commas to clarify meaning or avoid ambiguity

Year 5 Word Structure Standard(s) Introduced

SP5.1 –cious or –tious	vicious, precious, infectious, nutritious
SP5.2 Endings –cial and –tial	official, confidential, essential
SP5.3 Word ending –ant, -ance, -ancy, -ent, -ence/-ency	observant, observance, expectant, innocent, decent, assistant, obedient
SP5.4 Words ending –able and –ible	adorable, applicable, considerable, changeable, possible
SP5.5 Adding suffixes beginning with vowel letters to words ending –fer	transferred, reference, transference
SP5.7 Words with 'ei' after 'c'	deceive, conceive, ceiling

SP5.6 Use of hyphen

Key Vocabulary for Teaching and Learning	
	relative clause, modal verb, relative pronoun, parenthesis, bracket, dash, determiner, cohesion, ambiguity

Reading Comprehension & Immersion → Gathering & Capturing Content → Composing Text

YEAR 5	STANDARDS-BASED ENGLISH UNIT OF WORK
Genre/Text-Type:	
Title(s):	
Summer Term & Approximate Date Span:	

Embedded Standards for ALL units of work

Reading Comprehension	Composition
(a) Continue to read and discuss an increasingly wide range of fiction, poetry, plays and non-fiction and reference books or textbooks	(a) Use dictionaries to check spelling and meaning of words
(b) Reading books that are structured in different ways and reading for a range of purposes	(b) Use the first three or four letters of a word to check spelling, meaning or both of these in a dictionary
(c) Increasing familiarity with a wide range of books, including myths, legends and traditional tales, modern fiction, fiction from our literary heritage, and books from other cultures and traditions	(c) Use a thesaurus
	(d) Noting and developing initial ideas, drawing on reading and research where necessary
(d) Recommending books that they have read to their peers, giving reason for their choices	(e) Draft and write selecting appropriate grammar and vocabulary, understanding how such choices can change and enhance meaning
(e) Identifying and discussing themes and conventions in and across a wide range of writing	(f) Précising longer passages
(f) Learning a wider range of poetry by heart	(g) Assessing effectiveness of own writing and others'
(g) Preparing poems and plays to read aloud and to perform, showing understanding through intonation, tone and volume so that meaning is clear to the audience	(h) Proposing changes to grammar, vocabulary and punctuation to enhance effects and clarify meaning
	(i) Proof-read for spelling and punctuation errors
(h) Explain and discuss their understanding of what they have read, including through formal presentations and debates, maintaining a focus on topic and using notes where necessary	(j) Perform their own compositions, using appropriate intonation, volume and movement so meaning is clear

Year 5 Standards

SS5.1 Relative clauses beginning with *who, which, where, why, whose, that,* or an omitted relative pronoun	TS5.1 Devices to build cohesion within a paragraph (e.g. *then, after that, this, firstly*)	P5.1 Brackets, dashes or commas to indicate parenthesis
SS5.2 Indicating degrees of possibility using modal verbs (e.g. *might, should, will, must*) or adverbs (e.g. *perhaps, surely*)	TS5.2 Linking ideas across paragraphs using adverbials of time (e.g. *later*), place (e.g. *nearby*) and number (e.g. *secondly*)	P5.2 Use of commas to clarify meaning or avoid ambiguity

Year 5 Word Structure Standard(s) Introduced

SP5.1 –cious or –tious	vicious, precious, infectious, nutritious
SP5.2 Endings –cial and –tial	official, confidential, essential
SP5.3 Word ending –ant, -ance, -ancy, -ent, -ence/-ency	observant, observance, expectant, innocent, decent, assistant, obedient
SP5.4 Words ending –able and –ible	adorable, applicable, considerable, changeable, possible
SP5.5 Adding suffixes beginning with vowel letters to words ending –fer	transferred, reference, transference
SP5.7 Words with 'ei' after 'c'	deceive, conceive, ceiling

SP5.6 Use of hyphen

Key Vocabulary for Teaching and Learning	relative clause, modal verb, relative pronoun, parenthesis, bracket, dash, determiner, cohesion, ambiguity

Reading Comprehension & Immersion → Gathering & Capturing Content → Composing Text

Year 6 Standards-Based Unit Plan

A single unit plan is provided for Year 6 to be used as the basis for medium-term planning across an academic year. There are few new word structure standards to be secured during Year 6 because the vast majority of these should have been achieved as children progressed through Key Stage 2 making it unnecessary to lock these into unit plans in the way this was done for Key Stage 1 and Year 3 to Year 5. Teachers in Year 6 will also need to have flexibility to address any areas of weakness in word-level work in preparing children for end of Key Stage 2 Tests.

Genre/Text-Type:
Title(s):
Autumn / Spring / Summer Term & Approximate Date Span:

STANDARDS-BASED ENGLISH UNIT OF WORK

Embedded Standards for ALL units of work

Reading Comprehension	Composition
(a) Continue to read and discuss an increasingly wide range of fiction, poetry, plays and non-fiction and reference books or textbooks **(b)** Reading books that are structured in different ways and reading for a range of purposes **(c)** Increasing familiarity with a wide range of books, including myths, legends and traditional tales, modern fiction, fiction from our literary heritage, and books from other cultures and traditions **(d)** Recommending books that they have read to their peers, giving reason for their choices **(e)** Identifying and discussing themes and conventions in and across a wide range of writing **(f)** Learning a wider range of poetry by heart **(g)** Preparing poems and plays to read aloud and to perform, showing understanding through intonation, tone and volume so that meaning is clear to the audience **(h)** Explain and discuss their understanding of what they have read, including through formal presentations and debates, maintaining a focus on topic and using notes where necessary	**(a)** Use dictionaries to check spelling and meaning of words **(b)** Use the first three or four letters of a word to check spelling, meaning or both of these in a dictionary **(c)** Use a thesaurus **(d)** Noting and developing initial ideas, drawing on reading and research where necessary **(e)** Draft and write selecting appropriate grammar and vocabulary, understanding how such choices can change and enhance meaning **(f)** Précising longer passages **(g)** Assessing effectiveness of own writing and others' **(h)** Proposing changes to grammar, vocabulary and punctuation to enhance effects and clarify meaning **(i)** Proof-read for spelling and punctuation errors **(j)** Perform their own compositions, using appropriate intonation, volume and movement so meaning is clear

Year 6 Word Structure Standard Introduced

SP6.1 Words containing letter string 'ough'	ought, bought, thought, rough, touch, although, through
SP6.2 Words with 'silent letters'	doubt, island, lamb, solemn, thistle, knight

SP6.3 Homophones and other words that are often confused

SS6.1 Use of the **passive voice** to affect the presentation of information in a **sentence** SS6.2 Expanded **noun phrases** to convey complicated information concisely SS6.3 The difference between structures typical of informal speech and structures appropriate for formal speech and writing (such as the use of question tags, e.g. *He's your friend, isn't he?*, or the use of the **subjunctive** in some very formal writing and speech)	TS6.1 Linking ideas across paragraphs using a wider range of **cohesive devices**: semantic **cohesion** (e.g. repetition of a **word** or phrase), grammatical connections (e.g. the use of **adverbials** such as *on the other hand*, *in contrast*, or *as a consequence*), and **ellipsis** TS6.2 Layout devices, such as headings, sub-headings, columns, bullets, or tables, to structure text	P6.1 Use of the semi-colon, colon and dash to mark the boundary between independent **clauses** (e.g. It's raining; I'm fed up.) P6.2 Use of the colon to introduce a list P6.3 **Punctuation** of bullet points to list information P6.4 How hyphens can be used to avoid ambiguity (e.g. *man eating shark* versus *man-eating shark*, or *recover* versus *re-cover*)
Key Vocabulary for Teaching and Learning	active and passive voice, subject and object, hyphen, colon, semi-colon, bullet points, synonym and antonym	

Reading Comprehension & Immersion → Gathering & Capturing Content → Composing Text

Introducing Standards-Based Writing Assessment Records

Assessing writing, which many schools will do each half term, must be against grade-level standards. The Standards-Based Writing Assessment Records provided in this book have been developed as documents to support scrutiny of individual children's written work.

Each Standards-Based Writing Assessment Record includes benchmarks. These have been derived from aligning standards in the National Curriculum programme of study against the most recently published descriptors for Level 2 through to Level 6 (Standards and Testing Agency, 2013). It is not intended that these are used to give a National Curriculum level or sublevel. The benchmarks offer further details on what a standard entails to support classroom teachers in deciding whether there is sufficient evidence in children's work to award Emerging, Expected or Exceeding (see Chapter 2). When the benchmarks have been met and an abundance of evidence accumulated to show achievement of a standard has been collected, the completion of the Assessment Record is simple. Shorthand codes can be inserted into cells as shown in this example.

Standards	Benchmarks	Achievement					
		Au1	Au2	Sp1	Sp2	Su1	Su2
SS1.1 How words can combine to make sentences	Past and present tense generally consistent Sentences often brief, starting with simple subject/verb (may include some variation through use of adverbs/simple noun phrases)	EM	EM	EM	E	E	E
P1.1 Separation of words with spaces		WB	EM	EM	E	E	EX
P1.2 Use of capital letters, full stops, question and exclamation marks to demarcate sentences	Sentences sometimes demarcated by capital letters and full stops, use of exclamation or question marks Capital letters used for names and personal pronouns	EM	EM	EM	EM	EM	E
SS1.2 Joining words and joining sentences using *and*	Primarily simple and compound sentences working towards grammatical accuracy Clauses and sentences linked with 'and'	WB	EM	EM	EM	E	E

Reaching an overall judgement on whether or not children have met grade-level standards at the end of the year is likely to pose a challenge. This is going to be a matter of professional judgement and the evidence available for scrutiny, involving moderation activities within a school or between local schools who have formed clusters to mutually support one another. Any exemplification of grade-level written work produced by the Department of Education as part of supporting end of Key Stage 2 Teacher Assessment will act as a key resource in determining whether children are performing at the expected level of proficiency.

To state the obvious, individual children show different profiles of strengths and areas for development. Making a summative judgement using the Standards-Based Writing Assessment Records will involve consistency in practice across Key Stage 1 and 2. School management and leadership teams will need to set clear boundaries for what constitutes children achieving the vast majority of grade-level standards and are therefore deemed to be in the category of Expected or Exceeding. This is no less problematic when forming summative judgements in Mathematics or Science.

YEAR 1 STANDARDS-BASED WRITING ASSESSMENT RECORD

Spelling

S1.1 Words containing phonemes already taught	Au2	Sp2	Su2
S1.2 Common exception words	Au2	Sp2	Su2

Word Structure

WS1.1 Regular plural noun suffixes –s or –es	Au2	Sp2	Su2
WS1.2 Suffixes that can be added to verbs –ing, -ed and -er	Au2	Sp2	Su2
WS1.3 Prefix un- to change meaning of verbs and adjectives (negation-unkind-or undoing-untie)	Au2	Sp2	Su2

Handwriting

H1.1 Begin to form lower-case letters in the correct direction, starting and finishing in the right place	Au2	Sp2	Su2
H1.2 Forms capital letters	Au2	Sp2	Su2

Grammar and Punctuation Key Stage 1

Standards	Benchmarks	Achievement					
		Au1	Au2	Sp1	Sp2	Su1	Su2
SS1.1 How words can combine to make sentences	Past and present tense generally consistent Sentences often brief, starting with simple subject/verb (may include some variation through use of adverbs/simple noun phrases)						
P1.1 Separation of words with spaces							
P1.2 Use of capital letters, full stops, question and exclamation marks to demarcate sentences	Sentences sometimes demarcated by capital letters and full stops, use of exclamation or question marks Capital letters used for names and personal pronouns						
SS1.2 Joining words and joining sentences using *and*	Primarily simple and compound sentences working towards grammatical accuracy Clauses and sentences linked with 'and'						
T TS1.1 Sequencing sentences to form short narratives	Simple opening and ending Some attempt to organise and group related ideas together Some attempt to sequence events or ideas Related sentences linked by pronouns or simple time connectives						
Writing for Effect	Some awareness of purpose with ideas and content generally relevant to task, e.g. informative points in a report; memories in recount; sequence of events in stories- possible repetitive or sparse with limited awareness of the reader Viewpoint may be indicated by simple comment or action Some detail included through adventurous word choice appropriate to task						

YEAR 2 STANDARDS-BASED WRITING ASSESSMENT RECORD

Spelling

S2.1 Accurate spelling of common exception words	Au2	Sp2	Su2
S2.2 Correct spelling of words with contracted forms (P2.3)	Au2	Sp2	Su2

Word Structure

WS2.1 Formation of nouns using suffixes –ness and –er	Au2	Sp2	Su2
WS2.2 Formation of adjectives using suffixes –ful and –less	Au2	Sp2	Su2
WS2.3 Use of suffixes –er and –est to form comparison of adjectives and verbs	Au2	Sp2	Su2

Handwriting

H2.1 Forms lower case letters of the correct size relative to one another	Au2	Sp2	Su2
H2.2 Uses some of the diagonal and horizontal strokes needed to join letters and understand which letters, when adjacent to one another, are best left unjoined	Au2	Sp2	Su2
H2.3 Write capital letters and digits of the correct size, orientation and relationship to one another and to lower case letters	Au2	Sp2	Su2
H2.4 Use spacing between words that reflects the size of letters	Au2	Sp2	Su2

Grammar and Punctuation Key Stage 1

Standards	Benchmarks	Achievement					
		Au1	Au2	Sp1	Sp2	Su1	Su2
SS1.1 Subordination (when, if, because) and coordination (or, and, but) used	May include some complex sentences (when/because/if), but may be repetitive						
SS2.3 Sentences with different forms: statement, question, exclamation and command							
P2.1 Use of capital letters, full stops, question marks and exclamation marks to demarcate sentences	Full stops, capital letters, exclamation and question marks mostly accurate						
P2.2 Commas used to separate items in a list	Most accurate; some inverted commas for speech might be evident						
P2.3 Apostrophes to mark contracted forms in spelling	Apostrophe used for contracted form in spelling mostly accurate						
TS2.1 Correct choice and consistent use of present tense and past tense throughout writing TS2.1 Use of the continuous form of verbs in the present and past tense to mark actions in progress	Tense generally consistent and appropriate to task, including modals (can/will) Tense generally consistent and appropriate to task, including modals (can/will) Continuous form of verbs in past and present tense used correctly						
Brief introduction and/or ending usually signalled Simple text structure with an attempt to organise related ideas in sections or paragraphs Some attempt to sequence ideas logically Simple adverbials/pronouns may link sentences, sections or paragraphs Some linking of events and ideas although flow may be disjointed or disrupted							
Writing for Effect		Some awareness of purpose through selection of relevant content and an attempt to interest the reader Features of writing generally appropriate to selected task, e.g. use of dialogue in story; use of first person for recount; use of imperative in instructions Content may be imbalanced, e.g. led predominantly by dialogue Viewpoint (opinion, attitude, position) is expressed, but may not be maintained Some detail/description of events or ideas expanded through vocabulary (simple adverbs, adjectives) or explanation with some vocabulary selected for effect or appropriateness to task					

YEAR 3 STANDARDS-BASED WRITING ASSESSMENT RECORD

Spelling

S3.1 Use prefixes and suffixes and show understanding of how to add them	Au2	Sp2	Su2
S3.2 Spell homophones correctly	Au2	Sp2	Su2
S3.3 Spell often misspelt words correctly	Au2	Sp2	Su2

Word Structure

WS3.1 Formation of nouns using a range of prefixes (such as super-, anti-, auto-)	Au2	Sp2	Su2
WS3.2 Use of determiners (a, an) according to whether the next word begins with a vowel or a consonant	Au2	Sp2	Su2

Handwriting

H3.1 Uses diagonal and horizontal strokes that are needed to join letters and understand which letters, when adjacent to one another, are best left unjoined	Au2	Sp2	Su2
H3.2 Legibility, consistency and quality of handwriting, e.g. by ensuring that the downward strokes of letters are parallel and equidistant; that lines of writing are spaced sufficiently so that ascenders and descenders of letters do not touch	Au2	Sp2	Su2

Grammar and Punctuation Key Stage 1

Standards	Benchmarks	Achievement					
		Au1	Au2	Sp1	Sp2	Su1	Su2
GP3.1 Range of sentences with more than one clause by using wider range of conjunctions (when, if, because, although) SS3.1 Expressing time and cause using conjunctions (when, so, before, after, while, because), adverbs (then, next soon, therefore) and prepositions (before, after, during, in, because of)	Sentences mostly grammatically sound Correct use of subordination Some variety in subordinating connectives, e.g. because, if, which (because the rain can damage it/which was strange/if she could) Some variation in sentence structure through a range of openings, e.g. adverbials (some time later/as we ran/once we had arrived), subject reference (they/the boys/our gang), speech						
GP3.2 Use perfect form of verbs to mark relationships of time and cause (TS3.3)	Security of tense and person Tense choice appropriate with verb forms varied and generally accurate						
GP3.3 Choose nouns or pronouns appropriately for clarity and cohesion GP3.4 Choose nouns or pronouns appropriately to avoid ambiguity and repetition (TS3.1)	Connections within and between paragraphs generally maintained through use of on-going references, e.g. pronouns, adverbials and connectives						
P3.1 Begin to use inverted commas to punctuate direct speech	Most sentences correctly demarcated, e.g. some commas mark phrases or clauses; apostrophes mark contractions. If used, inverted commas demarcate the beginning and end of direct speech, correct on most occasions						
TS3.1 Use of paragraphs to group related material	Appropriate opening and closing, which may be linked Organisation through sequencing or logical transition, e.g. simple chronological stages, ideas grouped by related points, subheadings.						
CW3.4 In narratives, creating settings, characters and plot	Related events or ideas organised into paragraphs or sections to support content of writing in different text types						
CW3.6 In non-narrative material, use simple organisational devices such as headings and subheadings (TS3.2)	Connections within and between paragraphs generally maintained through use of on-going references, e.g. pronouns, adverbials and connectives Paragraphs extended and developed around topic, main point, idea or event (with explanation, contrast and additional detail)						
Writing for Effect	Clear purpose and relevant content for reader Features of text-type/genre are evident (tense and verb form, layout, formality) Balance between action and dialogue or fact and comment Viewpoint is established and maintained (contrasting attitudes/opinions may be presented) Ideas and events developed through some deliberate selection of phrases and vocabulary (technical terminology, vivid language, word choice for effect or emphasis) Some use of stylistic features support purpose, e.g. formal/informal vocabulary; appropriate use of similes						

YEAR 4 STANDARDS-BASED WRITING ASSESSMENT RECORD

Spelling

S4.1 Use prefixes and suffixes and show understanding of how to add them	Au2	Sp2	Su2
S4.2 Spell homophones correctly	Au2	Sp2	Su2
S4.3 Spell often misspelt words correctly	Au2	Sp2	Su2

Word Structure

WS4.1/P4.2 The grammatical difference between plural and possessive –s evident	Au2	Sp2	Su2
WS4.2 Standard English forms for verb inflections used instead of local spoken forms used throughout	Au2	Sp2	Su2

Handwriting

H4.1 Uses diagonal and horizontal strokes that are needed to join letters and understand which letters, when adjacent to one another, are best left unjoined	Au2	Sp2	Su2
H4.2 Legibility, consistency and quality of handwriting, e.g. by ensuring that the downward strokes of letters are parallel and equidistant; that lines of writing are spaced sufficiently so that ascenders and descenders of letters do not touch	Au2	Sp2	Su2

Grammar and Punctuation Key Stage 1

Standards	Benchmarks	Achievement					
		Au1	Au2	Sp1	Sp2	Su1	Su2
GP4.1 Range of sentences with more than one clause by using wider range of conjunctions (when, if, because, although)	Sentences mostly grammatically sound Correct use of subordination Some variety in subordinating connectives, e.g. because, if, which						
GP4.2 Use perfect form of verbs to mark relationships of time and cause	Security of tense and person Tense choice appropriate with verb forms varied and generally accurate						
GPS4.3 Choose nouns or pronouns appropriately for clarity and cohesion GPS4.4 Choose nouns or pronouns appropriately to avoid ambiguity and repetition (TS4.2)	Connections within and between paragraphs generally maintained through use of on-going references, e.g. pronouns, adverbials and connectives						
P4.1 Use of inverted commas to punctuate direct speech	Most sentences correctly demarcated, e.g. some commas mark phrases or clauses; apostrophes mark contractions. If used, inverted commas demarcate the beginning and end of direct speech, correct on most occasions						
P4.3 Use of commas after fronted adverbials	Some variation in sentence structure through a range of openings, e.g. adverbials, subject reference (they/the boys/our gang), speech						
TS4.1 Use of paragraphs to organise ideas around a theme	Appropriate opening and closing, which may be linked Organisation through sequencing or logical transition, e.g. simple chronological stages, ideas grouped by related points, subheadings.						
CW4.4 In narratives, creating settings, characters and plot	Related events or ideas organised into paragraphs or sections to support content of writing in different text types						
CW4.6 In non-narrative material, use simple organisational devices such as headings and subheadings	Connections within and between paragraphs generally maintained through use of on-going references, e.g. pronouns, adverbials and connectives Paragraphs extended and developed around topic, main point, idea or event						
Writing for Effect	Clear purpose and relevant content for reader Features of text-type/genre are evident (tense and verb form, layout, formality) Balance between action and dialogue or fact and comment Viewpoint is established and maintained (contrasting attitudes/opinions may be presented) Ideas and events developed through some deliberate selection of phrases and vocabulary (technical terminology, vivid language, word choice for effect or emphasis) Some use of stylistic features support purpose, e.g. formal/informal vocabulary; appropriate use of similes						

YEAR 5 STANDARDS-BASED WRITING ASSESSMENT RECORD

Spelling

S5.1 Prefixes and suffixes	Au2	Sp2	Su2
S5.2 Spell words with 'silent' letters (knight, psalm, solemn)	Au2	Sp2	Su2
S5.3 Correct spelling of homophones	Au2	Sp2	Su2

Word Structure

WS5.1 Converting nouns or adjectives into verbs using suffixes (-ate, -ise, -ify)	Au2	Sp2	Su2
WS5.2 Verb prefixes (dis-, de-, mis-, over- and re-)	Au2	Sp2	Su2

Handwriting

H5.1 Chooses which shape of a letter to use when given choices and deciding, as part of their personal style, whether or not to join specific letters	Au2	Sp2	Su2
H5.2 Chooses writing implement that is best suited to task (e.g. quick notes, letters)	Au2	Sp2	Su2

Grammar and Punctuation Key Stage 1

Standards	Benchmarks	Achievement					
		Au1	Au2	Sp1	Sp2	Su1	Su2
SS5.1 Relative clauses beginning with *who, which, where, why, whose, that,* or an omitted relative pronoun	Variety in sentence length, structure and subject to help expand ideas, convey issues/facts or provide emphasis, detail and description						
SS5.2 Indicating degrees of possibility using modal verbs (e.g. *might, should, will, must*) or adverbs (e.g. *perhaps, surely*)	Different sentence types (questions, direct and reported speech, commands used appropriately) Emphasis created through word order and accurate use of verb phrases, including passive voice where appropriate A range of verb forms develops meaning and appropriate tense choice is maintained Modifiers contribute to shades of meaning (e.g. adverbs)						
P5.1 Brackets, dashes or commas to indicate parenthesis	Range of punctuation used almost always correctly, e.g. commas mark phrases and clauses, brackets and dashes						
P5.2 Use of commas to clarify meaning or avoid ambiguity							
WC5.6 & TS5.1 Devices used to build cohesion used within a paragraph (then, after that, this, firstly)	Some shaping of paragraphs may be evident to highlight or prioritise information, provide chronological links, build tension or interject comment and reflection						
WC5.6 & TS5.2 Linking ideas across paragraphs using adverbials of time (later), place (nearby) and number (secondly)	Overall organisation of text is supported by paragraphs or sections which enable coherent development and control of content across the text Relationships between paragraphs or sections give structure to the whole text, e.g. links make structure between topics clear; connections between opening and ending A range of cohesive devices used to develop or elaborate ideas both within and between paragraphs, e.g. pronouns; adverbials; connectives; subject-specific vocabulary; phases or chains of reference Sequencing and structured organisation of paragraphs and/or sections contributes to overall effectiveness of text Information/events developed in depth within some paragraphs and/or sections						
Writing for Effect WC5.1 Identifying the audience for and purpose of the writing, selecting the appropriate form and using other similar writing as models for their own WC5.4 In narrative, describe settings, characters and atmosphere integrating dialogue to convey character and advance the action WC5.7 Uses further organisational and presentational devices to structure text and to guide the reader (headings, subheadings and underlining)	Purpose of writing is clear and generally maintained with some effective selection and placing of content to inform/engage the reader Features of selected form are clearly established, e.g. appropriate selection and variation of tense; choice of person; level of formality; adaptation of content for genre and audience Content is balanced and controlled with some effective selection and ordering of text to engage the reader, e.g. placement of significant ideas/event for emphasis; reflective comment; opinion; dialogue Established and controlled viewpoint with some development of opinion, attitude, position or stance Ideas and events developed through elaboration, nominalisation and imaginative detail, Vocabulary predominantly appropriate to text type and genre; precise word choice may create impact and augment meaning Varied stylistic features may support both purpose and effect, e.g. alliteration, metaphors, puns and emotive phrases						

YEAR 6 STANDARDS-BASED WRITING ASSESSMENT RECORD

Spelling

S6.1 Prefixes and suffixes	Au2	Sp2	Su2
S6.2 Spell words with 'silent' letters (knight, psalm, solemn)	Au2	Sp2	Su2
S6.3 Correct spelling of homophones	Au2	Sp2	Su2

Word Structure

WS6.1 Vocabulary typical of informal speech and vocabulary appropriate for formal writing (e.g 'said' verses 'reported', 'alleged' or 'claimed' in formal text)	Au2	Sp2	Su2

Handwriting

H6.1 Chooses which shape of a letter to use when given choices and deciding, as part of their personal style, whether or not to join specific letters	Au2	Sp2	Su2
H6.2 Chooses writing implement that is best suited to task (e.g. quick notes, letters)	Au2	Sp2	Su2

Grammar and Punctuation Key Stage 1

Standards	Benchmarks	Achievement					
		Au1	Au2	Sp1	Sp2	Su1	Su2
SS6.1 & GP6.2 Use of passive voice to affect presentation of information in a sentence	Controlled use of a variety of simple and more complex sentences contributes to clarity of purpose and overall effect on reader						
SS6.2 & GP6.3 Expanded noun phrases to convey complicated information concisely	Subordinating connectives may be manipulated for emphasis or to nominalise for succinctness (Because of that, he failed)						
SS6.3 & GP6.1 Difference in structures used in informal and formal writing (such as question tags and subjunctive)	Verb forms are mostly controlled and selected to convey precision of meaning. Modifiers are used to qualify, intensify or emphasise (exceptional results, insignificant amount). A range of sentence features are used to give clarity or emphasis of meaning (fronted adverbials, complex noun phrases and prepositional phrases. Syntax and full range of punctuation are consistently accurate in a variety of sentence structures with occasional errors in ambitious structures						
P6.1 & GP6.9 Use of semi-colon, colon and dash to mark boundary between independent clauses (It's raining: I'm fed up)	Syntax and full range of punctuation are consistently accurate in a variety of sentence structures with occasional errors in ambitious structures						
P6.2&3 & GP6.10&11 Use of colon to introduce a list and punctuation of bullet points to list information	Syntax and full range of punctuation are consistently accurate in a variety of sentence structures with occasional errors in ambitious structures						
P6.4 & GP6.8 Hyphens to avoid ambiguity ('man eating shark' verses 'man-eating shark')	Syntax and full range of punctuation are consistently accurate in a variety of sentence structures with occasional errors in ambitious structures						
TS6.1 Linking ideas across paragraphs using a wider range of cohesive devices: semantic cohesion (repetition of word or phrase), grammatical connections (use of adverbials: on the other hand, in contrast, as a consequence) and ellipsis (WC6.6)	Overall organisation of the text is controlled to take account of reader's possible reaction, question or opinion. A range of features are used to inform the reader of the overall direction of the writing (opening paragraph clearly introduces main themes or creates interest; withholding of information for effect; paragraph or sentence markers; references or links information and ideas across text)						
WC6.4 In narrative, describe settings, characters and atmosphere integrating dialogue to convey character and advance the action	Some paragraphs and/or sections are shaped and developed to support meaning and purpose, e.g. prioritising subjects, events, ideas that are developed in greater detail and depth						
WC6.7 Uses further organisational and presentational devices to structure text and to guide the reader (headings, subheadings and underlining) TS6.2 Use layout devices, such as headings, subheadings, columns, bullets or tables to structure text	A range of cohesive devices contribute to the effect of the text on the reader and the placing of emphasis for impact, e.g. precise adverbials as sentence starters; a range of appropriate connectives; subject-specific vocabulary; select use of pronoun referencing; complex noun phrases; prepositional phrases						

Writing for Effect

WC6.1 Identifying the audience for and purpose of the writing, selecting the appropriate form and using other similar writing as models for their own

Controlled use of a variety of simple and more complex sentences contributes to clarity of purpose and overall effect on reader
A range of sentence features are used to give clarity or emphasis of meaning (fronted adverbials, complex noun phrases and prepositional phrases
Subordinating connectives may be manipulated for emphasis or to nominalise for succinctness (Because of that, he failed)
Verb forms are mostly controlled and selected to convey precision of meaning
Modifiers are used to qualify, intensify or emphasise (exceptional results, insignificant amount)
Syntax and full range of punctuation are consistently accurate in a variety of sentence structures with occasional errors in ambitious structures

Chapter 8: A Standards-Based Model for Science

In this final chapter, a standards-based model for Science is provided through a sequence of medium-term plans. Each of the unit plans corresponds to the curriculum and assessment mapping contained in Chapter Two. Working and thinking scientifically standards for Key Stage 1, Lower Key Stage 2 and Upper Key Stage 2 are indicated on each unit plan. Where they appear in bold font, it indicates an end of phase expectation for achievement. It is envisaged that classroom teachers will embed these standards into their teaching sequences to ensure a balance within and between units of work.

Standards from the revised National Curriculum are featured in the medium-term plans with benchmarks or components given opposite them. These have been generated through alignment of the programme of study with pre-existing units from the Qualification and Curriculum Agency (QCA) Scheme of Work. Some standards will not be fully deconstructed into their components. There are two reasons for this. First of all, not all standards have antecedents in the QCA Scheme of Work. Secondly, classroom teachers need to gain experience of unpicking standards as part of their own planning and assessment practice. However, the majority of the medium-term plans presented in this chapter reduce some of the workload involved when unravelling the scope of standards in Science. Several medium-term plans provide spaces for teachers to include their own annotations and ideas for developing a teaching sequence. It is recognised that revision will need to be included as part of most units in Year 6 to assist with teacher assessment at the end of Key Stage 2 and in the event of a school being selected for the sampling tests. As a result, many of the medium-term plans are templates to facilitate this.

The unit plans also include some teaching and learning activities suggested in medium-term plans produced by the QCA. It will be noticed that only selected activities from the latter organisation's scheme have been replicated here. They are intended as an orientation to what teachers may wish to include in their teaching sequences rather than offering a prescription of content and how to deliver it to children.

For a reader interested in how to track learning and achievement of grade-level standards in Science, end of unit tracking grids and summative assessment could be created using a format similar to the examples provided for Mathematics as supplementary materials towards the end of this book.

When developing the medium-term plans contained in this chapter, congruency between standards, teaching and assessment must be explicit. Chapter Three covered the importance of breaking standards into the components of what children need to learn and ensuring this is sequenced logically in teaching sequences. The use of Assessment Plans, which was discussed in Chapter Five, is also relevant when using the following unit plans.

Year 1 Science Unit Plans

Year 1 Autumn 1		SCIENCE UNIT OF WORK: EVERDAY MATERIALS
Thinking and Working Scientifically Standards	**Content Standards for Science**	**Benchmarks**
ScKS1.1 Asking simple questions ScKS1.2 Observing closely, using simple equipment ScKS1.3 Performing simple tests ScKS1.4 Using observations and ideas to suggest answers to questions	EM1.1 Distinguish between an object and the material from which it is made EM1.2 Identify and name a variety of everyday materials, including wood, plastic, glass, metal, water and rock EM1.3 Describe the simple properties of a variety of everyday materials EM1.4 Compare and group together a variety of everyday materials on the basis of their simple physical properties EM1.5 Find out how the shapes of solid objects made from some materials can be changed by squashing, bending, twisting and stretching	There are many materials and these can be named and described
		Every material has many properties which can be recognised using our senses and described using appropriate vocabulary
		Record observations of materials
		Ask questions and to explore materials and objects using appropriate senses, making observations and communicating these
		There are many materials and these can be named and described
		Objects are made from materials, and different, everyday objects can be made from the same materials
		Materials can be used in a variety of ways
		Materials can be sorted in a variety of ways according to their properties
		Group materials together and make a record of groupings
Key Vocabulary for Teaching and Learning	Names of materials e.g. metal, plastic, wood, paper, glass, clay, rock, fabric, sand; Words used to describe materials e.g. hard, soft, rough, smooth, shiny, dull, magnetic, transparent, bendy, waterproof, strong; Words and phrases for making comparisons e.g. the same as, different from, harder, smoother; Words which may have different meanings in a non-science context e.g. group, material; Expressions giving reasons using 'because'	
Benchmarks	**Qualification and Curriculum Authority (QCA) Teaching Activities**	
There are many materials and these can be named and describedEvery material has many properties which can be recognised using our senses and described using appropriate vocabulary Record observations of materials	Ask children to handle a variety of objects and collections of objects e.g. spoons, keys, wooden objects, papers, fabrics and ask them to describe them e.g. hard, soft, shiny, dull, bendy. Introduce words children are not familiar with. Record e.g. by writing descriptions round a picture of the object.	
Ask questions and to explore materials and objects using appropriate senses, making observations and communicating these There are many materials and these can be named/described	Ask children to suggest other senses they could use to find out what objects are like. Use feely bags or a blindfold game to encourage children to use senses of touch, hearing and smell to describe or identify materials. Ask children who are not blindfolded to ask questions e.g. Is it hard, smooth, rough? Does it make a noise? Present children with a collection of familiar materials e.g. wood, metals, plastic, clay, sand to observe. Talk about what the materials are like and name them. Ask children to go on a material hunt inside/outside the classroom and identify other objects made of the same material. Record results by drawing in groups with labels.	
Objects are made from materials, and different, everyday objects can be made from the same materials Materials can be used in a variety of ways Materials can be sorted in a variety of ways according to their properties	Make a display of wooden objects choosing attractive or unusual objects, if possible. Invite children to add to the display. Discuss where the material to make the objects came from. Ask children to choose an object they particularly like and to use as many words as they can to describe it e.g. how it feels, looks. Build up collections e.g. of plastic objects, metal objects, glass objects. Label each set. Use simple reference books to find out more about each material.	

Thinking and Working Scientifically Standards	Content Standards for Science	Benchmarks
ScKS1.1 Asking simple questions ScKS1.2 Observing closely, using simple equipment ScKS1.3 Performing simple tests ScKS1.4 Using observations and ideas to suggest answers to questions	LT1.2 Observe and name a variety of sources of light, including electric lights, flames and the Sun LT1.2 Associate shadows with a light source being blocked by something	Light is essential for seeing things
		When it is dark other senses can be used to help us find things and identify things
		There are many sources of light
		Light sources vary in brightness
		Observe and make comparisons of sources of light
		Sources of light show up best at night-time
		The Sun is the source of light for the Earth
		It is dangerous to look at the Sun because it is so bright
		Shadows are formed when light travelling from a source is blocked
		Shadows are formed when objects block light from the Sun
		Shadows are similar in shape to the objects forming them

Key Vocabulary for Teaching and Learning	Words and phrases related to light and dark e.g. bright, light, dark, black, night, day, reflect, reflective strip; Names of light sources e.g. torch, warning light, Sun, candle, lantern; Words and phrases used to make comparisons e.g. darker/darkest, bright/brighter/brightest; Expressions giving reasons using 'because'.

Benchmarks	Qualification and Curriculum Authority (QCA) Teaching Activities
Light is essential for seeing things When it is dark other senses can be used to help us find things and identify things There are many sources of light Light sources vary in brightness Observe and make comparisons of sources of light	Create a 'dark area' in the classroom or visit a room in the school which can be darkened with curtains or blinds. Ask children to find a particular child or item in the dark room. Gradually increase the light. Ask children to say when they can use their sense of sight to identify the child or item. Ask children to say how they tried to find the object and what they do if they wake up in a dark room. If necessary, prompt them to think about using other senses Take the children on a walk round the school to look for sources of light e.g. computer light, warning lights on switches. Ask them to think of as many light sources as they can. Make a collection of light sources or, using pictures, make a collage showing a variety of light sources. Ask children to compare the light from different sources.
Objects cannot be seen in darkness	Present children with a 'black box' which has a small peephole in one end and a larger hole covered with cardboard in the top. Ask children to explore the 'black box' to find out if they can see an object when there is no light (cardboard over the hole) and when there is light. Give children torches of different brightness and ask them to find out what is in the box.
The Sun is the source of light for the Earth It is dangerous to look at the Sun because it is so bright Shadows are formed when light travelling from a source is blocked Shadows are formed when objects block light from the Sun Shadows are similar in shape to the objects forming them	On a day when there is sunshine with some clouds, take the children into the playground and ask them to decide without looking at the Sun when it goes behind (or emerges from) a cloud. Ask children to explain how they can tell. Explore shadow formations using torches and other light sources. Introduce idea of light travelling from a source by shining a powerful torch beam through a comb with widely spaced teeth or a cardboard tube, showing the beam is blocked and doesn't bend around corners. Children explore shadows of themselves in different positions. Record shadows on playground using chalk and observe how they change position and shape during day.
Opaque materials do not let light through Transparent materials let a lot of light through	Predict which materials (opaque, transparent and translucent) allow light through.

Thinking and Working Scientifically Standards	Content Standards for Science	Benchmarks
ScKS1.1 Asking simple questions ScKS1.2 Observing closely, using simple equipment ScKS1.3 Performing simple tests ScKS1.4 Using observations and ideas to suggest answers to questions	PL1.1 Identify and name a range of common plants, including garden plants, wild plants and trees, and those classified as deciduous and evergreen PL1.2 Identify and describe the basic structure of a variety of common flowering plants, including roots, stem/trunk, leaves and flowers	There are different plants in the immediate environment
		Make careful observations of one or two plants and of where they grow and to communicate these
		Plants grow
		Plants have leaves, stems and flowers
		Plants have roots
		Observe and compare the roots of different plants
		Plants provide food for humans

Key Vocabulary for Teaching and Learning	Words and phrases for making comparisons e.g. tall/taller/tallest, like, similar to, different from; Words relating to plants e.g. branch, flower, root, stem, seeds, seedlings, plants, leaf, weed ; Words and phrases relating to living and non-living things e.g. living, non-living, alive, not alive, dead, healthy.

Benchmarks	Qualification and Curriculum Authority (QCA) Teaching Activities
There are different plants in the immediate environment Make careful observations of one or two plants and of where they grow and to communicate these Plants grow Plants have leaves, stems and flowers Plants have roots Observe and compare the roots of different plants	Take children for a walk around the school and challenge them to find (but not pick or pull up) plants growing in as many different places as they can. Ask them for their ideas about why plants grow where they do. Have a prepared, large, outline plan of the area visited and ask children to stick labels or pictures of plants where they were found. Ask children to suggest why we grow plants. Show children some planted seedlings or with the children plant quick-growing seeds. Ask children to suggest how they will change as they grow. Help children to look after and to observe the seedlings at regular intervals over the next week and to record, in drawings, how they have changed. As children observe the seedlings, consolidate knowledge of names of the parts of the plant.

Thinking and Working Scientifically Standards	Content Standards for Science	Benchmarks
ScKS1.1 Asking simple questions ScKS1.2 Observing closely, using simple equipment ScKS1.3 Performing simple tests ScKS1.4 Using observations and ideas to suggest answers to questions	AH1.1 Identify and name a variety of common animals that are birds, fish, amphibians, reptiles, mammals and invertebrates AH1.2 Identify and name a variety of common animals that are carnivores, herbivores and omnivores AH1.3 Describe and compare the structure of a variety of common animals (birds, fish, amphibians, reptiles, mammals and invertebrates, and including pets) AH1.4 Identify, name, draw and label the basic parts of the human body and say which part of the body is associated with each sense	Observe and recognise some simple characteristics of animals
		The group of living things called animals includes humans
		Humans are more like each other than they are like other animals
		Living things in the locality can be grouped according to observable similarities and differences
		Humans have bodies with similar parts
		Humans have bodies with similar parts
		We have five senses which allow us to find out about the world

Key Vocabulary for Teaching and Learning	Words naming features of animals and plants e.g. feathers, fur, shell, branch: Comparative expressions e.g. long, longer, longest, small, smaller, smallest, similar to, different from; Expressions making generalisations e.g. 'we all...', 'most have...'; Expressions of time related to change; Words relating to their senses e.g. sense, eye, sight, see, ear, hearing, smell, nose, touch, feel; Words for parts of the body of humans and other animals e.g. leg, wing, arm, beak; Words and phrases relating to living and non-living things e.g. alive, living, not alive, human, animal

Benchmarks	Qualification and Curriculum Authority (QCA) Teaching Activities
Observe and recognise some simple characteristics of animals and plants The group of living things called animals includes humans	Review children's understanding by presenting them with a collection of pictures and specimens of animals and plants e.g. bee, spider, worm, mealworm, snail, dog, horse, bird, snake, crocodile, butterfly, whale, grass, ivy, holly, cherry tree, daffodil, oak tree, human and ask them to group them into animals and plants. Elicit simple ideas about the groupings e.g. the plants have green parts, the animals all move. Ask children explicitly about some items e.g. a green animal.
Living things in the locality can be grouped according to observable similarities and differences	Give children a collection of pictures of animals (including humans) found in the local environment and ask them to find different ways of sorting them.
Humans have bodies with similar parts We have five senses which allow us to find out about the world	Play 'Simon says' with emphasis on naming parts and on identifying all humans have the same parts. Ask children to name and locate parts of the body using drawings and labels. Ask children questions about the five senses and where the sense organs are located in the body.

Year 1 Summer 1		SCIENCE UNIT OF WORK: SEASONAL CHANGES

Thinking and Working Scientifically Standards	Content Standards for Science	Benchmarks
ScKS1.1 Asking simple questions ScKS1.2 Observing closely, using simple equipment ScKS1.3 Performing simple tests ScKS1.4 Using observations and ideas to suggest answers to questions	E&S1.1 Observe changes across the four seasons E&S1.2 Observe and describe weather associated with the seasons and how day length varies	

Key Vocabulary for Teaching and Learning	

Standards/Benchmarks	Indicative Teaching & Learning Activities

Year 2 Science Unit Plans

Year 2 Autumn 1		SCIENCE UNIT OF WORK: USES OF EVERYDAY MATERIALS
Thinking and Working Scientifically Standards	**Content Standards for Science**	**Benchmarks**
ScKS1.1 Asking simple questions	EM2.1 Identify and compare the uses of a variety of everyday materials, including wood, metal, plastic, glass, brick/rock, and paper/cardboard	There is a range of materials with different characteristics
ScKS1.2 Observing closely, using simple equipment		Some materials occur naturally and some do not
ScKS1.3 Performing simple tests		Some naturally occurring materials are treated (shaped, polished) before they are used
ScKS1.4 Using observations and ideas to suggest answers to questions		Names of some naturally occurring materials
	EM2.2 Compare how things move on different surfaces	Objects made from some materials can be altered by squashing, bending, twisting and stretching
ScKS1.5 Gathering and recording data to help in answer questions		Sometimes pushes and pulls change the shape of objects
		Pushes or pulls can make things speed up or slow down or change direction
		Explain how to make familiar objects move faster or slower
		Describe ways of making materials or objects change, using appropriate vocabulary
		Explore materials using appropriate senses and making observations and simple comparisons
		Identify a range of common materials and that the same material is used to make different objects
		Recognise properties such as hardness, strength and flexibility and compare materials in terms of these properties
		Materials are suitable for making a particular object because of their properties and that some properties are more important than others when deciding what to use
Key Vocabulary for Teaching and Learning	Names of a variety of materials e.g. wood, metal, leather, plastic, clay and groups of material e.g. natural, manufactured; Words giving ways of changing materials e.g. squash, bend, twist, stretch, heat, cool, freeze, melt, boil; Words which have a different meaning in other contexts e.g. fair, material; Expressions of comparison e.g. warm/warmer/warmest; Expressions of reason using 'because'; Expressions making predictions; Words describing the characteristics of materials e.g. strong, hard, flexible, absorbent, transparent; Nouns and related verbs e.g. comparison/compare, description/describe; words related to movement e.g. direction, distance, force; comparative expressions e.g. further, furthest, fast, faster, fastest, slow, slower, slowest, higher	

Benchmarks	Qualification and Curriculum Authority (QCA) Teaching Activities
There is a range of materials with different characteristics Some materials occur naturally and some do not Some naturally occurring materials are treated (shaped, polished) before they are used Names of some naturally occurring materials	Present children with a careful selection of materials, some of which are found naturally and some of which are not e.g. twigs, unpolished/unfinished wood, sand, rocks, water, bone, clay, sheep's wool, glass, plastic, paper, cardboard and ask them to sort the materials into those which are found naturally and those which are not. Show children objects e.g. a wooden ruler or chair, a woollen jersey, a stone lampstand and talk to them about how the natural material was altered in making the object and why people might want to do this. Ask children to use simple secondary sources to find out how some materials e.g. glass, paper, earthenware are made from naturally occurring materials. Challenge children to classify materials by making a collage using only naturally occurring or only not naturally occurring materials.
Identify a range of common materials and that the same material is used to make different objects Recognise properties such as hardness, strength and flexibility and compare materials in terms of these properties Materials are suitable for making a particular object because of their properties and that some properties are more important than others when deciding what to use	Ask children to do a survey around the school of materials that have been used for particular purposes e.g. wood for floors, plastic for guttering, metal for door handles, plastic for electric sockets, gold for rings. Ask children to say how they know or what helped them to decide that a particular object is made of a particular material. Ask children to explain their classification of 'difficult' objects e.g. plastic with a wood grain. Ask children to describe a material so that others can identify it, using terms e.g. transparent, strong, hard, flexible. With the children, draw up a table or simple database of properties of materials e.g. wood, glass, metal, rubber, plastic, wool, cotton, ceramics. Present children with a series of objects or pictures e.g. a wooden chair, plastic bottle, paper towel, woollen jersey or show a video footage illustrating different materials being used. Ask children why each material was used to make the object and ask them to suggest and evaluate an alternative material.
Sometimes pushes and pulls change the shape of objects Pushes or pulls can make things speed up or slow down or change direction Suggest questions about ways in which different objects move	Present children with a collection of materials. Ask children to explore how to make a variety of shapes. Present children with a collection of toy cars and ask them how to make them move faster, slower, or change direction Ask children to think about toy cars rolling on a flat surface and to suggest a question they might explore

217

Thinking and Working Scientifically Standards	Content Standards for Science	Benchmarks
ScKS1.1 Asking simple questions **ScKS1.2 Observing closely, using simple equipment** **ScKS1.3 Performing simple tests** **ScKS1.4 Using observations and ideas to suggest answers to questions** **ScKS1.5 Gathering and recording data to help in answer questions**	SND2.1 Observe and name a variety of sources of sound, noticing we hear with our ears SND2.2 Recognise that sounds get fainter as the distance from the sound source increases	There are many different sources of sounds
		Explore sounds using their sense of hearing
		There are many different ways of making sounds
		There are many ways of describing sounds
		We hear with our ears
		Some sounds can be heard from a long distance
		Sounds seem louder the nearer you are to the source
		Sounds get fainter as they travel away from a source

Key Vocabulary for Teaching and Learning	Words describing sounds or ways of making sounds e.g. high, low, loud, quiet, shake, pluck, rattle, ring, silence, direction; Words and phrases for making comparisons e.g. louder, quieter, further away, nearer; Near synonyms e.g. soft/quiet, noise/sound; Words which have different meanings in other contexts e.g. low, high, soft.

Benchmarks	Qualification and Curriculum Authority (QCA) Teaching Activities
We hear with our ears Some sounds can be heard from a long distance Sounds seem louder the nearer you are to the source Sounds get fainter as they travel away from a source	Ask children to draw a picture or describe how they think we hear. Carry out a number of short activities e.g. ask them to point to where a sound is coming from; using ear muffs over both or one ear see if children can hear as well as with both ears which will test their ideas. Ask children which sounds they can hear from far away eg thunder, ambulance/police sirens, shouting and whether they are louder if they are nearer. Ask children to describe what it is like to be near a very loud sound. Ask children to think about how far away they can hear sounds e.g. in the hall, can they hear someone talking at the other end? Can they hear someone talking at the other end of the playground? Take children into a hall (or playground on a still day) and explore with them whether they can hear a quiet sound e.g. a buzzer at one end from the other. Explore a number of alternative ways of finding out e.g. moving towards, away from the sound, using different sources of sound, placing the sound source at one end, one side, in the middle of the hall

Thinking and Working Scientifically Standards	Content Standards for Science	Benchmarks
ScKS1.1 Asking simple questions

ScKS1.2 Observing closely, using simple equipment

ScKS1.3 Performing simple tests

ScKS1.4 Using observations and ideas to suggest answers to questions

ScKS1.5 Gathering and recording data to help in answer questions | ALT2.1 Explore and compare the difference between things that are living, dead, and things that have never been alive

ALT2.2 Identify that most living things live in habitats to which they are suited and describe how different habitats provide for the basic needs of different kinds of animals and plants, and how they depend on each other

ALT2.3 Identify and name a variety of plants and animals in their habitats, including micro-habitats

ALT2.4 Describe how animals obtain their food from plants and other animals, using the ideas of a simple food chain, and name and identify different sources of food | Identify different types of habitat |
		Different animals are found in different habitats
		Observe the conditions in a local habitat and make a record of the animals found
		Use keys to identify local plants or animals
		Animals and plants in a local habitat are interdependent
		Identify the structure of a food chain in a specific habitat
		Animals are suited to the habitat in which they are found
		Most food chains start with a green plant

Key Vocabulary for Teaching and Learning	Words related to life processes e.g. nutrition; Words relating to habitats and feeding relationships e.g. habitat, condition, organism, predator, prey, producer, consumer, food chain, key; Words which have a different meaning in other contexts e.g. producer, consumer, key, condition; Expressions making generalisations and comparisons.

Benchmarks	Qualification and Curriculum Authority (QCA) Teaching Activities
Identify different types of habitat

Different animals are found in different habitats | Introduce children to the word 'habitat' using pictures to illustrate meaning. Explain the meaning of 'habitat'.

Using pictures of places in the immediate locality or similar to those in the locality as stimuli, ask children to predict where a particular organism will be found |
| Observe the conditions in a local habitat and make a record of the animals found

Use keys to identify local plants or animals | Ask children to observe and describe the conditions e.g. light, water, soil, shade, temperature |
| Identify the structure of a food chain in a specific habitat

Animals are suited to the habitat in which they are found

Most food chains start with a green plant | Review habitats with children and ask them to say which organisms are found in a specific habitat. Challenge children to identify the food of specific animals, some of which eat plants and some of which eat animals. Introduce terms 'predator' and 'prey' and start by considering pairs e.g. plant and one animal or two animals. |

Thinking and Working Scientifically Standards	Content Standards for Science	Benchmarks
ScKS1.1 Asking simple questions **ScKS1.2 Observing closely, using simple equipment** **ScKS1.3 Performing simple tests** **ScKS1.4 Using observations and ideas to suggest answers to questions** **ScKS1.5 Gathering and recording data to help in answer questions**	**Animals, including humans** AH2.1 Notice that animals, including humans, have offspring which grow into adults AH2.2 Find out about and describe the basic needs of animals, including humans, for survival (water, food and air) AH2.3 Describe the importance for humans of exercise, eating the right amounts of different types of food, and hygiene **Plants** P2.1 Observe and describe how seeds and bulbs grow into mature plants P2.2 Find out and describe how plants need water, light and a suitable temperature to grow and stay healthy	Animals reproduce and change as they grow older
		Humans need water and food to stay alive
		We eat different kinds of food
		Sometimes we eat a lot of some food and not very much of others
		To stay healthy, we need an adequate and varied diet
		We need exercise to stay healthy
		Green plants need light to grow
		Plants need healthy roots, leaves and stems to grow well
		Plants need water, but not unlimited water for healthy growth
		Plant growth is affected by temperature

Key Vocabulary for Teaching and Learning	Words related to plants (branch, root, seedling, root, stem, bulb, seed, leaf)

Benchmarks	Qualification and Curriculum Authority (QCA) Teaching Activities
Animals reproduce and change as they grow older	Use secondary sources or first-hand observation of animal young growing into adults.
Plants need leaves in order to grow well Plants need water, but not unlimited water, for healthy growth Plants need light for healthy growth Plant growth is affected by temperature	Introduce the idea of a plant as an organism in which different parts e.g. leaf, stem and root all need to work properly if the plant is to grow well. Present children with similar plants of the same species e.g. geranium and ask them to suggest how these could be used to find out whether plants need leaves to grow well. Respond to children's suggestions or remove many of the leaves from one plant, keep both in the same place and water equally. Remind children that plants need water and ask them whether they think the more water they have the better they will grow. Show children a planted seedling e.g. bean and ask how they could use this and similar seedlings to investigate the question. Take children to look at grass that has been covered or show them a plant that has been in the dark and ask them to describe and explain what has happened.

Year 3 Science Unit Plans

Year 3 Autumn 1		SCIENCE UNIT OF WORK: ROCKS
Thinking and Working Scientifically Standards	**Content Standards for Science**	**Benchmarks**
ScLK1.1 Asking relevant questions ScLK1.2 Setting up simple practical enquires, comparative and fair tests ScLK1.3 Making accurate measurements using standard units, using a range of equipment for example thermometers and data loggers ScLK1.4 Gathering, recording, classifying and presenting data in a variety of ways to help in answering questions ScLK1.5 Recording findings using simple scientific language, drawings, labelled diagrams, bar charts and tables ScLK1.6 Reporting on findings from enquiries, including oral and written explanations, displays or presentations of results and conclusions ScLK1.7 Using results to draw simple conclusions and suggest improvements, new questions and predictions for setting up further tests ScLK1.8 Identifying differences, similarities or changes related to simple scientific ideas and processes ScLK1.9 Using straightforward scientific evidence to answer questions or to support their findings	EM3.1 Compare and group together different kinds of rocks on the basis of their simple physical properties EM3.2 Describe in simple terms how fossils are formed when things that have lived are trapped within rock EM3.3 Recognise that soils are made from rocks and organic matter	Rocks are used for a variety of purposes
		Rocks can be grouped according to observable characteristics
		Observe and compare rocks
		Rocks are chosen for particular purposes because of their characteristics
		Beneath all surfaces there is rock
		Differences between rocks can be identified by testing
		There are different kinds of soil depending on the rock from which they come

Key Vocabulary for Teaching and Learning	Names of different rocks and soils e.g. slate, marble, chalk, granite, sand, clay; Words relating to rocks and soils e.g. rock, stone, pebble, texture, absorbent; expressions of reason using 'because'.
Benchmarks	**Qualification and Curriculum Authority (QCA) Teaching Activities**
There are different kinds of soil depending on the rock from which they come Rocks can be grouped according to observable characteristics Observe and compare rocks Differences between rocks can be identified by testing	Show a video footage or a series of pictures showing different soils. Ask children to compare these with a sample of soil from the local environment. Show a series of pictures e.g. cliffs, quarries, mountains with rock faces, fields/moors with rocky outcrops, muddy fields, streets and ask children to point out where the rocks are. Ask them to suggest why they can see rocks in some pictures but not in others. Present children with a collection of rocks to observe and group in terms of texture e.g. size, shape and arrangement of particles and appearance e.g. range of colours. Compare rocks in terms of how easily they are worn away. Help children to carry out a 'rubbing' test to compare how well different rocks withstand being ground down, and record results. Help children test for differences in permeability by dropping small quantities of water on to rocks and observing whether it remains on the surface or not.

Thinking and Working Scientifically Standards	Content Standards for Science	Benchmarks
ScLK1.1 Asking relevant questions	LT3.1 Notice that light is reflected from surfaces LT3.3 Find patterns that determine the size of shadows	When the Sun is behind them their shadow is in front
ScLK1.2 Setting up simple practical enquires, comparative and fair tests		The Sun appears to move across the sky in a regular way every day
ScLK1.3 Making accurate measurements using standard units, using a range of equipment for example thermometers and data loggers		The Sun appears highest in the sky at midday
ScLK1.4 Gathering, recording, classifying and presenting data in a variety of ways to help in answering questions		The higher the Sun appears in the sky the shorter the shadow
ScLK1.5 Recording findings using simple scientific language, drawings, labelled diagrams, bar charts and tables		Shadows of objects in sunlight change over the course of the day
ScLK1.6 Reporting on findings from enquiries, including oral and written explanations, displays or presentations of results and conclusions		Shadows change in length and position throughout the day
ScLK1.7 Using results to draw simple conclusions and suggest improvements, new questions and predictions for setting up further tests		
ScLK1.8 Identifying differences, similarities or changes related to simple scientific ideas and processes		
ScLK1.9 Using straightforward scientific evidence to answer questions or to support their findings		

Key Vocabulary for Teaching and Learning	Words and phrases relating to light and shadow formation e.g. transparent, opaque, shadow, block, direction, light travels; Expressions of reason using 'because'; Expressions of comparison e.g. shortest, highest; Expressions making generalisations.

Benchmarks	Qualification and Curriculum Authority (QCA) Teaching Activities
When the Sun is behind them their shadow is in front

The Sun appears to move across the sky in a regular way every day

The Sun appears highest in the sky at midday

The higher the Sun appears in the sky the shorter the shadow | Take the children out in the playground on a sunny day and ask them to mark the direction their shadow is pointing in and the direction of the Sun. Remind them of the dangers of looking at the Sun. Ask children to explain what these marks show. Set up a shadow stick in the playground and mark south, east and west in relation to it. At regular times e.g. 9.00, 12.00, 15.00 over a period of several days mark the direction and length of the shadow and the direction of the Sun. |

Thinking and Working Scientifically Standards	Content Standards for Science	Benchmarks
ScLK1.1 Asking relevant questions ScLK1.2 Setting up simple practical enquires, comparative and fair tests ScLK1.3 Making accurate measurements using standard units, using a range of equipment for example thermometers and data loggers ScLK1.4 Gathering, recording, classifying and presenting data in a variety of ways to help in answering questions ScLK1.5 Recording findings using simple scientific language, drawings, labelled diagrams, bar charts and tables ScLK1.6 Reporting on findings from enquiries, including oral and written explanations, displays or presentations of results and conclusions ScLK1.7 Using results to draw simple conclusions and suggest improvements, new questions and predictions for setting up further tests ScLK1.8 Identifying differences, similarities or changes related to simple scientific ideas and processes ScLK1.9 Using straightforward scientific evidence to answer questions or to support their findings	PL3.1 Identify and describe the functions of different parts of flowering plants: roots, stem, leaves and flowers PL3.2 Explore the requirements of plants for life and growth (air, light, water, nutrients from the soil, and room to grow) and how they vary from plant to plant PL3.3 Investigate the way in which water is transported within plants PL3.4 Explore the role of flowers in the life cycle of flowering plants, including pollination, seed formation and seed dispersal	Flowering plants reproduce
		Seeds can be dispersed in a variety of ways
		Make careful observations of fruits and seeds, to compare them and use results to draw conclusions
		That many fruits and seeds provide food for animals including humans
		Consider conditions that might affect germination and plan how to test them
		Seeds need water and warmth (but not light) for germination
		The life cycle of flowering plants including pollination, fertilisation, seed production, seed dispersal and germination

Key Vocabulary for Teaching and Learning	Words and phrases associated with life processes e.g. reproduction, life cycle Names for parts of a flower e.g. stamen, style, stigma, sepal, petal, ovary, pollen Names for processes related to life cycles and associated verbs e.g. reproduction/reproduce, germination/germinate, pollination/pollinate, fertilisation/fertilise, dispersal/disperse; Descriptions and explanations using a sequence of ideas.

Benchmarks	Qualification and Curriculum Authority (QCA) Teaching Activities
Seeds can be dispersed in a variety of ways Make careful observations of fruits and seeds, to compare them and use results to draw conclusions Many fruits and seeds provide food for animals including humans	Help children to make a collection of fruits with seeds e.g. apple, tomato, cherry, strawberry, avocado, mango and some seed cases and seeds which are not fleshy fruits e.g. wheat, maize, dandelion, poppy, winged seed cases (ash and sycamore) together with pictures of the parent plant. Talk with the children about seed dispersal and use observation and secondary sources to find out and record how the seeds are dispersed including the role of humans and other animals in the process. Using examples or pictures ask children to suggest how an unfamiliar seed is dispersed. Ask children to suggest why plants produce so many seeds.
Consider conditions that might affect germination and plan how to test them Seeds need water and warmth (but not light) for germination	Remind children that once seeds have been dispersed they need to germinate.
Life cycle of flowering plants including pollination, fertilisation, seed production, seed dispersal and germination	Review with children their knowledge of flower structure, pollen dispersal, pollination, fertilisation, and seed development and dispersal. Ask children to choose a familiar plant and introduce the term 'life cycle', create a display sheet to illustrate the complete life cycle of the plant. With the children compare the life cycles of different plants pointing out similarities e.g. in the processes and differences e.g. in the types of fruit or the mechanism for seed dispersal.

| Year 3
Spring 2	SCIENCE UNIT OF WORK: ANIMALS INCLUDING HUMANS

Thinking and Working Scientifically Standards	Content Standards for Science	Benchmarks
ScLK1.1 Asking relevant questions

ScLK1.2 Setting up simple practical enquires, comparative and fair tests

ScLK1.3 Making accurate measurements using standard units, using a range of equipment for example thermometers and data loggers

ScLK1.4 Gathering, recording, classifying and presenting data in a variety of ways to help in answering questions

ScLK1.5 Recording findings using simple scientific language, drawings, labelled diagrams, bar charts and tables

ScLK1.6 Reporting on findings from enquiries, including oral and written explanations, displays or presentations of results and conclusions

ScLK1.7 Using results to draw simple conclusions and suggest improvements, new questions and predictions for setting up further tests

ScLK1.8 Identifying differences, similarities or changes related to simple scientific ideas and processes

ScLK1.9 Using straightforward scientific evidence to answer questions or to support their findings | AH3.1 Identify that animals, including humans, need the right types and amounts of nutrition, and that they cannot make their own food, they get nutrition from what they eat

AH3.3 Identify that humans and some animals have skeletons and muscles for support, protection and movement | Make and record relevant observations of bones and skeletons |
		Human skeletons are internal and grow as humans grow
		The skeleton supports the body
		Animals with skeletons have muscles attached to the bones
		A muscle has to contract (shorten) to make a bone move
		Muscles act in pairs
		When someone is exercising or moving fast, the muscles work hard
		All animals, including humans, need to feed

Key Vocabulary for Teaching and Learning	Words relating to skeletons and muscles *e.g. ribs, spine, skull, contract, relax, vertebrate*; Nouns and related verbs *e.g. contraction, contract*

Standards/Benchmarks	Qualification and Curriculum Authority (QCA) Teaching Activities
Human skeletons are internal and grow as humans grow	Discuss relative sizes of bones in people.
Discuss how the size of parts of the body *e.g. length of forearm, circumference of head* changes as they grow.
The skeleton supports the body	Observe some invertebrates *e.g. snails and worms* and compare the body of the invertebrate (its lack of rigidity) with the human body.
Animals with skeletons have muscles attached to the bones
A muscle has to contract (shorten) to make a bone move
Muscles act in pairs	Use secondary sources to illustrate muscles and movement. Explain muscle contraction as an active process and relaxation as being passive. Ask children to explore their own muscles moving *e.g. in their arms* and what this feels like. Demonstrate movement by using models illustrating muscles and ask children to explain what the models show.

Thinking and Working Scientifically Standards	Content Standards for Science	Benchmarks
ScLK1.1 Asking relevant questions ScLK1.2 Setting up simple practical enquires, comparative and fair tests ScLK1.3 Making accurate measurements using standard units, using a range of equipment for example thermometers and data loggers ScLK1.4 Gathering, recording, classifying and presenting data in a variety of ways to help in answering questions ScLK1.5 Recording findings using simple scientific language, drawings, labelled diagrams, bar charts and tables ScLK1.6 Reporting on findings from enquiries, including oral and written explanations, displays or presentations of results and conclusions ScLK1.7 Using results to draw simple conclusions and suggest improvements, new questions and predictions for setting up further tests ScLK1.8 Identifying differences, similarities or changes related to simple scientific ideas and processes ScLK1.9 Using straightforward scientific evidence to answer questions or to support their findings	FM3.1 Notice that some forces need contact between two objects and some forces act at a distance FM3. 2 Observe how magnets attract or repel each other and attract some materials and not others FM3.3 Compare and group together a variety of everyday materials on the basis of whether they are attracted to a magnet, and identify some magnetic materials FM3.4 Describe magnets as having two poles FM3.5 Predict whether two magnets will attract or repel each other, depending on which poles are facing	There are forces between magnets and that magnets can attract (pull towards) and repel (push away from) each other
		Make generalisations about what happens when magnets are put together
		Make and test predictions about whether materials are magnetic or not
		Magnets attract some metals but not others and that other materials are not attracted to magnets

Key Vocabulary for Teaching and Learning	Names for some metals e.g. iron, copper, aluminium; Terms relating to magnets e.g. attract, repel, magnetic, non-magnetic, attraction, repulsion; Nouns and related verbs e.g. attraction/attract, repulsion/repel; Expressions making generalisations.

Benchmarks	Qualification and Curriculum Authority (QCA) Teaching Activities
Make and test predictions about whether materials are magnetic or not Magnets attract some metals but not others and that other materials are not attracted to magnets	Present children with a collection of materials, including materials found in and around the classroom, and ask them to suggest which are magnetic and how they can find out whether they are right. When children consider their results, they should be asked to group the materials into magnetic and non-magnetic and to make a relevant generalisation.

Year 4 Science Unit Plans

Year 4 Autumn 1	SCIENCE UNIT OF WORK: STATES OF MATTER	
Thinking and Working Scientifically Standards	**Content Standards for Science**	**Benchmarks**
ScLK1.1 Asking relevant questions

ScLK1.2 Setting up simple practical enquires, comparative and fair tests

ScLK1.3 Making accurate measurements using standard units, using a range of equipment for example thermometers and data loggers

ScLK1.4 Gathering, recording, classifying and presenting data in a variety of ways to help in answering questions

ScLK1.5 Recording findings using simple scientific language, drawings, labelled diagrams, bar charts and tables

ScLK1.6 Reporting on findings from enquiries, including oral and written explanations, displays or presentations of results and conclusions

ScLK1.7 Using results to draw simple conclusions and suggest improvements, new questions and predictions for setting up further tests

ScLK1.8 Identifying differences, similarities or changes related to simple scientific ideas and processes

ScLK1.9 Using straightforward scientific evidence to answer questions or to support their findings | EM4.1 Compare and group materials together, according to whether they are solids, liquids or gases

EM4.2 Observe that some materials change state when they are heated or cooled, and measure the temperature at which this happens in degrees Celsius

EM4.3 Identify the part played by evaporation and condensation in the water cycle and associate the rate of evaporation with temperature | Identify solids and liquids

There are liquids other than water

Liquids do not change in volume when they are poured into a different container

The same material can exist as both solid and liquid

Liquids can be changed to a solid by cooling and this is freezing or solidifying

A solid can be changed to a liquid by heating and this is melting

Different solids melt at different temperatures

Melting and solidifying or freezing are changes that can be reversed and are the reverse of each other

Evaporation is when a liquid turns to a gas

Explain 'disappearance' of water in a range of situations as evaporation

Liquids other than water evaporate

Explain everyday examples of 'drying' in terms of factors affecting evaporation

Condensation is when a gas turns to a liquid

Condensation is the reverse of evaporation

Air contains water vapour and when this hits a cold surface it may condense

The boiling temperature of water is 100°C

Water evaporates from oceans, seas and lakes, condenses as clouds and eventually falls as rain

Water collects in streams and rivers and eventually finds its way to the sea

Evaporation and condensation are processes that can be reversed

Interpret the water cycle in terms of the processes involved |
| **Key Vocabulary for Teaching and Learning** | Terms relating to states of matter e.g. solid, liquid, melt, freeze, solidify; Expressions for making suggestions using 'if', 'might', 'could'; Descriptions using a sequence of ideas; Words and phrases related to changes of state e.g. evaporation, condensation, boiling temperature, state, change of state, water cycle, conditions, solid, liquid, gas; Names of processes and verbs related to them e.g. condensation/condense, evaporation/evaporate, melting/melt, freezing/freeze, solidification/solidity; Expressions for generalising and summarising. | |

Benchmarks	Qualification and Curriculum Authority (QCA) Teaching Activities
Identify solids and liquids There are liquids other than water Observations and measurements of volume recording them in tables and using them to draw conclusions Liquids do not change in volume when they are poured into a different container	Present children with additional items for the collection including liquids of differing viscosity and ask them to divide them into two groups only. If necessary supplement the examples with pictures. Discuss the groupings with the children introducing the terms 'solid' and 'liquid' and ask children to re-group the items in this way. Ask children to write down or draw in as many ways as possible how the solids and liquids are different from each other and how they are similar. It may be helpful to ask questions e.g. Are all the liquids colourless? What happens to the liquid if you change the container it is in? Can you spill the solids? What happens if you tilt the bottle the liquids are in? Draw children's attention to particular properties. Extend the activity by presenting children with some 'difficult' items e.g. cotton wool, sponge, sand, rice and ask them to classify these as solids or liquids. Ask children to explore and describe how powders and solids consisting of many small pieces e.g. rice, salt, sand are different or similar to liquids e.g. by tilting jars containing these, by trying to use sand to turn a water wheel, by sieving through gauze.
The same material can exist as both solid and liquid Liquids can be changed to a solid by cooling and this is freezing or solidifying A solid can be changed to a liquid by heating and this is melting Different solids melt at different temperatures Melting and solidifying or freezing are changes that can be reversed and are the reverse of each other	Ask children to suggest when they have seen water freezing, and what conditions are necessary for this to happen. Ask them to suggest how to make ice melt. Elicit examples of other familiar materials melting or solidifying e.g. wax running down the side of a candle, chocolate melting etc, and let children explore what happens to wax if it is held in the hand or put in a warm place. Ask children how to keep familiar materials e.g. ice, chocolate, butter from melting and help them to relate these to temperature. Use secondary sources to illustrate molten metals or molten lava and emphasise that many materials have to be heated before they melt. Ask children to use secondary sources to find out more about melting metals and to record information about why this is important.
Liquids other than water evaporate Explain everyday examples of 'drying' in terms of factors affecting evaporation Condensation is when a gas turns to a liquid Condensation is the reverse of evaporation Air contains water vapour and when this hits a cold surface it may condense	Demonstrate using e.g. nail varnish, correction fluid, other liquids evaporate. Ask children to explain why they can smell e.g. perfume, aftershave, natural gas from a distance. Show pictures of appliances e.g. hairdryers, tumble dryers, rotary clothes line and ask children to explain how these help to make things 'dry' more quickly. Record explanations in writing e.g. in an advertisement for a particular sort of appliance. Demonstrate an example of condensation e.g. steam from a kettle hitting a cold surface and discuss with children what happens to water vapour when it cools down. Discuss with children where in their homes they see water collecting on surfaces e.g. in the kitchen, bathroom. Introduce the words 'condense' and 'condensation'. Demonstrate what happens when ice cubes are placed in the centre of cling film covering a container of hot/warm water. Ask children to feel the cling film to see how warm it is in different places and to observe the size of the droplets. Ask children to illustrate in diagrams and annotate to explain what happens. Show children examples of condensation where there is no obvious source of water vapour e.g. breathing on a cold window pane, droplets of water collecting on a metal glass containing mixture of ice and water, droplets of water collecting on a can of soft drink from the freezer. Ask children where they think the water came from and to record in a drawing with annotation.
Water evaporates from oceans, seas and lakes, condenses as clouds and eventually falls as rain Water collects in streams and rivers and eventually finds its way to the sea Evaporation and condensation are processes that can be reversed Interpret the water cycle in terms of the processes involved	Ask children a question about our water e.g. Where does our bath water come from? Visit a water works or use secondary sources to show where our water supply comes from. Help children to see the relationship to earlier work on evaporation and condensation and to use what they know to build up the water cycle from first principles.

Thinking and Working Scientifically Standards	Content Standards for Science	Benchmarks
ScLK1.1 Asking relevant questions **ScLK1.2 Setting up simple practical enquires, comparative and fair tests** **ScLK1.3 Making accurate measurements using standard units, using a range of equipment for example thermometers and data loggers** **ScLK1.4 Gathering, recording, classifying and presenting data in a variety of ways to help in answering questions** **ScLK1.5 Recording findings using simple scientific language, drawings, labelled diagrams, bar charts and tables** **ScLK1.6 Reporting on findings from enquiries, including oral and written explanations, displays or presentations of results and conclusions** **ScLK1.7 Using results to draw simple conclusions and suggest improvements, new questions and predictions for setting up further tests** **ScLK1.8 Identifying differences, similarities or changes related to simple scientific ideas and processes** **ScLK1.9 Using straightforward scientific evidence to answer questions or to support their findings**	SND4.1 Identify how sounds are made, associating some of them with something vibrating SND4.2 Find patterns between the pitch of a sound and features of the object that produced it SND4.3 Find patterns between the volume of a sound and the strength of the vibrations that produced it	Sounds are made when objects or materials vibrate Vibrations from sound sources travel through different materials to the ear Some materials are effective in preventing vibrations from sound sources reaching the ear The term 'pitch' describes how high or low a sound is Pitch of a drum depends on tightness of the skin Pitch of a stringed instrument depends on length, thickness and tightness Suggest how to change pitch Sounds can be made by air vibrating Volume is how loud or quiet a sound is Stronger vibrations produce louder sounds
Key Vocabulary for Teaching and Learning	Words related to sounds *e.g. pitch, loudness, vibration, muffle,* tuning; Near synonyms *e.g. quiet, soft, noise,* sound; Nouns and related adjectives *e.g. loudness, loud, tension,* tight; Expressions of contrast *e.g. this sound is loud and high, this is loud and* low; Generalisations about relationships between variables *e.g. If I tighten the drum skin the pitch will go up.*	

Benchmarks	Qualification and Curriculum Authority (QCA) Teaching Activities
Sounds are made when objects or materials vibrate Vibrations from sound sources travel through different materials to the ear	Demonstrate to children a number of examples of sounds associated with visible vibrations. Ask children to listen carefully for sounds they can hear which are made outside the classroom. Include sounds that they regularly hear through walls/doors.
Some materials are effective in preventing vibrations from sound sources reaching the ear	Discuss with children why sometimes it is important to prevent sounds travelling. Ask them to suggest how this is done *e.g. earmuffs, earplugs, soft floor coverings.* Walk around the school to see where sounds *e.g. footsteps* are loud and where they are not. Ask children to describe what they observed.
The term 'pitch' describes how high or low a sound is The pitch of a drum depends on its size and the tightness of its skin	Ask children to demonstrate playing a range of musical instruments or show children a video of a band or orchestra playing. Talk with children about sounds made by individual instruments and help them to describe the pitch of sounds. Ask children to play a number of drums to show how the pitch of a drum varies with size and, if possible, how it can be changes by tightening the skin.

Thinking and Working Scientifically Standards	Content Standards for Science	Benchmarks
ScLK1.1 Asking relevant questions **ScLK1.2 Setting up simple practical enquires, comparative and fair tests** **ScLK1.3 Making accurate measurements using standard units, using a range of equipment for example thermometers and data loggers** **ScLK1.4 Gathering, recording, classifying and presenting data in a variety of ways to help in answering questions** **ScLK1.5 Recording findings using simple scientific language, drawings, labelled diagrams, bar charts and tables** **ScLK1.6 Reporting on findings from enquiries, including oral and written explanations, displays or presentations of results and conclusions** **ScLK1.7 Using results to draw simple conclusions and suggest improvements, new questions and predictions for setting up further tests** **ScLK1.8 Identifying differences, similarities or changes related to simple scientific ideas and processes** **ScLK1.9 Using straightforward scientific evidence to answer questions or to support their findings**	ALT4.1 Identify and name a variety of living things (plants and animals) in the local and wider environment, using classification keys to assign them to groups ALT4.2 Recognise that environments are constantly changing and that this can some times pose dangers to living things	

Key Vocabulary for Teaching and Learning	

Standards/Benchmarks	Indicative Teaching and Learning Activities

Year 4 Spring 2	SCIENCE UNIT OF WORK: ANIMALS INCLUDING HUMANS

Thinking and Working Scientifically Standards	Content Standards for Science	Benchmarks
ScLK1.1 Asking relevant questions	AH4.1 Describe the simple functions of the basic parts of the digestive system in humans	
ScLK1.2 Setting up simple practical enquires, comparative and fair tests		
ScLK1.3 Making accurate measurements using standard units, using a range of equipment for example thermometers and data loggers	AH4.2 Identify the different types of teeth in humans and their simple function	
ScLK1.4 Gathering, recording, classifying and presenting data in a variety of ways to help in answering questions	AH4.3 Construct and interpret a variety of food chains, identifying producers, predators and prey	
ScLK1.5 Recording findings using simple scientific language, drawings, labelled diagrams, bar charts and tables		
ScLK1.6 Reporting on findings from enquiries, including oral and written explanations, displays or presentations of results and conclusions		
ScLK1.7 Using results to draw simple conclusions and suggest improvements, new questions and predictions for setting up further tests		
ScLK1.8 Identifying differences, similarities or changes related to simple scientific ideas and processes		
ScLK1.9 Using straightforward scientific evidence to answer questions or to support their findings		

Key Vocabulary for Teaching and Learning	
Benchmarks	Indicative Teaching and Learning Activities

Thinking and Working Scientifically Standards	Content Standards for Science	Benchmarks
ScLK1.1 Asking relevant questions ScLK1.2 Setting up simple practical enquires, comparative and fair tests ScLK1.3 Making accurate measurements using standard units, using a range of equipment for example thermometers and data loggers ScLK1.4 Gathering, recording, classifying and presenting data in a variety of ways to help in answering questions ScLK1.5 Recording findings using simple scientific language, drawings, labelled diagrams, bar charts and tables ScLK1.6 Reporting on findings from enquiries, including oral and written explanations, displays or presentations of results and conclusions ScLK1.7 Using results to draw simple conclusions and suggest improvements, new questions and predictions for setting up further tests ScLK1.8 Identifying differences, similarities or changes related to simple scientific ideas and processes ScLK1.9 Using straightforward scientific evidence to answer questions or to support their findings	ELEC4.1 Identify common appliances that run on electricity ELEC4.2 Construct a simple series electrical circuit, identifying and naming its basic parts, including cells, wires, bulbs, switches and buzzers ELEC4.3 Identify whether or not a lamp will light in simple series circuit based on whether or not the lamp is part of a complete loop with battery ELEC4.4 Recognise that a switch opens and closes a circuit and associate this with whether or not a lamp lights in simple series circuit ELEC4.5 Recognise some common conductors and insulators and associate metals with being good conductors	A circuit needs a power source
		A complete circuit is needed for a device to work
		Circuits powered by batteries can be used for investigation and experiment, appliances connected to the mains must not
		Some materials are better conductors of electricity than others
		Metals are good conductors of electricity, most other materials are not and that metals are used for cables and wires, plastics are used to cover wires and as covers for plugs and switches
		A switch can be used to make or break a circuit to turn things on or off (using both batteries or mains)

Key Vocabulary for Teaching and Learning	Words and phrases relating to electrical circuits *e.g. battery, bulb, buzzer, motor, break, electrical conductor, electrical* insulator; Names of types of material *e.g. metal,* plastic; Expressions used to make generalisations; Expressions for making suggestions using 'if', 'might', 'could'.

Benchmarks	Qualification and Curriculum Authority (QCA) Teaching Activities
Some materials are better conductors of electricity than others Metals are good conductors of electricity, most other materials are not and that metals are used for cables and wires, plastics are used to cover wires and as covers for plugs and switches	Ask children what materials are used to make electric circuits and ask them to suggest why this is. Ask children how they could test their ideas *e.g. by inserting different materials into a complete circuit with a bulb, motor or a buzzer and observing whether the device will still work.* Record where conductors and where insulators are useful.
A switch can be used to make or break a circuit to turn things on or off (using both batteries or mains)	Demonstrate switches on familiar devices (mains and battery driven) and how they can be used to turn the devices on and off. Ask children to make simple switches *e.g. from paper clips, foil, drawing pins* and incorporate them into circuits with bulbs or buzzers. Elicit children's ideas about the function of switches,

231

Year 5 Science Unit Plans

Year 5 Autumn 1		SCIENCE UNIT OF WORK: PROPERTIES OF EVERYDAY MATEIALS AND CHANGES (REVERSIBLE & IRREVERSIBLE)
Thinking and Working Scientifically Standards	**Content Standards for Science**	**Benchmarks**
ScUK1.1 Planning enquiries, including recognising and controlling variables where necessary ScUK1.2 Taking measurements, using a range of scientific equipment, with increasing accuracy and precision ScUK1.3 Recording data and results of increasing complexity using scientific diagrams and labels, classification keys, tables, bar and line graphs, and models ScUK1.4 Reporting findings from enquiries, including oral and written explanations of results, explanations involving causal relationship and conclusions ScUK1.5 Presenting findings in written form, displays and other presentations ScUK1.6 Using test results to make predictions to set up further comparative and fair tests ScUK1.7 Using simple models to describe scientific ideas ScUK1.8 Identifying scientific evidence that has been used to support or refute ideas or arguments	EM5.1 Compare and group together everyday materials based on evidence from comparative and fair tests, including their hardness, solubility, conductivity (electrical and thermal) and response to magnets EM5.2 Understand how some materials will dissolve in liquid to form a solution, and describe how to recover a substance from a solution EM5.3 Use knowledge of solids, liquids and gases to decide how mixtures might be separated, including through filtering EM5.4 Give reasons, based on evidence from comparative and fair tests, for the particular uses of everyday materials, including metals, wood and plastic EM5.5 Demonstrate that dissolving, mixing and changes of state are reversible changes EM5.6 Explain that some changes result in the formation of new materials, and that this kind of change is not usually reversible, including changes associated with burning, oxidisation, and the action of acid on bicarbonate of soda	Heating some materials can cause them to change and this may or may not be reversible
		Cooling some materials can cause them to change and this may or may not be reversible
		When materials are burned, new materials are formed
		Changes that occur when most materials are burned are not reversible
		Some changes that occur when materials are mixed cannot be easily reversed
		Solids can be mixed and that it is often possible to get the original materials back
		Choose appropriate apparatus for separating a mixture of solids
		Changes occur when some solids are added to water
		When solids do not dissolve or react with the water they can be separated by filtering
		Choose apparatus to separate an undissolved solid from a liquid
		Some solids dissolve in water to form solutions and that although the solid cannot be seen it is still present
		When solids dissolve a clear solution is formed, the solid cannot be separated by filtering
		Predict whether salt or sugar can be separated from a solution by filtering and to test the prediction to see if it was correct
Key Vocabulary for Teaching and Learning	Terms relating to states of matter and to separation *eg solid, liquid, melt, dissolve, solution, filter, undissolved, dissolved;* Expressions for making suggestions using 'if', 'might', 'could'; Descriptions using a sequence of ideas.	

Benchmarks	Qualification and Curriculum Authority (QCA) Teaching Activities
Solids can be mixed and that it is often possible to get the original materials back Choose appropriate apparatus for separating a mixture of solids	Demonstrate different sized solid particles are separable by sieving. Challenge children to separate a mixture of *e.g. sand, rice, dried peas and paper clips using their own techniques and to explain why these worked.*
Changes occur when some solids are added to water When solids do not dissolve or react with the water they can be separated by filtering Choose apparatus to separate an undissolved solid from a liquid Some solids dissolve in water to form solutions and that although the solid cannot be seen it is still present When solids dissolve a clear solution is formed, the solid cannot be separated by filtering Predict whether salt or sugar can be separated from a solution by filtering and to test the prediction to see if it was correct When liquid evaporates from a solution, the solid is left behind	Children to explore what happens when a range of materials *e.g. salt, instant coffee, sugar, flour, powder paint, chalk, sand, glass beads or marbles, plaster of Paris,* are mixed with water and to group the solids according to what happens, recording their results in a table. Children suggest and try out how they could get marbles or sand back from the mixture with water. Discuss why marbles can be separated from water by coarse sieves but sand cannot. Ask for suggestions of how to modify the apparatus to get sand back possibly illustrating ideas using tea bags or coffee filters. Children try out apparatus and materials *eg muslin, paper towels, gauze bandage, blotting paper, fabrics* they have suggested and describe and explain what they did. Remind children that when salt and sugar are added to water clear solutions are obtained, and if necessary show them this again. Ask children to say what they think has happened to the salt and sugar, remind them *e.g. of adding sugar to tea or salt to cooking vegetables* and to suggest how they could find out *e.g. by tasting the solution.* Ask children to predict whether salt or sugar can be separated by filtration. Discuss what they would need to do to find out whether their prediction is correct and help them to decide how to do this. Find out by testing whether their prediction is correct or not.
Heating some materials can cause them to change and this may or may not be reversible Cooling some materials can cause them to change and this may or may not be reversible When materials are burned, new materials are formed Changes that occur when most materials are burned are not reversible Some changes that occur when materials are mixed cannot be easily reversed	Demonstrate or show pictures or film footage of what happens when a range of materials burn. Discuss what is made and ask the children if they think other materials are made that they can't see. Talk about how they would know if a gas were made when they can't see it. Discuss everyday examples of burning, such as natural gas in cookers, bonfires, fires and barbeques. Discuss safety in relation to burning and point out that new materials are made and they may be harmful.

Thinking and Working Scientifically Standards	Content Standards for Science	Benchmarks
ScUK1.1 Planning enquiries, including recognising and controlling variables where necessary ScUK1.2 Taking measurements, using a range of scientific equipment, with increasing accuracy and precision ScUK1.3 Recording data and results of increasing complexity using scientific diagrams and labels, classification keys, tables, bar and line graphs, and models ScUK1.4 Reporting findings from enquiries, including oral and written explanations of results, explanations involving causal relationship and conclusions ScUK1.5 Presenting findings in written form, displays and other presentations ScUK1.6 Using test results to make predictions to set up further comparative and fair tests ScUK1.7 Using simple models to describe scientific ideas ScUK1.8 Identifying scientific evidence that has been used to support or refute ideas or arguments	FO5.1 Explain that unsupported objects fall towards the earth because of the force of gravity acting between the Earth and falling object FO5.2 Identify the effects of air resistance, water resistance and friction, that act between moving surfaces FO5.3 Understand that force and motion can be transferred through mechanical devices such as gears, pulleys, levers and springs	Springs are used in a variety of ways
		When a spring is stretched or compressed upward, it exerts a downward force on whatever is compressing or stretching it, and that when an elastic band is stretched downward, it exerts an upward force on whatever is stretching it
		Forces act in particular directions
		Several forces may act on one object
		The Earth and objects are pulled towards each other; this gravitational attraction causes objects to have weight
		Use a forcemeter carefully, interpreting the scale correctly
		Weight is a force and is measured in newtons
		Represent the direction of forces using arrows
		When an object is submerged in water, the water provides an upward force (upthrust) on it
		Air resistance slows moving objects
		Force between two moving surfaces in contact is called friction
		Friction can be useful
		Water resistance slows an object moving through water

Key Vocabulary for Teaching and Learning	Words relating to forces and the measurement of forces *e.g. weight, gravity, upthrust, newton, forcemeter*. Near synonyms *eg still, stationary, at rest, not moving*: Generalisations about patterns in behaviour & descriptions and explanations involving a sequence of ideas.

Benchmarks	Qualification and Curriculum Authority (QCA) Teaching Activities
Springs are used in a variety of ways When a spring is stretched or compressed upward, it exerts a downward force on whatever is compressing or stretching it, and that when an elastic band is stretched downward, it exerts an upward force on whatever is stretching it Forces act in particular directions	Children to make a list of examples of where springs are used at school or at home. Ask children to pull springs and elastic bands and to push springs and to describe the direction of the force on their hands. Show children how to make a catapult or 'push meter' using elastic bands to propel a toy car or weighted container along a flat surface and ask them to predict what will happen if the bands are stretched by different amounts. Help children to decide how to test their predictions.
The Earth and objects are pulled towards each other; this gravitational attraction causes objects to have weight Use a forcemeter carefully, interpreting the scale correctly Weight is a force and is measured in newtons Represent the direction of forces using arrows When an object is submerged in water, the water provides an upward force (upthrust) on it Air resistance slows moving objects Air resistance is a force that slows objects moving through air When an object falls, air resistance acts in the opposite direction to the weight	Show children examples of objects which have clearly identifiable and familiar forces acting on them *e.g. an object suspended from an elastic band, an object suspended from a spring, an object resting on a strong spring, a paper clip hanging from a magnet.* Ask children to say what forces are acting on each object. Ask children to draw diagrams showing the direction of the forces with arrows and to label these. Ask children to use a forcemeter to weigh a series of objects suspended in air and then suspended in water. Remind children of the previous activity and of air resistance as a force and ask children to explore how spinners weighted with paper clips fall when dropped. Ask them to suggest a question/investigate a question.
Force between two moving surfaces in contact is called friction Friction can be useful Water resistance slows an object moving through water	Talk with children about surfaces between which there is low or high friction and make a list showing everyday situations where high friction is helpful *e.g. tyres on cars and bicycles, goal keeper's gloves, tying shoe laces* and everyday situations where low friction is useful *e.g. skating, playground slides.* Ask children to describe what it is like to walk through water *e.g. in a swimming pool* and to suggest why it is difficult. Elicit their ideas about why fish and boats can move through water. If necessary prompt them to think about shape. Show children a tall cylinder filled with water and talk with them about what they could do, using this apparatus and a small piece of plasticine, to find out which shapes move easily through water.

Year 5 Spring 1		SCIENCE UNIT OF WORK: ALL LIVING THINGS
Thinking and Working Scientifically Standards	**Content Standards for Science**	**Benchmarks**
ScUK1.1 Planning enquiries, including recognising and controlling variables where necessary ScUK1.2 Taking measurements, using a range of scientific equipment, with increasing accuracy and precision ScUK1.3 Recording data and results of increasing complexity using scientific diagrams and labels, classification keys, tables, bar and line graphs, and models ScUK1.4 Reporting findings from enquiries, including oral and written explanations of results, explanations involving causal relationship and conclusions ScUK1.5 Presenting findings in written form, displays and other presentations ScUK1.6 Using test results to make predictions to set up further comparative and fair tests ScUK1.7 Using simple models to describe scientific ideas ScUK1.8 Identifying scientific evidence that has been used to support or refute ideas or arguments	ALT5.1 Explain differences in the life cycles of a mammal, an amphibian, an insect and a bird ALT5. 2 Describe the life process of reproduction in some plants and animals	The life cycle of flowering plants including pollination, fertilisation, seed production, seed dispersal and germination
		Adults have young and that these grow into adults which in turn produce young
		If living things did not reproduce they would eventually die out
Key Vocabulary for Teaching and Learning	Words and phrases associated with life processes *e.g. reproduction, life cycle;* Names for parts of a flower *e.g. stamen, style, stigma, sepal, petal, ovary,* pollen; Names for processes related to life cycles and associated verbs *e.g. reproduction/reproduce, germination/germinate, pollination/pollinate, fertilisation/fertilise, dispersal/disperse;* Descriptions and explanations using a sequence of ideas.	
Benchmarks	**Qualification and Curriculum Authority (QCA) Teaching Activities**	
Plants produce flowers which have male and female organs, seeds are formed when pollen from the male organ fertilises the ovum (female) The life cycle of flowering plants including pollination, fertilisation, seed production, seed dispersal and germination	Review with children their knowledge of flower structure, pollen dispersal, pollination, fertilisation, and seed development and dispersal. Ask children to choose a familiar plant and introduce the term 'life cycle', create a display sheet to illustrate the complete life cycle of the plant.	

Thinking and Working Scientifically Standards	Content Standards for Science	Benchmarks
ScUK1.1 Planning enquiries, including recognising and controlling variables where necessary	AH5.1 Describe the changes as humans develop from birth to old age	Adults have young and that these grow into adults which in turn produce young
		Human young are dependent on adults for a relatively long period
ScUK1.2 Taking measurements, using a range of scientific equipment, with increasing accuracy and precision		
ScUK1.3 Recording data and results of increasing complexity using scientific diagrams and labels, classification keys, tables, bar and line graphs, and models		
ScUK1.4 Reporting findings from enquiries, including oral and written explanations of results, explanations involving causal relationship and conclusions		
ScUK1.5 Presenting findings in written form, displays and other presentations		
ScUK1.6 Using test results to make predictions to set up further comparative and fair tests		
ScUK1.7 Using simple models to describe scientific ideas		
ScUK1.8 Identifying scientific evidence that has been used to support or refute ideas or arguments		

Key Vocabulary for Teaching and Learning	
Benchmarks	Qualification and Curriculum Authority (QCA) Teaching Activities
Adults have young and that these grow into adults which in turn produce young Human young are dependent on adults for a relatively long period	Talk with children about the growth and development of humans and discuss different stages *e.g. babyhood, childhood, adolescence, adulthood.* Ask children to devise a time line to demonstrate stages in the growth and development of humans and talk with them about the relative lengths of each stage.

Thinking and Working Scientifically Standards	Content Standards for Science	Benchmarks
ScUK1.1 Planning enquiries, including recognising and controlling variables where necessary ScUK1.2 Taking measurements, using a range of scientific equipment, with increasing accuracy and precision ScUK1.3 Recording data and results of increasing complexity using scientific diagrams and labels, classification keys, tables, bar and line graphs, and models ScUK1.4 Reporting findings from enquiries, including oral and written explanations of results, explanations involving causal relationship and conclusions ScUK1.5 Presenting findings in written form, displays and other presentations ScUK1.6 Using test results to make predictions to set up further comparative and fair tests ScUK1.7 Using simple models to describe scientific ideas ScUK1.8 Identifying scientific evidence that has been used to support or refute ideas or arguments	E&S5.1 Describe the movement of the Earth relative to the Sun in the solar system E&S5.2 Describe the movement of the Moon relative to the Earth E&S5.3 Describe the Sun, Earth and Moon as approximately spherical bodies E&S5.4 Use the idea of the Earth's rotation to explain day and night	The Sun, Earth and Moon are approximately spherical
		The relative sizes of the Sun, Moon and Earth
		The Sun appears to move across the sky over the course of a day
		It is the Earth that moves, not the Sun, and the Earth spins on its axis once every 24 hours
		It is daytime in the part of the Earth facing the Sun and night-time in the part of the Earth away from the Sun
		The Earth takes a year to make one complete orbit of the Sun, spinning as it goes
		The Sun rises in the general direction of the East and sets in the general direction of the West
		Present times of sunrise and sunset in a graph and to recognise trends and patterns in the data
		The Moon takes approximately 28 days to orbit the Earth
		The different appearance of the Moon over 28 days provides evidence for a 28-day cycle
Key Vocabulary for Teaching and Learning	Words and phrases related to the shape and movement of the Earth and Moon *e.g. sphere, revolve, orbit, spin, rotate, axis, sunrise, sunset, north, south, east, west;* Nouns and associated adjectives *e.g. sphere/spherical;* Words and phrases which have similar but distinct meanings *e.g. rotate around, rotate on its axis, spin, orbit;* Expressions for generalising and summarising; Descriptions and explanations involving a sequence of ideas.	

Benchmarks	Qualification and Curriculum Authority (QCA) Teaching Activities
The Sun, Earth and Moon are approximately spherical It is sometimes difficult to collect evidence to test scientific ideas and that evidence may be indirect	Use secondary sources and models and ask children whether these suggest the bodies are flat or spherical. Find out some earlier ideas about whether the Earth was flat or spherical and what evidence people used to support their ideas.
The relative sizes of the Sun, Moon and Earth	Put Earth, Moon and Sun in order of size by selecting from a range of spheres *e.g. football, beach ball, tennis ball, pea, ball bearing, peppercorn, tiny beads about 1/4 size of pea, table tennis ball.* Explain to children that if a pea represents the Earth then the beach ball represents the Sun and the bead the Moon. Ask three children to hold the three spheres and position them in the classroom to give an idea of their relative distances apart.
It is the Earth that moves, not the Sun, and the Earth spins on its axis once every 24 hours It is daytime in the part of the Earth facing the Sun and night-time in the part of the Earth away from the Sun	Use secondary sources to illustrate the Earth spinning on its axis. Show children a model of the process. Ask children to show others how night and day arise from the Earth spinning on its axis.
The Earth takes a year to make one complete orbit of the Sun, spinning as it goes The Moon takes approximately 28 days to orbit the Earth The different appearance of the Moon over 28 days provides evidence for a 28-day cycle	Discuss with children their understanding of a 'year'. Illustrate that the appearance of the Moon changes in a regular manner over a period of approximately 28 days. Model the Moon's orbit round the Earth. Ask children to describe the movement of the Moon *e.g. as it goes round the Earth it turns so that the same side always faces the Earth.*

Year 6 Science Unit Plans

Year 6 Autumn 2		SCIENCE UNIT OF WORK: LIGHT
Thinking and Working Scientifically Standards	Content Standards for Science	Benchmarks
ScUK1.1 Planning enquiries, including recognising and controlling variables where necessary ScUK1.2 Taking measurements, using a range of scientific equipment, with increasing accuracy and precision ScUK1.3 Recording data and results of increasing complexity using scientific diagrams and labels, classification keys, tables, bar and line graphs, and models ScUK1.4 Reporting findings from enquiries, including oral and written explanations of results, explanations involving causal relationship and conclusions ScUK1.5 Presenting findings in written form, displays and other presentations ScUK1.6 Using test results to make predictions to set up further comparative and fair tests ScUK1.7 Using simple models to describe scientific ideas ScUK1.8 Identifying scientific evidence that has been used to support or refute ideas or arguments	LT6.1 Understand light appears to travel in straight lines LT6.2 Use the idea light travels in straight lines to explain that objects are seen because they give out or reflect light into the eye LT6.3 Explain that we see things because light travels from light sources to our eyes or from light sources to objects and then to our eyes LT6.4 Use the idea that light travels in straight lines to explain why shadows have the same shape as the objects that cast them, and to predict the size of shadows when the position of the light source changes	Light travels from a source
		We see because light from the source enters our eyes
		Light from an object can be reflected by a mirror, the reflected light enters our eyes and we see the object
		The direction of a beam or ray of light travelling from a source can be indicated by a straight line with an arrow
		When a beam of light is reflected from a surface, its direction changes
		Shiny surfaces reflect light better than dull surfaces
		Identify factors which might affect the size and position of the shadow of an object
		Investigate how changing one factor causes a shadow to change
Key Vocabulary for Teaching and Learning	Words and phrases related to shadow formation and reflection e.g. opaque, reflect, reflection, light beam, mirror, light travelling; Expressions making generalisations about patterns in results; Descriptions and explanations involving a sequence of ideas.	
Benchmarks	Qualification and Curriculum Authority (QCA) Teaching Activities	
Light from an object can be reflected by a mirror, the reflected light enters our eyes and we see the object When a beam of light is reflected from a surface, its direction changes Identify factors which might affect the size and position of the shadow of an object Investigate how changing one factor causes a shadow to change	Children to explore what they can see with a mirror by posing questions *e.g. Can you see behind you? Can you make a beam of light move round the classroom?* Ask children to think of other questions to explore and to record and explain their observations in drawing and writing. Help children to represent the direction of a light beam using straight lines with arrows Demonstrate to children, in a relatively dark area, what happens when a torch with a powerful beam is placed on a piece of white paper and shone at a mirror. Ask children to trace the path of the beam and of the reflected beam and to explore what happens when the light hits the mirror at different angles Remind children of shadow formation using an opaque object *e.g. a cardboard figure.* Ask them to explore ways in which the shadow of the figure can be made to change. Ask children to suggest questions they could investigate *e.g. What happens to the size of the shadow when you move the figure nearer the light?*	

Thinking and Working Scientifically Standards	Content Standards for Science	Benchmarks
ScUK1.1 Planning enquiries, including recognising and controlling variables where necessary **ScUK1.2 Taking measurements, using a range of scientific equipment, with increasing accuracy and precision** **ScUK1.3 Recording data and results of increasing complexity using scientific diagrams and labels, classification keys, tables, bar and line graphs, and models** **ScUK1.4 Reporting findings from enquiries, including oral and written explanations of results, explanations involving causal relationship and conclusions** **ScUK1.5 Presenting findings in written form, displays and other presentations** **ScUK1.6 Using test results to make predictions to set up further comparative and fair tests** **ScUK1.7 Using simple models to describe scientific ideas** **ScUK1.8 Identifying scientific evidence that has been used to support or refute ideas or arguments**	ALT6.1 Describe how living things are classified into broad groups according to common observable characteristics and based on similarities and differences, including plants, animals and microorganisms ALT6.2 Give reasons for classifying plans and animals based on specific characteristics	
Key Vocabulary for Teaching and Learning		
Benchmarks	Indicative Teaching and Learning Activities	

Thinking and Working Scientifically Standards	Content Standards for Science	Benchmarks
ScUK1.1 Planning enquiries, including recognising and controlling variables where necessary **ScUK1.2 Taking measurements, using a range of scientific equipment, with increasing accuracy and precision** **ScUK1.3 Recording data and results of increasing complexity using scientific diagrams and labels, classification keys, tables, bar and line graphs, and models** **ScUK1.4 Reporting findings from enquiries, including oral and written explanations of results, explanations involving causal relationship and conclusions** **ScUK1.5 Presenting findings in written form, displays and other presentations** **ScUK1.6 Using test results to make predictions to set up further comparative and fair tests** **ScUK1.7 Using simple models to describe scientific ideas** **ScUK1.8 Identifying scientific evidence that has been used to support or refute ideas or arguments**	AH6.1 Identify and name the main parts of the human circulatory system and explain the functions of the heart, blood vessels and blood. AH6.2 recognise the impact of diet, exercise, drugs and lifestyle on the way their bodies function AH6.3 Describe the ways in which nutrients an water are transported within animals, including humans	

Key Vocabulary for Teaching and Learning	
Benchmarks	**Indicative Teaching and Learning Activities**

Thinking and Working Scientifically Standards	Content Standards for Science	Benchmarks
ScUK1.1 Planning enquiries, including recognising and controlling variables where necessary	EV6.1 Recognise that living things produce offspring of the same kind, but normally offspring vary and are not identical to their parents	
ScUK1.2 Taking measurements, using a range of scientific equipment, with increasing accuracy and precision	EV6.2 Recognise that living things have changed over time and that fossils provide information about living things that inhabited the Earth millions of years ago	
ScUK1.3 Recording data and results of increasing complexity using scientific diagrams and labels, classification keys, tables, bar and line graphs, and models	EV6.3 Identify how animals and plants are adapted to suit their environment in different ways and that adaptation may lead to evolution	
ScUK1.4 Reporting findings from enquiries, including oral and written explanations of results, explanations involving causal relationship and conclusions		
ScUK1.5 Presenting findings in written form, displays and other presentations		
ScUK1.6 Using test results to make predictions to set up further comparative and fair tests		
ScUK1.7 Using simple models to describe scientific ideas		
ScUK1.8 Identifying scientific evidence that has been used to support or refute ideas or arguments		

Key Vocabulary for Teaching and Learning	
Benchmarks	Indicative Teaching and Learning Activities

Year 6 Summer 2	SCIENCE UNIT OF WORK: ELECTICITY

Thinking and Working Scientifically Standards	Content Standards for Science	Benchmarks
ScUK1.1 Planning enquiries, including recognising and controlling variables where necessary **ScUK1.2 Taking measurements, using a range of scientific equipment, with increasing accuracy and precision** **ScUK1.3 Recording data and results of increasing complexity using scientific diagrams and labels, classification keys, tables, bar and line graphs, and models** **ScUK1.4 Reporting findings from enquiries, including oral and written explanations of results, explanations involving causal relationship and conclusions** **ScUK1.5 Presenting findings in written form, displays and other presentations** **ScUK1.6 Using test results to make predictions to set up further comparative and fair tests** **ScUK1.7 Using simple models to describe scientific ideas** **ScUK1.8 Identifying scientific evidence that has been used to support or refute ideas or arguments**	ELEC6.1 Associate the brightness of a lamp or the volume of a buzzer with the number and voltage of cells used in the circuit ELEC6.2 Compare and give reasons for variations in how components function, including the brightness of bulbs, the loudness of buzzers and the on/off position of switches ELEC6.3 Use recognised symbols when representing a simple circuit in a diagram	There are conventional symbols for components in circuits and these can be used to draw diagrams of circuits
		Circuit diagrams using symbols can be understood by anyone who knows the symbols and can be used for constructing and interpreting circuits
		Brightness of bulbs in a circuit can be changed
		Brightness of bulbs in a circuit can be changed by changing wires in a circuit (thickness/length), number of cells and their voltage

Key Vocabulary for Teaching and Learning	

Benchmarks	Qualification and Curriculum Authority (QCA) Teaching Activities
There are conventional symbols for components in circuits and these can be used to draw diagrams of circuits Circuit diagrams using symbols can be understood by anyone who knows the symbols and can be used for constructing and interpreting circuits	Review factors that change brightness of bulbs, speed or motors and so on. Discuss conventional symbols for circuit diagrams. Children draw circuit diagrams for others to construct from diagram.

Supplementary Resources & Materials

Selecting Materials to Support the Standards-Based Curriculum for England

As with any new initiative or development in education, a range of commercial products come onto the market. Not all products, materials and resources will be fully aligned to a standards-based model and promote the necessary congruency at classroom level. It is therefore essential to carefully evaluate products. Examine any claims to be matched or aligned to the National Curriculum by using the following questions. They are not exhaustive, but offer a framework for deciding on whether or not a financial investment is going to enhance a standards-based curriculum or compromise its integrity.

The main focus of evaluating materials is the extent to which they align teaching, learning and assessment. Keep in mind the concept of congruency introduced in Chapter One.

Teaching, Learning and Assessment	
	Do the materials contain the important concepts contained in the National Curriculum?
	To what extent do the materials or products address the depth and breadth of grade-level standards?
	Is the suggested teaching sequence logical and progressive?
	To what extent do the materials, resources or products include frequent assessment opportunities?
	Where assessment materials are included as part of a product, do they promote multiple measures?
	If assessment materials are included, are they valid and reliable? This was a key issue raised in Chapter Four when assessing without National Curriculum levels was considered.

How strongly is congruency between standards, teaching, learning and assessment promoted?

Content and Presentation

Is the content accurate?

How consistent is the content with standards in the National Curriculum? For example, is the pitch and expectation appropriately aligned to grade-level standards?

Does any background material provided for teachers support the development of subject-knowledge, appropriate selection of pedagogical approaches and signal common misconceptions that may need to be addressed?

Are the materials written so they are accessible to children?

If resource sheets or textbooks are included, are instructions for tasks and activities clear for teachers and children?

Are there any ethnic, cultural, racial, economic or gender biases in the materials?

Where additional resources are required beyond the product, are these specified clearly to aid teachers in preparing teaching and learning activities?

Example of Year-on-Year Tracking Without National Curriculum Levels

In this example, each child's overall achievement of grade-level standards at the end of each year group can be tracked. A profile of how a child has progressed from their starting point against National Curriculum standards in Year 1 through to Year 6. Below, it is possible to see that Child A started with a low baseline and exceeded expectations by the end of Year 6. It is possible to say teaching and learning has been highly effective in supporting an individual who could have underachieved. Child B could be considered as having coasted through Key Stage 1 and Key Stage 2 despite the individual leaving Key Stage 2 with the expected body of knowledge to make them ready for secondary education. Child C has been at risk of underachievement, but made more rapid and sustained progress in Upper Key Stage 2.

Such a means of tracking cohorts as they move through the school could be devised for English (reading and writing as separate strands, perhaps), Mathematics and Science.

	Year 1	Year 2	Year 3	Year 4	Year 5	Year 6
Child A	WB	EM	E	E	EX	EX
Child B	E	E	E	EM	E	E
Child C	EM	EM	EM	EM	E	E

An alternative would be to work with percentages of children on-track against grade-level standards as they move through each year group.

	Year 1	Year 2	Year 3	Year 4	Year 5	Year 6
Reading	54%	60%	65%	72%	72%	80%
Writing	52%	55%	60%	65%	70%	80%
Mathematics	65%	70%	60%	55%	50%	60%
Science	75%	75%	70%	78%	80%	80%

The tracking could be adapted to show percentages at Well Below, Emerging, Expected and Exceeding so impact of teaching can be analysed in greater detail. Names of children could be inserted below each percentage to closely monitor individuals. This could be done along the lines of the tracking grids against grade-level standards in Mathematics contained in these supplementary materials.

Tracking Grid for Year 1 Conquering Primary Maths

This example of a tracking grid is design to monitor children's progress through *Conquering Primary Maths*. The percentage of children at each stage of achievement in relation to a benchmark can be inserted into the appropriate row and column. Beneath this, the names of children can be included to help explicitly identify those who may require intervention.

Tracking Year 1 Achievement by CPM Benchmarks				
Autumn 1	**% Well Below**	**% Emerging**	**% Expected**	**% Exceeding**
Comparisons: Ordering- taller, shorter, longer, above, below, to the right, to the left, behind, between				
Comparison of sets: more, less, equal, many, few				
Number pictures: less than, more than, equal to, not equal to < > = ≠				
Identifying, writing and using 0 and 1; number line				
Identifying, writing and using 2; number line (write and use + - and =)				
Comparisons: Number pictures and balancing equations and inequalities (2>1 and 1<2)				
2D Shapes: Square, Rectangle, Triangle and Circle Ordering and arranging objects and shapes in pattern				

Autumn 2	% Well Below	% Emerging	% Expected	% Exceeding
Writing and using 3; number line, practise < > + - = (number bonds within)				
Writing and using 4; number line, practise < > + - = (number bonds within)				
Writing and using 5; number line, practise < > + - = (number bonds within)				
Writing and using 6; number line, practise < > + - = (number bonds within)				
Writing and using 7; number line, practise < > + - = (number bonds within)				
Writing and using 8; number line, practise < > + - = (number bonds within)				

Spring 1	% Well Below	% Emerging	% Expected	% Exceeding
Revision and Practise: 0, 1, 2, 3, 4, 5 6, 7 and 8				
Writing and using 9 number line, practise < > + - = (number bonds within)				
Writing and using 10 number line, practise < > + - = (number bonds within)				
Revision and Practise: 0 to 10 and mathematical symbols (number bonds within)				
Sequence events in chronological order				
Days, weeks, months and years				
Measure and record time				
Tell the time (hour and half past hour)				

Spring 2	% Well Below	% Emerging	% Expected	% Exceeding
Revision and practice: 0 to 10				
Extending the number line 0-20				
Number bonds and sums to 11				
Number bonds and sums to 12				
Number bonds and sums to 13				
Number bonds and sums to 14				
Compare and describe length/height				
Compare and describe mass/weight				
Compare and describe capacity/volume				
Measure and record lengths/heights				
Measure and record mass/weight				
Measure and record capacity/volume				

Summer 1	% Well Below	% Emerging	% Expected	% Exceeding
Number bonds and sums to 15				
Number bonds and sums to 16 & 17				
Number bonds and sums to 18 & 19				
Number bonds and sums to 20				
Counting, read and write numbers to 100 in numerals				
Money-denominations				
Turns				

Summer 2	% Well Below	% Emerging	% Expected	% Exceeding
Count, read and write numbers to 100 in numerals				
Count in multiples of one, two, fives and tens				
Solve multiplication and divisions using objects and arrays				
Fractions: Halves and Quarters				

Example End of Year 1 Tracking in Mathematics

The tracking grid provided here is intended for use at the end of Year 1. It can be used to show the percentage of children achieving each grade level standard in the Mathematics programme of study in the National Curriculum. Those individuals who are Well Below, Emerging or Exceeding could be underneath the numerical representation of achievement. This would allow school leadership and management to identify appropriate intervention required in Year 2 for those at risk of not meeting grade-level standards by the end of Key Stage 1. By noting the names of individuals who are Well Below, Emerging or Exceeding can help the next teacher begin to formulate a plan for what content needs revision and anticipate how to respond to more able children's learning needs. A similar format could be constructed for Year 2 through to Year 6.

End of Year 1 Achievement of National Curriculum Standards in Mathematics

	% Well Below	% Emerging	% Expected	% Exceeding
NPV1.1 Count to and across 100, forwards and backwards, beginning with 0 or 1, or from any given number				
NPV1.2 Count, read and write numbers to 100 in numerals, count in different multiples including ones, twos, fives and tens				
NPV1.3 given a number, identify one more and one less				
NVP1.4 identify and represent numbers using concrete objects and pictorial representations including the number line, and use the language of: equal to, more than, less than (fewer), most, least				
NPV1.5 read and write numbers from 1 to 20 in digits and words				
AS1.1 Read, write and interpret mathematical statements involving addition (+), subtraction (-) and equals (=) signs				
AS1.2 Represent and use number bonds and related subtraction facts within 20				
AS1.3 Add and subtract one-digit and two-digit numbers to 20 (9 + 9, 18 - 9), including zero				
AS1.4 Solve simple one-step problems that involve addition and subtraction, using concrete objects and pictorial representations, and missing number problems				
MD1.1 Solve simple one-step problems involving multiplication and division, calculating the answer using concrete objects, pictorial representations and arrays with the support of the teacher.				
M1.1 Compare, describe and solve practical problems for lengths and heights (e.g. long/short, longer/shorter, tall/short, double/half)				

M1.2 Compare, describe and solve practical problems for mass or weight (e.g. heavy/light, heavier than, lighter than)				
M1.3 Compare, describe and solve practical problems for capacity/volume (full/empty, more than, less than, quarter)				
M1.4 Compare, describe and solve practical problems for time (quicker, slower, earlier, later				
M1.5 Measure and begin to record lengths and heights				
M1.6 Measure and begin to record mass/weight				
M1.7 Measure and begin to record capacity and volume				
M1.8 Measure and begin to record time (hrs, mins, secs)				
M1.9 Recognise and know the value of different denominations of coins and notes				
M1.10 Sequence events in chronological order using language such as: before and after, next, first, today, yesterday, tomorrow, morning, afternoon and evening				
M1.11 Recognise and use language relating to dates, including days of the week, weeks, months and years				
M1.12 Tell the time to the hour and half past the hour and draw the hands on a clock face to show these times.				
GPS1.1 2-D shapes (e.g. rectangles (including squares), circles and triangles)				
GPD1.1 order and arrange combinations of objects and shapes in patterns				
GPD1.2 Describe position, directions and movements, including half, quarter and three-quarter turns.				
F1.1 Recognise, find and name a half as one of two equal parts of an object, shape or quantity				
F1.2 Recognise, find and name a quarter as one of four equal parts of an object, shape or quantity				

Notes

Example Year 3 Summative Tracking in Mathematics

Year 3 Conquering Primary Maths: Summative Assessment				
Standards in Mathematics	% WB	% EM	% E	% EX
NPV3.2 Recognise the place value of each digit in a three-digit number (hundreds, tens, ones)				
Children				
NPV3.3 Compare and order numbers up to 1000				
Children				
NPV3.5 Read and write numbers to at least 1000 in numerals and in words				
Children				
NPV3.1 Count from 0 in multiples of 4, 8, 50 and 100; finding 10 or 100 more or less than a given number				
Children				
NPV3.6 Solve number problems and practical problems involving these ideas				
Children				
NPV3.4 Identify, represent and estimate numbers using different representations				
Children				

GPS3.1 Draw 2-D shapes and make 3-D shapes using modelling materials; recognise 3-D shapes in different orientations; and describe them with increasing accuracy				
Children				
M3.2 Measure the perimeter of simple 2-D shapes				
Children				
AS3.1 Add and subtract mentally a three-digit number and ones				
Children				
AS3.2 Add and subtract mentally a three-digit number and tens				
Children				
AS3.3 Add and subtract a three-digit number and hundreds				
Children				
AS3.4 Add and subtract numbers with up to three digits, using the efficient written methods of columnar addition and subtraction				
Children				
AS3.5 Estimate the answer to a calculation and use inverse operations to check answers				
Children				

AS3.6 Solve problems, including missing number problems, using number facts, place value, and more complex addition and subtraction				
Children				
M3.3 Add and subtract amounts of money to give change, using both £ and p in practical contexts				
Children				
MD3.1 Recall and use multiplication and division facts for the 3, 4 and 8 multiplication tables				
Children				
MD3.2 Write and calculate mathematical statements for multiplication and division using the multiplication tables that they know, including for two-digit numbers times one-digit numbers, using mental and progressing to efficient written methods				
Children				
MD3.3 Solve problems, including missing number problems involving multiplication and division including integer scaling problems and correspondence problems in which n objects are connected to m objects				
Children				

D3.1 Interpret and present data using bar charts, pictograms and tables				
Children				
D3.1 Solve one-step and two-step questions such as 'How many more?' and 'How many fewer?' using information presented in scaled bar charts and pictograms and tables				
Children				
F3.1 Count up and down in tenths; recognise that tenths arise from dividing an object into 10 equal parts and in dividing one-digit numbers or quantities by 10				
Children				
F3.2 Recognise, find and write fractions of a discrete set of objects: unit fractions and non-unit fractions with small denominators				
Children				
F3.3 Recognise and use fractions as numbers: unit fractions and non-unit fractions with small denominators				
Children				
F3.4 Recognise and show, using diagrams, equivalent fractions with small denominators				
Children				

F3.5 Add and subtract fractions with the same denominator within one whole				
Children				
F.3.6 Compare and order unit fractions with the same denominator				
Children				
F3.7 Solve problems that involve all of the above				
Children				
GPS3.2 Recognise angles as a property of shape and associate angles with turning				
Children				
GPS3.3 Identify right angles, recognise that two right angles make a half-turn, three make three quarters of a turn and four a complete turn; identify whether angles are greater than or less than a right angle				
Children				
GPS3.4 Identify horizontal, vertical, perpendicular and parallel lines in relation to other lines				
Children				
M3.1 Measure, compare, add and subtract: lengths (m/cm/mm); mass (kg/g); volume/capacity (l/ml)				
Children				

M3.4 Tell and write the time from an analogue clock, including using Roman numerals from I to XII, and 12-hour and 24- hour clocks				
Children				
M3.5 Estimate and read time with increasing accuracy to the nearest minute; record and compare time in terms of seconds, minutes, hours and o'clock; use vocabulary such as a.m./p.m., morning, afternoon, noon and midnight				
Children				
M3.6 Know the number of seconds in a minute and the number of days in each month, year and leap year				
Children				
M3.7 Compare durations of events, for example to calculate the time taken by particular events or tasks				
Children				

Example End of Unit Tracking Sheet in Mathematics

Tracking grids to monitor achievement by each unit of work can be devised. Here, a Year 2 example is provided for Unit 2F Money and Data. The format is applicable to Year 3 through to Year 6. By using end of unit tracking grids, school leadership and management are able to frequently monitor how children in a cohort are progressing towards grade-level standards during an academic year. Not unlike the other examples of tracking given previously, percentages can be given as well as the names of individual children who are Well Below, Emerging and so on in relation to specific grade-level standards. Tracking grids required at the end of each unit of work can also assist with reporting to parents frequently as part of informal discussions or consultation evenings.

Year 2 Conquering Primary Maths Summer 2	Unit 2F Money and Data Tracking Sheet			
Standards in Mathematics	**% WB**	**% EM**	**% E**	**% EX**
F2.1 Recognise, find, name and write fractions (third, quarter and three-quarters) of length, shape, set of objects or quantity				
Children				
F2.2 Write simple fractions and recognise the equivalence of two quarters and one half				
Children				
GPD2.2 Use mathematical vocabulary to describe position, direction and movement, including distinguishing between rotation as a turn and in terms of right angles for quarter, half and three- quarter turns (clockwise and anti-clockwise), and movement in a straight line				
Children				

Annex 1: Guided Reading Records

Guided Reading Planning and Assessment Record: Key Stage 1 (Year 1)

Word Reading

WR1.1 Apply phonic knowledge and skills as the route to decode words

WR1.2 Read accurately by blending sounds in unfamiliar words containing GPC that have been taught

WR1.3 Read common exception words, noting unusual correspondences between spelling and sound and where these occur in the word

WR1.4 Read words containing taught GPCs and –s, -es, -ing, -ed, -er and –est endings

WR1.5 Read other words of more than one syllable that contain taught GPC

WR1.6 Read words with contractions (I'm, I'll and we'll) and understand that the apostrophe represents the omiited letter(s)

WR1.7 Read aloud accurately books that are consistent with their developing phonic knowledge

WR1.8 Re-read these books to build up their fluency and confidence in word reading

Reading Comprehension

Making Connections	EXPECTED: Relates background knowledge and experience to text
	EXCEEDING: Uses background knowledge to enhance comprehension and interpretation. Makes text-to-text and text-to-self connections; uses author schema with familiar text to make predictions

Questioning

EXPECTED: Asks questions relevant to text; can answer questions

EXCEEDING: Asks questions to enhance meaning; can easily answer questions; beginning awareness of different question types

Visualisation

EXPECTED: Describes some sensory images tied directly to the text

EXCEEING: Describes own sensory images; images can be elaborated from the literal text and demonstrated using any modality

Determining Importance

EXPECTED: Identifies some concepts in text as more important to text meaning (characters, plot, main idea or setting)

EXCEEDING: Identifies words, characters and/or events as more important to overall meaning; makes some attempt to explain reasoning

Comprehension Monitoring

EXPECTED: Identifies difficulties and articulates need to solve problem; does not articulate what the problem is

EXCEEDING: Identifies location and type of difficulty and articulates the need to solve the problem

Inferring

EXPECTED: Draws conclusions and makes predictions that are consistent with text and background knowledge

EXCEEDNG: Draws conclusions and makes predictions using examples from the text

Synthesis

EXPECTED: Retells most key elements in sequence

EXCEEDING: Retells elements of the text in logical sequence; may include some extension to overall theme, message or background knowledge

Group Target(s):	Dates:	Texts:
		Age-appropriate level for E and EX

Teaching Sequence: (1) Introduction/Strategy Check/Comprehension Focus (2) Independent Reading (*Not a 'round robin'*) (3) Returning to Text (5) Responding to Text (6) Follow Up/Next Steps

Names	Word Reading	Reading Comprehension
Individual targets		

Guided Reading Planning and Assessment Record: Key Stage 1 (Year 2)

Word Reading

WR2.1 Continue to apply phonic knowledge and skills as the route to decode words until automatic decoding has become embedded and reading is fluent

WR2.2 Read accurately be blending the sounds in words that contain the graphemes taught so far, especially recognition of alternative sounds for graphemes

WR2.3 Read accurately words of two or more syllables that contain the same GPCs as above

WR2.4 Read words containing common suffixes

WR2.5 Read further common exception words, noting unusual correspondence between spelling and sound and where these occur in words

WR2.6 Read most words quickly and accurately when they have been frequently encountered without overt sounding and blending

WR2.7 Read aloud books closely matched to their improving phonic knowledge, sounding out unfamiliar words accurately, automatically and without undue hesitation

WR2.8 Re-read books to build up fluency and confidence in word reading

Reading Comprehension

Making Connections	EXPECTED: Uses background knowledge to enhance comprehension and interpretation. Makes text-to-text and text-to-self connections; uses author schema with familiar text to make predictions

Questioning

EXPECTED: Asks questions to enhance meaning; can easily answer questions; beginning awareness of different question types

Visualisation

EXPECTED: Describes own sensory images; images can be elaborated from the literal text and demonstrated using any modality

Determining Importance

EXPECTED: Identifies words, characters and/or events as more important to overall meaning; makes some attempt to explain reasoning

Comprehension Monitoring

EXPECTED: Identifies location and type of difficulty and articulates the need to solve the problem

Inferring

EXPECTED: Draws conclusions and makes predictions using examples from the text

Synthesis

EXPECTED: Retells elements of the text in logical sequence; may include some extension to overall theme, message or background knowledge

Group Target(s):	Dates:	Texts: *Age-appropriate level for E and EX*

Teaching Sequence: (1) Introduction/Strategy Check/Comprehension Focus (2) Independent Reading (*Not a 'round robin'*) (3) Returning to Text (5) Responding to Text (6) Follow Up/Next Steps

Names *Individual targets*	Word Reading	Reading Comprehension

Guided Reading Planning and Assessment Record: Lower Key Stage 2 (Year 3)
Word Reading

WR3.1 Apply growing knowledge of root words, prefixes and suffixes (etymology and morphology) to read aloud and understand meaning of new words they meet

WR3.2 Read exception words, noting the unusual correspondence between spelling and sound and where these occur in the word

Reading Comprehension

Making Connections

EXPECTED: Relates background knowledge and experience to text

EXCEEDING: Uses background knowledge to enhance comprehension and interpretation. Makes text-to-text and text-to-self connections; uses author schema with familiar texts to make predictions

Questioning

EXPECTED: Asks questions relevant to text; can answer questions

EXCEEDING: Asks questions to enhance meaning derived; can easily answer questions; beginning awareness of different types of questions

Visualisation

EXPECTED: Describes some sensory images tied directly to text or description of the picture constructed in text

EXCEEING: Describes own sensory images; images can be elaborated from the literal text and demonstrated using any modality

Determining Importance

EXPECTED: Identifies some concepts in text as more important to text meaning (character, plot, main idea or setting)

EXCEEDING: Identifies words, characters and/or events as more important to overall meaning; makes some attempt to explain reasoning

Comprehension Monitoring

EXPECTED: Identifies difficulties and articulates need to solve problem; does not necessarily articulate what the problem is

EXCEEDING: Identifies location and type of difficulty and articulates need to solve the problem

Inferring

EXPECTED: Draws conclusions and makes predictions that are consistent with text and background knowledge

EXCEEDNG: Draws conclusions and makes predictions using examples from text

Synthesis

EXPECTED: Retells most key elements in sequence

EXCEEDING: Retells elements of the text in logical sequence; may include some extension to overall message or theme

Group Target(s):	Dates:	Texts: *Age-appropriate level for E and EX*

Teaching Sequence: (1) Introduction/Strategy Check/Comprehension Focus (2) Independent Reading (*Not a 'round robin'*) (3) Returning to Text (5) Responding to Text (6) Follow Up/Next Steps

Names *Individual targets*	Word Reading	Reading Comprehension

Guided Reading Planning and Assessment Record: Lower Key Stage 2 (Year 4)

Word Reading

WR4.1 Apply growing knowledge of root words, prefixes and suffixes (etymology and morphology) to read aloud and understand meaning of new words they meet

WR4.2 Read exception words, noting the unusual correspondence between spelling and sound and where these occur in the word

Reading Comprehension

Making Connections

EMERGING: Relates background knowledge and experience to text

EXPECTED: Uses background knowledge to enhance comprehension and interpretation. Makes text-to-text and text-to-self connections; uses author schema with familiar texts to make predictions

Questioning

EMERGING: Asks questions relevant to text; can answer questions

EXPECTED: Asks questions to enhance meaning derived; can easily answer questions; beginning awareness of different types of questions

Visualisation

EMERGING: Describes some sensory images tied directly to text or description of the picture constructed in text

EXPECTED: Describes own sensory images; images can be elaborated from the literal text and demonstrated using any modality

Determining Importance

EMERGING: Identifies some concepts in text as more important to text meaning (character, plot, main idea or setting)

EXPECTED: Identifies words, characters and/or events as more important to overall meaning; makes some attempt to explain reasoning

Comprehension Monitoring

EMERGING: Identifies difficulties and articulates need to solve problem; does not necessarily articulate what the problem is

EXPECTED: Identifies location and type of difficulty and articulates need to solve the problem

Inferring

EMERGING: Draws conclusions and makes predictions that are consistent with text and background knowledge

EXPECTED: Draws conclusions and makes predictions using examples from text

Synthesis

EMERGING: Retells most key elements in sequence

EXPECTED: Retells elements of the text in logical sequence; may include some extension to overall message or theme

Group Target(s):	Dates:	Texts: *Age-appropriate level for E*

Teaching Sequence: (1) Introduction/Strategy Check/Comprehension Focus (2) Independent Reading (*Not a 'round robin'*) (3) Returning to Text (5) Responding to Text (6) Follow Up/Next Steps

Names *Individual targets*	Word Reading	Reading Comprehension

Guided Reading Planning and Assessment Record: Upper Key Stage 2 (Year 5)

Word Reading

WR5.1 Apply knowledge of root words, prefixes and suffixes (etymology and morphology) to read aloud and understand meaning of new words

Reading Comprehension

Making Connections	EXPECTED: Relates background knowledge an experience to text and expands the interpretations of text using schema; may discuss schema related to author/text structure EXCEEDING: Explains how schema enriches interpretation of text and begins to make connections beyond life experience and immediate text

Questioning

EXPECTED: Asks questions to deepen meaning of text; may explain how the questions enhance comprehension (metacognition)
EXCEEDING: Uses questions to challenge the text (author's purpose, theme or point of view)

Visualisation

EXPECTED: Describes own mental images, usually visual; images are somewhat elaborated from literal text
EXCEEDING: Creates and describes multi-sensory images that extend and enrich the text and can explain how those images enhance comprehension

Determining Importance

EXPECTED: Identifies words, characters and/or overall meaning and makes some attempt to explain reasoning
EXCEEDING: Identifies at least one key concept, idea or theme in overall text meaning and clearly explains why

Comprehension Monitoring

EXPECTED: Identifies problem at word, sentence or schema level; can articulate and use a strategy to fix comprehension breakdown, usually at word or sentence level
EXCEEDING: Identifies at least one strategy to build meaning when comprehension breaks down; can articulate which strategies are most important for a given text

Inferring

EXPECTED: Draws conclusions and/or makes predictions and can explain the source of the conclusion or prediction
EXCEEDING: Develops predictions, interpretations and/or conclusions about the text and the reader's background knowledge or ideas and beliefs

Synthesis

EXPECTED: Stops frequently to reflect on text meaning; uses own schema and story elements to enhance meaning; may identify key theme
EXCEEDING: Stops frequently to reflect on text meaning; relates to the story or genre in a personal way; can identify key theme(s); may articulate how this process has created new meaning upon completion of text

Group Target(s):	Dates:	Texts: *Age-appropriate level for E and EX*

Teaching Sequence: (1) Introduction/Strategy Check/Comprehension Focus (2) Independent Reading (*Not a 'round robin'*) (3) Returning to Text (5) Responding to Text (6) Follow Up/Next Steps

Names *Individual targets*	Word Reading	Reading Comprehension

WR6.1 Apply knowledge of root words, prefixes and suffixes (etymology and morphology) to read aloud and understand meaning of new words

Reading Comprehension

Making Connections	EXPECTED: Explains how schema enriches interpretation of text and begins to make connections beyond life experience and immediate text

Questioning

EXPECTED: Uses questions to challenge the text (author's purpose, theme or point of view)

Visualisation

EXPECTED: Creates and describes multi-sensory images that extend and enrich the text and can explain how those images enhance comprehension

Determining Importance

EXPECTED: Identifies at least one key concept, idea or theme in overall text meaning and clearly explains why

Comprehension Monitoring

EXPECTED: Identifies at least one strategy to build meaning when comprehension breaks down; can articulate which strategies are most important for a given text

Inferring

EXPECTED: Develops predictions, interpretations and/or conclusions about the text and the reader's background knowledge or ideas and beliefs

Synthesis

EXPECTED: Stops frequently to reflect on text meaning; relates to the story or genre in a personal way; can identify key theme(s); may articulate how this process has created new meaning upon completion of text

Group Target(s):	Dates:	Texts: *Age-appropriate level for E*

Teaching Sequence: (1) Introduction/Strategy Check/Comprehension Focus (2) Independent Reading (*Not a 'round robin'*) (3) Returning to Text (5) Responding to Text (6) Follow Up/Next Steps

Names *Individual targets*	Word Reading	Reading Comprehension

Reading Comprehension	
Making Connections	
Questioning	
Visualisation	
Determining Importance	
Comprehension Monitoring	
Inferring	
Synthesis	

Group Target(s):	Dates:	Texts: *Age-appropriate level for E*

Teaching Sequence: (1) Introduction/Strategy Check/Comprehension Focus (2) Independent Reading (*Not a 'round robin'*) (3) Returning to Text (5) Responding to Text (6) Follow Up/Next Steps

Names *Individual targets*	Word Reading	Reading Comprehension

Glossary

Alignment

The direct link between standards, teaching and assessment. This link occurs in the classroom as well as in the form of a through-line between statutory requirements in the National Curriculum and a local-articulated curriculum influencing what occurs at the chalkface.

All Children

A term used to convey the fact that the revised National Curriculum raises expectations for every child in state education. This is regardless of gender, sexuality, ethnicity and socioeconomic disadvantage. Some children will have special educational needs or face extreme adversities. Their individual needs will need to be taken into account and accommodations made.

Analytic Rubric or Scoring

Performance on different dimensions or criteria is assessed. A child's achievement on one dimension can be assessed or an overall judgement made on learning across all criteria included in the rubric.

Assessment

A process where learning is quantified, described and information on achievement against grade-level standards gathered. Assessment can also indicate where teaching needs to be improved to impact more profoundly on learning.

Assessment Plan

A document where choices for assessing learning are made in relation to standards or specific criteria linked to a standard. This is the equivalent of short-term planning driven by assessment for learning, but formalises it.

Assessment Tools or Strategies

This refers to what children produce to show learning in relation to a standard and the means by which classroom teachers will determine if a child is meeting expectations. These include short answer tasks, products and performances. Rubrics, checklists and answer keys are used to analyse learning against standards.

Authentic Assessment	Assessments that have authenticity are based on what a child can do in a variety of contexts at different points in an academic year. Authentic assessment demonstrates children can apply knowledge and understanding acquired.
Baseline	The collection of evidence against which future performance can be measured. At school-level, achievement of National Curriculum grade-level standards at Year 1 can be used to determine how well children progress as they move through a school. At classroom level, pre-assessment before a unit of work provides the baseline against which the impact of teaching on learning can be shown.
Benchmark	These are the components of a grade-level standard identified through unpicking these to determine the depth and breadth of learning encoded in a general curricular statement.
Classroom Assessment	See **School-Based Assessment**
Closed Response Tasks	Items in a closed response task have one right answer. They typically involve yes or no, true or false and multiple choice. This type of task should only be used to assess specific knowledge and understanding that children have acquired.
Cognitive Demand	The complexity of intellectual activity required by a task or encoded within a standard.
Common Core Standards	The term used in the United States of America for educational standards. Common Core Standards, formed by government and education leaders, compare well with standards in other high-performing countries.
Congruency	A core principle in a standards-based curriculum. It refers to ensuring teaching and assessment are focused on children learning what is necessary to meet grade-level standards set down in the National Curriculum.
Constructed Responses	Constructed response tasks or items require children to generate their own answer. A constructed response can be a short answer in written or oral form, a product or performance. These are more authentic assessments than closed response tasks.

Construct Validity	An assessment measuring what it claims to measure. Validity is associated with **Reliability**.
Content Validity	The extent to which content of an assessment task represents what has been taught.
Conventional Approach	An approach where a topic is selected from the curriculum that is taught and then assessed before moving on to the next topic. It contrasts with a standards-based model. See **Standards-Based Curriculum**.
Conquering Primary Maths	The name given to the collection of standards-based unit plans and overviews for each year group contained in *Towards a Standards-Based Curriculum*.
Criteria	These specify the characteristics of standards used to assess children's work and learning. When criteria are defined to create a scale showing different proficiencies, a rubric or scoring guide can be created. See **Rubrics**.
Criterion-Referenced Assessment	A child's performance is compared against the standards and descriptions of what expected achievement involves. Standards-based or (school-based assessment) are criterion-referenced. **See School-Based Assessment**.
Curriculum and Assessment Mapping	A school's long-term plan stipulating what children will learn and when. Mapping builds an assessment framework into the curriculum. It is expected that what should be taught in a half term block will be assessed within that time frame.
Data	Data refers to records of observations and assessment information enabling inferences to be drawn on how well children are meeting grade-level standards.
Data Rich	Records of learning and performance at school-level and classroom level. Data provides information to influence planning and decision-making. Data rich is the state of possessing evidence, but not necessarily using this to impact on teaching and learning. See **Information Rich**.
Diagnostic Assessment	An assessment identifying what a child does know or does not know. Diagnostic assessment reveals what a child is able to do and what he or she is not yet able to do.

Formative Assessment	This is also referred to as 'assessment for learning'. Formative assessment provides data that informs how teaching sequences progress to ensure all children meet grade-level standards.
Generalised Rubric	A rubric that can be used to assess the quality of products or performances where the same criteria always apply.
Holistic Scoring	Issuing an overall score or judgement. This is of particular relevance when assessing writing and reading.
Information Rich	This term refers to how data, evidence and records of learning, are used in decision-making to improve pedagogical approaches and the quality of teaching received by children within and between classes.
Inter-Rater Reliability	Human error can be made when making a judgement on a child's achievement and learning. Having more than one teacher assessing the evidence for a judgement can lead to greater consistency.
Learning Outcome(s)	Statements describing the essential aim for learning in the classroom. They state what an individual should be able to demonstrate by the end of a specified time frame.
Metacognition	An individual's awareness of what they know and how they came to know it. Metacognition is the process by which children are conscious of their own knowledge and the processes by which they can learn and resolve difficulties or confusion.
Multiple Measures	Providing more than one way for children to demonstrate they are achieving grade-level standards. In order to take multiple measures of learning, multiple opportunities for children to show what they can do are necessary. For example, open-ended and closed tasks or eliciting constructed and selected responses.
On-Demand Assessment	Assessment occurring at a predetermined time. This form of assessment must be completed in a set amount of time under certain conditions. End of Key Stage 2 testing is an example of on-demand assessment as is the Phonic Screening Test for Year 1 children.
Open-Ended Tasks	An activity with no single correct answer or response.

This type of task determines what children know and how learning is applied to a new context or situation. This type of task would generally be considered an authentic assessment. See **Authentic Assessment**.

Outcomes-Based Education	The focus is on assessing what has been learned rather than being driven solely by the need for curriculum coverage.
Pace Setting	Ensuring that curriculum and assessment mapping indicates what is taught, assessed and when this is expected to occur. Unit plans or medium-term planning will contain clusters of standards to be met within a specified time frame. Classroom teachers therefore need to manage teaching and learning time effectively in order to maintain the pace of learning required in academic year.
Performance Gap	The difference between what children can presently do and the expected level of performance or proficiency.
Reliability	Consistency in judgements made about what children have achieved. See **Inter-Rater Reliability**.
Rubric	One form of scoring a child's performance. A quality rubric consists of a measurement scale involving clear criteria and performance descriptors for each point on the scale. See **Generalised Rubric** and **Task-Specific Rubric**.
Scale	This is a continuum. There are several types of scales. In a rubric, a scale is created to show differences in proficiency against criteria.
Schema or Schematics	The cognitive framework that helps an individual to organise and interpret information.
School-Based Assessment	Criteria for assessment are taken directly from standards and their associated components or benchmarks. See **Criterion-Referenced Assessment**.
Scoring Guides	Assessment tools used to determine how a child's learning relates to grade-level standards. Examples of scoring guides include answer keys, observation schedules, checklists and different types of rubrics.
Short-Cycle Assessment	This operates frequently during a unit of work. Assessment tasks are set ahead of a teaching sequence

commencing and relate to specific standards or components needed to demonstrate achievement of a standard. Short-cycle assessment involves planning assessment, gathering evidence of learning, interpreting what the evidence indicates and making decisions on what is taught next and to whom. Also see **Assessment Plans**.

Standards-Based

A clear relationship exists between teaching and learning activities, classroom resources and assessments in relation to standards forming the curriculum. See **Alignment** and **Congruency**.

Standards-Based Assessment

See **School-Based Assessment**.

Standards-Based Curriculum

The curriculum states what all children must know, understand and be able to do. These statements are known as standards. Standards form the basis for what is taught and, consequently, what gets assessed. An alternative term for a standards-based curriculum is a standards-based system.

Standards-Based Reform

A term used in the United States of America from the 1990s onwards. It refers to a shift towards the curriculum making what children are expected to know, understand and be able to do explicit. Assessment aligns to these standards and is used to hold schools to account for how well children achieve expectations. Within England, the National Curriculum for 2014 can be viewed as a standards-based reform.

Standards-Based Reporting

Achievement is reported and recorded against grade-level standards that have been taught and assessed.

Standards-Based Unit Plan

All teaching, learning and assessment relate to one another. They are designed to lead children to achievement of specified standards. A standards-based unit plan can be referred to as a medium-term plan.

Task-Specific Rubric

Scoring guidelines that have been devised for a particular task. The criteria in a task-specific rubric describe what a child must demonstrate to be working at an expected level of proficiency. The language used in this type of rubric will be specific to the task and the grade-level standards underpinning the activity.

Taxonomies of the Cognitive Domain	A hierarchy of knowledge and understanding. Lower-order thinking is associated with the ability to recall information. Higher-order thinking involves the ability to evaluate and apply learning.
Test	A set of items designed to tap into what a child knows or can do in relation to one or more areas related to standards.
Unpicking Standards	A process where an individual classroom teacher or group of teachers identify the components of a standard. The grade-level standard is broken down into smaller steps of learning that form the basis for progressive teaching sequences. The benchmarks or components are also included as part of assessment tasks and activities.
Validity	The extent to which an assessment actually measures what it claims to. See **Construct Validity** and **Content Validity**.

References

ALEXANDER, R. (2004) *Towards Dialogic Teaching: Rethinking classroom talk* (2nd ed.), Cambridge, Dialogos UK Ltd.

BISHOP, J., BRISTOW, J., CORIELL, B., JENSEN, M., JOHNSON, LURING, S., LYONS-TINSLEY, M., MEFFORD, M., NEU, G., SAMULSKI, E., WARNER, T., and WHITE. M. (2011) Assessment Outside the Bubble: Performance Assessment for Common Core State Standards, *Online submission, ERIC EBSCOhost.*

BROWN, G. T. L. (2011) School based assessment methods: Development and implementation, *Journal of Assessment Paradigms*, 1. 1, pp. 30-32.

CAIN, K. (2010) 'Reading for Meaning: The skills that support reading comprehension and its development' in Hall, K., Goswami, U., Harrison, C., Ellis, S. and Soler, J. (Eds.) *Interdisciplinary Perspectives on Learning to Read: Culture, Cognition and Pedagogy.* Oxon: Routledge, pp. 74-86.

CALIFORNIA ACADEMIC PARTNERSHIP PROGRAMME (CAPP) (2009) *Improving Standards-Based Instruction: An Interview With Trudy Schoneman, Institutional Leadership Initiative Director*, The California State University.

CENTRE FOR INNOVATION IN TEACHING MATHEMATICS (1995) *Mathematics Enhancement Programme (MEP)*, Plymouth: The University of Plymouth.

COALEY, K. (2010) *An Introduction to Psychological Assessment and Psychometrics*, London: SAGE Publications Limited.

DAS, J. P. and JANZEN, C. (2004) Learning Math: Basic concepts, maths difficulties, and suggestions for intervention, *Developmental Disabilities Bulletin*, 32. 2, pp. 191-205.

DEPARTMENT FOR EDUCATION (2011) *Review of the National Curriculum in England: What can we learn from the English, mathematics and science curricula of high-performing jurisdictions?* Department for Education (Research Report).

DEPARTMENT FOR EDUCATION (2013) *The National Curriculum in England: Framework document for consultation*, Department for Education.

DEPARTMENT FOR EDUCATION (July 2013) *The National Curriculum in England: Framework document for consultation*, Department for Education.

DEPARTMENT FOR EDUCATION (2010) *The Importance of Teaching*, London: Department for Education.

DEPARTMENT FOR EDUCATION AND EMPLOYMENT (1998) *The National Literacy Strategy: Framework for Teaching*, Suffolk: DfEE Publications.

DEPARTMENT FOR EDUCATION AND SKILLS (2006) *Primary Framework for Literacy and Mathematics*, Norwich: DfES Publications.

DEPARTMENT FOR CHILDREN, SCHOOLS AND FAMILIES (2009) *Getting to Grips with Assessing Pupils' Progress*, Nottingham, Department for Children, Schools and Families Publications.

EMERSON, J. and BABTIE, P. (2010) *The Dyscalculia Assessment*, London, Continuum International Publishing Group.

HALL, K. (2010) 'Significant Lines of Research in Reading Pedagogy' in Hall, K., Goswami, U., Harrison, C., Ellis, S. and Soler, J. (Eds.) *Interdisciplinary Perspectives on Learning to Read: Culture, Cognition and Pedagogy.* Oxon: Routledge, pp. 3-16.

JOHNSTON, P. and COSTELLO, P. (2009) 'Principles for Literacy Assessment' in Fletcher-Campbell, F., Soler, J. and Reid, G. (Eds.) *Approaching Difficulties in Literacy Development: Assessment, Pedagogies and Programmes*, London: Sage Publications Ltd, pp. 145-162.

KINTSCH, W. and RAWSON, K, A. (2007) 'Comprehension' in Snowling, M. J. and Hulme, C. (Eds.) *The Science of Reading: A Handbook*, Oxford: Blackwell Publishing, pp. 207-226.

KISPAL, A. (2008) *Inference Skills for Reading Literature Review.* National Foundation for Education Research: DCSF.

KLINGER, J., VAUGHN, S. and BOARDMAN, A (2007) *Teaching Reading Comprehension to Students with Learning Difficulties*, London: The Guildford Press.

MANSOR, A., ONG HEE, L., RASUL, M., RAOF, R. and YUSOFF, N (2013) The Benefits of School-Based Assessment, *Asian Social Science*, 9. 8, pp. 101-106.

MARMOLEJO-RAMOS, F., ELOSUA DE JUAN, M. R., GYGAX, P., MADDEN, C. J. AND ROA, S. M. (2009) Reading between the lines: The activation of background knowledge during text comprehension, *Pragmatics and Cognition*, 17. 1, pp. 77-107.

RAKOW, S. (2008) Standards-Based v. Standards-Embedded Curriculum: Not Just Semantics, *Gifted Child Today*, 31. 1, pp. 43-49.

RASSOOL, N. (2009) 'Literacy: In Search of a Paradigm' in Soler, J., Fletcher-Campbell, F. and Reid, G. (eds) *Understanding Difficulties in*

Literacy Development: Issues and Concepts, London, Sage Publications Ltd in association with The Open University, pp. 7-31.

SIZMUR, S. and SAINSBURY, M. (1997) Criterion Referencing and the Meaning of National Curriculum Assessment, *British Journal of Educational Studies*, 45. 2, pp. 123-140.

SMITH, K. (2010) 'Comprehension as a social act: Texts, contexts and readers' in Hall, K., Goswami, U., Harrison, C., Ellis, S. and Soler, J. (Eds.) *Interdisciplinary Perspectives on Learning to Read: Culture, Cognition and Pedagogy*. Oxon: Routledge, pp. 61-73.

SNOW, D., PFISTER, N., PRAIRIE, C., CARR, J., WEBER, S. and WALKER, D. (2001) *Using Standards In Your Classroom: A Teacher Resource Guide*, United States: The Vermont Department of Education.

STUART, M. (2003) Fine-tuning the National Literacy Strategy to ensure continuing progress in standards of reading in the UK: Some suggestions for change, School of Psychology and Humanities/Institute of Education, University of London, pp. 1-20.

STUART, M., STAINTHORP, R. and SNOWLING, M. (2008) Literacy as a complex activity: deconstructing the simple view of reading, *Literacy*, 42. 2, pp. 59-66.

THE SCHOOL INFORMATION (ENGLAND) (AMENDED) REGULATIONS 2012 (2012) *The National Archives,* Ref 2012. No 1124.

WADLINGTON, E. and WADLINGTON, P. (2008) Helping Students With Mathematical Disabilities to Succeed, *Preventing School Failure*, 53. 1, pp. 2-7.

WOODLEY, L. and FERGUSON, A. (2003) *Standards-Based Assessment: A Model,* Curriculum Services Canada.

Notes

Notes

Notes

Notes

Notes

Notes

Notes

Notes

Notes

Printed in Great Britain
by Amazon.co.uk, Ltd.,
Marston Gate.